Planning Cities People and Schools

Offering the overlooked but essential viewpoint of young people from low-income communities of color and their public schools, *Planning Cities With Young People and Schools* offers an urgently needed set of best-practice recommendations for urban planners to change the status quo and reimagine the future of our cities for and with young people. Working with more than 10,000 students over two decades from the San Francisco Bay Area, to New York, to Tohoku, Japan, this work produces a wealth of insights on issues ranging from environmental planning, housing, transportation, regional planning, and urban education.

Part I presents a theory of change for planning more equitable, youth-friendly cities by cultivating intergenerational communities of practice where young people work alongside city planners and adult professionals. Part II explores youth engagement in resilience, housing, and transportation planning through an analysis of literature and international examples of engaging children and youth in city planning. Part III speaks directly to practitioners, scholars, and students alike, presenting "Six Essentials for Planning Just and Joyful Cities" as necessary precursors to effective city planning with and for our most marginalized, children, youth, and public schools.

For academics, policy makers, and practitioners, this book raises the importance of education systems and young people as critical to urban planning and the future of our cities.

Deborah L. McKoy is the founding director of the UC Berkeley Center for Cities and Schools and adjunct professor in the Department of City and Regional Planning. Her research focuses on the intersection of city planning, public education, and young people's experience of place. Deborah has a PhD from UC Berkeley, an MPA from Columbia University, and a BA from University at Albany.

Amanda Eppley is the associate director of the UC Berkeley Center for Cities and Schools. Amanda is an experienced public school educator, and her research interests examine the reciprocal impacts of cities and schools for the social justice potential that emerges at their confluence. She has an MCP from UC Berkeley with a concentration in environmental planning and a BA in history and education from Swarthmore College.

Shirl Buss is the creative director of the UC Berkeley Center for Cities and Schools. As a designer, planner, and educator, she has directed programs, facilitated participatory design projects, and taught K–graduate students in universities, schools, museums, and informal settings for over 30 years. She holds an MArch and PhD from the UCLA Graduate School of Architecture and Urban Planning.

"From the first word, you realize this book is different. In centering justice and joy as the essential framework for youth engagement in planning cities, *Planning Cities With Young People and Schools* offers a brilliant and powerful youth-led antidote to business as usual in urban development. Inside are remarkable real-world examples that center the voices, knowledge, and perspectives of young people in our cities, especially students of color, living in low-income communities. An invaluable resource for every planner and community activist."

Charisma Acey, Professor of City and Regional Planning, UC Berkeley, California

"*Planning Cities With Young People and Schools* is a tremendous resource for those who seek to deepen youth engagement in civic life. The book utilizes concrete examples that illustrate how this is being done and show readers why this work is so important. For educators, planners, community activists, and youth workers, this book will be a source of information and inspiration."

Pedro Noguera, Dean of the USC Rossier School of Education, Los Angeles, California

"Youth deserve to feel a sense of joy, a sense of justice, especially in their cities – that closest form of democracy to each individual."

Mayor Libby Schaaf, Oakland, California

Planning Cities With Young People and Schools

Forging Justice, Generating Joy

Deborah L. McKoy,
Amanda Eppley, and Shirl Buss

NEW YORK AND LONDON

First published 2022
by Routledge
605 Third Avenue, New York, NY 10158

and by Routledge
4 Park Square, Milton Park, Abingdon, Oxon OX14 4RN

Routledge is an imprint of the Taylor & Francis Group, an informa business

Library of Congress Cataloging-in-Publication Data
A catalog record for this title has been requested

ISBN: 978-0-367-69434-0 (hbk)
ISBN: 978-0-367-69433-3 (pbk)
ISBN: 978-1-003-14177-8 (ebk)

DOI: 10.4324/9781003141778

Typeset in Optima
by Apex CoVantage, LLC

To the thousands of young people who have inspired us with their willingness to question, learn, and imagine together.

Contents

Figures and Images

Figures

Images

Acknowledgements

This book is premised in large part on the notion that learning (and social change) is not an individual act but rather engagement in social practice. Thus, it would only stand to reason that we recognize the many, many members of our intergenerational community of practice that made this book possible.

We start where Y-PLAN began in 2000, by recognizing and honoring the hundreds of UC Berkeley graduate and undergraduate students who took a chance and enrolled in an unusual city planning class that brought them into the heart of local public schools. Here they were invited to serve as "mentors" and to not just read about city planning and community engagement but learn by asking questions and seeing our cities through the eyes of their youngest residents.

Yet there would be no book, and no Y-PLAN, without the thousands of teachers, administrators, city planners, civic leaders, and over 10,000+ young people who opened their doors and hearts to our shared practice and work over these years. As we reimagined formal structures we turned school classrooms inside out, repositioning students as agents of change and cities as the text for learning. We all learned so much and were transformed in the process.

This book is also built on decades of scholarship at UC Berkeley and beyond, and we proudly stand on "the shoulders of giants" who were kind and generous enough to read chapters and share their wisdom. Karen Chapple, Chair of UC Berkeley's Department of City and Regional Planning, has served as a champion of the role of young people in city planning for many years, and her feedback on our manuscript was invaluable. Charles

Underwood's willingness to dig in, offer important insights to each chapter, and even suggest a new book title went beyond the call.

Being at UC Berkeley, we are fortunate to have the opportunity to work with many other scholars who also have supported our work over the years and provided valuable feedback on this book, including Charisma Acey, Robert Cervero, and Carolina Reid. Other critical sources of inspiration for the depth and development of so many central ideas of this book, over many years, include Ronald Ashford, Jean Lave, Pedro Noguera, and David Stern.

Recognizing the importance of both visual storytelling and attention to written detail to bring our theories and arguments to life for readers, we must thank our graphic design team, Renee Harcourt and Katherine Marr, and our research and editing team, Elena Eimert, Tira Okamoto, and Chris Stone.

Since our inception in 2004, the UC Berkeley Center for Cities and Schools (CC+S) and the Y-PLAN civic learning initiative that predates it by four years have been housed at the Institute of Urban and Regional Development with core support from the College of Environmental Design, the Department of City Planning, and the Graduate School of Education. We would also like to thank CC+S co-founder Jeffrey Vincent, who was an early Y-PLANner himself and has served as a thought partner and earlier contributor to this work.

The growth of Y-PLAN from a university-community collaboration in one West Oakland classroom to a global action research initiative has been possible through the brilliant work of many CC+S program directors and team members who brought powerful insights and talents into this work. We recognize and thank Ariel Bierbaum, Jessie Stewart, Myrna Ortiz Villar, Ciera Dudley, and many others.

Our funders and sponsors whose financial support made this book possible include UC Links, The California Endowment, Stuart Foundation, Walter and Elise Haas Fund, Kellogg Foundation, NYC Fund for Public Schools, The United States-Japan Council, Softbank Corporation, and more.

Our civic, school and district partners are too numerous to be adequately identified here yet we do wish to recognize and honor core partners including those in the cities of Berkeley, Dallas, Detroit, East Palo Alto, Los Angeles, New Orleans, New York City, Oakland, Richmond (CA), Sacramento, San Francisco, San Jose, San Rafael, and Washington DC. and well as global partners in Japan and China.

Each author also owes a personal debt of gratitude to our families and friends:

Deborah L. McKoy

I first thank my many inspiring, and provocative, UC Berkeley students who started me down this path. David, my love and bashert, thank you for keeping us going and laughing in this most unusual year – and always. Eli and Jackson, thank you for the motivating hugs before zoom school and belief in your mom. And, finally (though not exhaustively) I thank my mom, Judith, and my family, whose vision for the world, and belief in justice for everyone, young and old, will always be my greatest inspiration and North Star.

Amanda Eppley

For your love and support and for keeping me grounded and centered in this tumultuous year and always, thank you to my partner, John. For persistently and lovingly pushing me to find the good in everything while still seeking to improve it, thank you to my children, Chris and Lexi.

Shirl Buss

My deepest love and appreciation go to my dear partner, Leslie Stone, who has supported and celebrated my work for almost 30 years. Also, a huge shout out to Prescott Reavis, D'Sjon Dixon, and Megumi Inouye, my close colleagues, with whom I have shared inspiration, hope, and joy each time we engage in creative action with designers and dreamers of all ages.

Foreword

The world's cities, big and small, are the laboratories from which democracy, culture, and innovation have emerged over the millennia. These urban incubators offer tremendous opportunity not just for the talented to achieve their dreams, but also for the city's least advantaged residents to rise above their circumstances and prosper. Yet, the vitality and potential of cities conceal a darker reality, of entrenched inequality fueled by segregation, itself produced by the state (Rothstein, 2017). When neighborhoods are segregated by race and income, children end up in segregated schools, impeding their life chances.

Sociologists, educators, and urban planners, among others, have long sought approaches to address the issue of segregation and upward mobility for urban youth. Urban planning in particular sees itself as an interdisciplinary field that translates knowledge into action to produce more just and inclusive cities. Nonetheless, there are ongoing debates about whose knowledge and vision should produce our cities, and how to incorporate more diverse voices. The most cited article, by far, in the history of the *Journal of the American Planning Association* is Sherry Arnstein's "A Ladder of Citizen Participation" (1969), which pointed out that planners were often substituting token strategies of consultation for meaningful partnership and power sharing. Few would disagree that we have failed to integrate true collaboration and co-creation into the planning and governance of cities. And until we do so, it will be hard to break down entrenched patterns of segregation and exclusion in our neighborhoods and schools.

Into this stalemate, the Y-PLAN (Youth-Plan, Learn, Act, Now) action research initiative brings a truly interdisciplinary and empowering strategy to transform cities for and with justice and joy. Over 20 years ago, Dr. Deborah

L. McKoy brought her vision to the UC Berkeley Department of City and Regional Planning. Why not, she asked, bring together the immense talent of the students at the best public university planning program in the country with the low-income students from the communities of color surrounding the university to engage together in planning cities? This seed turned into a global program that has touched the lives of thousands and built an intergenerational community of practice.

This book tells the story of Y-PLAN and makes the case for how integrating young people into planning processes weaves justice and joy into the urban fabric. At a moment when the crisis of housing precarity is destabilizing families and neighborhoods, transportation systems are at the brink of collapse, and climate change threatens the planet itself, we need to transform our cities. *Planning Our Cities With and For Young People* shows how youth apply their lived experience of housing, transportation, climate, and other challenges to developing – and implementing – creative visions for more sustainable and inclusive cities. For a practitioner audience, McKoy, Eppley, and Buss also provide invaluable advice on how to build the stakeholder networks that support youth engagement in city planning.

Y-PLAN grew out of a particular urban context, the San Francisco Bay Area, that embraces experimentation yet is ravaged by inequality. Over the decades, this strategy has proven its effectiveness across many different contexts. Its stories and approach will inspire alike those who have long grappled with entrenched urban and educational problems and the young people who are just learning how to express their visions and make a difference. It is our hope that by listening to our young people, we will begin to co-create cities that truly belong to all of us.

Karen Chapple
Professor and Chair, Department of
City and Regional Planning, UC Berkeley

References

Arnstein, S. R. (1969). A Ladder of Citizen Participation. *Journal of the American Institute of Planners, 35*(4), 216–224.

Rothstein, R. (2017). *The Color of Law: A Forgotten History of How Our Government Segregated America*. Liveright Publishing.

Preface

On March 12, 2020, we were on the UC Berkeley campus preparing for classes that engage youth in city planning – both in the Department of City and Regional Planning and in dozens of K–12 schools. That day, the news broke that COVID-19 was forcing the campus and local schools to close for at least "two weeks." Everything changed in that moment. Our upcoming event to celebrate the 20th anniversary of our Y-PLAN (Youth-Plan, Learn, Act, Now) action research initiative came to a screeching, heartbreaking halt. Our UC Berkeley seminar shifted online, and our K–12 classrooms shut down temporarily. Our civic partners scrambled to construct Zoom workspaces in their homes, and our most disadvantaged young people, those with insufficient access to technology, Wi-Fi, healthy food, and quiet spaces to study, were pushed further still from opportunity. In the midst of that heartbreak, an invitation to write this book about the power and promise of engaging young people in city planning emerged.

Together, we shifted from designing event posters and presentations to taking a deep dive into the theoretical core of our work that has evolved over two decades. We asked ourselves: What key insights and experiences would be of most value to share with local communities, scholars, and young people?

This past year we took a journey back in time, while simultaneously reimagining what the future of our cities, and the role of young people, could be. The theoretical and practical insights laid out in this book emanated from the hundreds of communities and classrooms we've worked in, spanning from pre-school to college. As co-authors, we share a commitment to help move the deep engagement of young people from the margins of city planning into the core of research and practice in the field.

For over a year, each of us (joined by our colleagues of many years) pored over the Y-PLAN archives of program files, artifacts, and articles, and student-generated original poetry, interview and survey data, field notes, artistic designs, and proposals for change. We revisited documentation, videos, and photographs of young people and adults listening, debating, and learning from and with each other as they tackled our cities' greatest challenges – from resilience to climate change to affordable housing to accessible transportation.

We also enjoyed the chance to be students again ourselves, as we dug into a wide range of literature and research from best practices in the field for how young people interact with, and are impacted by, short and long-range planning for our cities. It was inspiring, and humbling, to learn more about dozens of other powerful examples of communities engaging young people in city planning and social change around the world. We saw parallels with our work and ways we can augment each other. Each initiative adds student voices and experiences to a growing body of theory and practice around the country and world. In this book, we aim to share our Y-PLAN methodology with the global community of scholars and practitioners, while encouraging future generations to appreciate and incorporate the power and promise of young people in planning our cities.

As this manuscript heads to publication, hope is emerging for recovery from the COVID-19 global pandemic, amidst the devastation that has impacted so many of our young people and their communities. Scientists have developed vaccines, governments have crafted roll-out plans, and teachers have again proven their unrelenting dedication to their students. It is with emerging hope for the future that we present this book, built upon over two decades of shared experiences and insights. We invite our readers to join us in our ongoing and deepening commitment to work with young people to forge justice while generating joy in all of our communities.

PART I

In Theory and Practice

- Big picture

Introduction

Planning Cities for Justice and Joy

It was May 19, 2014, a warm spring day in the nation's capital, and the event hall was buzzing with anticipation and excitement. Over 150 young people along with university students, civic leaders, educators, and parents from Detroit to Dallas, New Orleans to New York, and more[1] were anxiously awaiting the arrival of Shaun Donovan, the Secretary of the US Department of Housing and Urban Development (HUD). The previous day, the young people had participated in an inspiring session within the distinguished conference chambers of the Russell Senate Office Building on Capitol Hill in Washington, DC. There, at a lively, interactive poster session, they engaged in critical dialogue with peers and national leaders, educators, industry heads, architects, and city planners. All of the students had taken on tough challenges posed by their local civic clients (city planners, community leaders, and government agencies), and they were sharing and getting feedback on their research-based proposals to address those issues. Now, the students were excited to share their work with Secretary Donovan. They lined the perimeter of the hall, proudly displaying professional-quality posters showcasing their visions for change in their communities.

Two young women, students from a New Orleans high school, were sharing last-minute tips with a young man from Queens, NY: "I would start with this quote about your cool maps app to help disabled residents locate needed resources. . . . I hear the Secretary is big on technology!" Hustling to move a few things around on his presentation board, he responded, "Thanks, good idea. I really like your ideas for the Claiborne Corridor – cool to see how you are proposing to bring art and liveliness to New Orleans' streets . . . still recovering from Katrina."

DOI: 10.4324/9781003141778-2

Moments later, two Secret Service members entered the event hall, scanning everything top to bottom. One tapped his left earpiece, indicating approval for Secretary Donovan, our nation's City Planner in Chief, to enter. Instead of heading directly to the podium to deliver brief remarks and head out ceremoniously, he lingered. To the delight of the young planners in the room, the Secretary visited all nine of the kiosks featuring students' detailed proposals for the futures of their respective cities. Shifting in role and spirit from a formal Cabinet official to an interested, engaged participant, Donovan stopped to speak with as many students as possible. He asked about the challenges they were tackling, the research they had conducted, and their visions for healthier, more equitable, and resilient cities. He stayed for a few extra moments with the young planner from Queens, curious to learn more about his proposal to leverage technology to assist people with hearing loss to navigate the city.

Finally, satisfied that he had a good sense of the scope of the students' visions to meet a range of challenges in their communities, Donovan stepped up to the podium. He spoke passionately about the importance of building the capacity of young people to contribute effectively to the planning and policy-making process. Pausing for a moment, the Secretary deviated from his prepared remarks. He wanted to share how grateful he was to be at this UC Berkeley National Youth Planning Summit: "I am really touched by your ideas and commitment to your cities. . . . I wish I had this opportunity to develop my skills, leadership, and visioning abilities about my community when I was in high school."

With that, the Secret Service team signaled for the Secretary to wrap up, but Donovan waved them off. "I'd like to take a few questions before I leave," he said. The students eagerly lined up at a mic on the side of the room. A young man from the South Bronx spoke up somewhat shyly, "First, I want to thank you for being here today. But I have to ask, why are rents getting so high in the Bronx? My family can't afford to live there anymore." Nodding his head in agreement, Donovan responded:

> Thank you for asking such an important question. As former NYC Housing Commissioner, I know just how right you are and spent many years trying to fix this – but there is much work yet to be done. We need to hear your voices and stories. The work I am seeing here should inspire city planners and civic leaders to value and use youth insights to create more equitable and sustainable communities. We

> need YOU – and everyone in this room – to help us come up with new ideas to make the changes that are so needed and deserved in all our cities.

At this summit, as young people[2] from Detroit to New Orleans to Oakland collaborated with educators, city leaders, community activists, and university students and faculty, they demonstrated how disparate groups can work together as partners to plan and lead cities. Applying their own insights to rigorous professional tools and engagement processes empowered these students to grapple with complex planning challenges and offer their own unique ideas and actionable proposals for change. In turn, it showed the powerful results of embedding public schools and young people, especially those facing deep economic and racial inequities like that young planner from Bronx, NY, into the fabric of planning our cities.

Image 1.1 At the 2014 UC Berkeley National Youth Planning Summit in Washington, DC, young women from New Orleans share their proposals for the revitalization of the Claiborne Corridor with US Secretary of Housing and Urban Development Shaun Donovan.

Source: UC Berkeley Center for Cities and Schools.

This introductory chapter sets the context for engaging young people in city planning. It explores two central tenets – justice and joy – in concert with authentic youth engagement particularly (though not exclusively) from our most marginalized, disadvantaged communities and their public schools. Although urban planners often do not recognize young people and public schools as critical stakeholders in their cities or value their potential, they are poised to provide insightful local knowledge to inform practices and strategies for planning cities. Inclusion of these often overlooked but essential perspectives sharpen our capacity to plan cities that truly serve everyone's needs in terms of social, economic, and racial equity and personal fulfillment. This chapter brings together progressive notions of city planning and education to offer a research-driven, interdisciplinary lens through which to more effectively re-imagine and design our cities.

Demonstrating this shift within the evolving youth engagement research and practice is UC Berkeley's Y-PLAN (Youth-Plan, Learn, Act, Now) action research initiative. Since its inception in 2000, this work has centered youth engagement in city planning through an intergenerational community of practice partnering young people, primarily low-income young Black, Indigenous, People of Color (BIPOC) students, with adults as agents of change. Today's work on youth engagement in city planning builds on and amplifies many years of engaged scholarship and inspiring practices across the globe. This framing, addressed in more depth throughout the book, envisions the ascent of the tenets of justice and joy precipitated by planning cities with and for young people who currently have the fewest social and economic opportunities.

Critical Underlying Tenets: Justice and Joy

Many scholars recognize the imperative of "Just Cities" (Fainstein, 2010; Marcuse et al., 2009; Griffin et al., 2015). When combined with a second imperative for so many young people, that of joy, these two essential and complex concepts form the foundation of this book's overall analysis. Partnerships with children and youth over many decades reveal that young people have a keen pragmatic understanding of the need and desire for both justice and joy in their lives and are extremely interested in contributing to solutions for the future – their future – that incorporate these ideas.

Just Cities

In an interview arguing for a new framing for progressive city planning, Fainstein stated, "It is my hope to shift the conversation within discussions of planning and public policy toward the character of urban areas . . . and redirect practitioners from their obsession with economic development to a concern with social equity" (Negrete, 2011). Fainstein (2010) described a "Just City" in her seminal work of that name, as one that boasts "investment and regulation [that] would produce equitable outcomes rather than support those already well off" (p. 3). In this way, the resulting just city would center equitable outcomes and support the residents who need it the most. The Harvard Graduate School of Design activated the theoretical understanding of a just city into practice with the establishment of the Just City Lab. The Lab provides support for cities seeking to develop their own understanding and definition of a just city through design research and a set of resources such as an index of 50 values from acceptance and aspiration to power and resilience (*Design for the Just City*, 2018).

One underlying tenet of just cities is the imperative of racial and economic equity for all. As Blackwell (2015) stated, "reimagining cities without a front-and-center commitment to equity, including racial equity, is a recipe for failure" (p. 61). She additionally called on city leaders to recognize that "America's history of racial exclusion repeats and deepens itself as low-income people of color are displaced from newly chic neighborhoods, shut out of all but the lowest-wage jobs, and isolated in aging, disinvested communities" (p. 62). Glover Blackwell's statements align well with Fainstein's (2010) call for greater focus on three core principles of democracy, diversity, and equity. Moreover, they both reflect the sentiments and insights of many urban young people who face adversities and challenges often far more formidable than those encountered in the lived experience of adult professionals involved in planning and governing our cities and regions.

As Connolly and Steil (2009) argued, seeking out such an understanding of the city is in part seeking to "realize the transformative potential of urban theory" (p. 1). They began by examining the everyday reality of city life and then worked to find ways to "reshape that reality and re-imagine that life" (p. 1). This included recognizing the harm and injustices that have come from urbanization and "the violence, insecurity, exploitation, and poverty that characterize urban life for many, as well as the physical expressions of unequal access to social, cultural, political, and economic capital that arise from intertwined divisions between race, class, and gender categories" (Connolly & Steil, 2009, p. 1).

That unequal access along lines of race, class, and gender impacts young people as well as adults, and as such, planning for just cities must address them and their needs accordingly. In the Marcuse et al. (2009) collection of essays titled *Searching for the Just City: Debates in Urban Theory and Practice*, only one essay referred explicitly to the leadership role of young people (p. 177). Meanwhile, Fainstein (2010) recognized that, "education is a crucial aspect of policy to be considered under the rubric of a just city" (p. 7), but she suggested that inclusion of education into a just cities framing needed be done separately, at another time. This acknowledgment presents an opportunity to authentically and explicitly engage young people, especially those from low-income BIPOC communities, and the public schools they attend, in planning a just city.

Much can be gained when robust initiatives create the conditions for students to bring their experientially acquired sense of justice into specific on-the-ground projects in their communities. When invited to collaborate with city planners and policymakers, young people bring distinctive perspectives engendered by their everyday lives. They analyze challenges before them critically and emotionally, with acuity and depth, because they have lived them. Many have been directly impacted by lack of affordable housing and access to healthy food and know first-hand about poverty, urban violence, and the fallout of displacement. They know their communities are disproportionately harmed by environmental pollution and lack of access to open space and natural resources. Given a platform for their voices to be heard, young people speak of the important role of home, of connection to place, and of social ties that bind their communities. All of their insights are based upon hard-earned local knowledge, and all are critical to planning what are called "just cities."

Including young people on the road to just cities necessitates a shift in the existing relationships between them and those with power to make decisions and direct research. This inclusion is particularly important considering that low-income BIPOC youth often differ from their civic leaders not only in age, but also in race, ethnicity, and socioeconomic status. The lack of shared experiences and backgrounds contributes to a gap between perspective and understanding, between what they see in the world around them and how they interpret it, and ultimately, between urban policies and young people's everyday lives.

Joyful Cities

In addition to opening up a much-needed critical examination of the very meaning of a just city, leveraging an intergenerational community of practice can also contribute to a joyful city. This term is certainly less common than just cities in the city planning realm but weighs heavily on the minds and hearts of young people everywhere. Joy is central to understanding the power and promise of young people in planning cities. While largely defined in the field of psychology, and recognized as complex, joy is understood not as an individual experience, but one that is shared, social in nature, and reflective of the positive and negative realities of daily life (Strawn, 2020). Importantly for the work of planning cities, it is often at the core of the hopeful visions children and youth express for the future. Thus, joy becomes the second central tenet in meaningful city planning initiatives involving young people.

Young people are acutely aware of their lived experience and, unlike many adults with years (if not decades) of disappointment and frustration from not getting their basic needs met in their cities, they bring hope and a sense of joyful possibility when invited to the planning table. The former Mayor of Bogotá Enrique Penalosa is likely one of the most-well cited leaders in calling for cities to be designed for children. Penalosa explained in 2004 that "In Bogotá, our goal was to make a city for all the children. . . . If a city is good for children, it will be good for everybody else" (Walljasper, 2004, p. 1). Capturing his vision of cities planned for children as "Cities of Joy," the well-known non-profit organization, Project for Public Spaces, has focused attention to the role of joy and needs of children in planning our cities.

While explicitly calling for joy within cities is not common, there is a growing literature on the relationship between sustainability and an aligned concept: happiness. Cloutier and Pfeiffer (2015) presented a new framework for sustainable community development that focuses on improving outcomes for happiness as a core goal. This framework included engagement practices such as happiness visioning, public participation, systems planning, and other interventions supporting sustainability. The authors posited that happiness offers a measure focused on the quality of human life that is universally understood and one that may lead to a far more sustainable future for everyone.

Beyond sustainability, Ballas (2013) expanded this construct to incorporate what is recognized as a more "subjective" but equally important measure of a city and regions' overall quality of life. He examined geographical and socio-economic contextual factors of overall well-being with an important focus on the impact of social and spatial inequalities, social justice and the city (p. 545). One of his key determinants of happiness focused on a city's overall income inequality and child well-being. He pointed to the need to understand and incorporate the difficulties faced by children in the US compared to other nations. He concluded with a call for city planning research to play a larger role in the emerging interdisciplinary work of the "science of happiness" recognizing the powerful role of place, and different needs and preferences of populations from the elderly and young people to a city's overall well-being and quality of life.

O'Brien (2005) further linked happiness in cities with children when she asserted that "Children's experience of transportation, while walking to school, is that of wonder, discovery, adventure, connection, and happiness" (p. 100). She also developed the idea of working toward "sustainable happiness," calling on city planners to better understand how a city focused on the pursuit of happiness "does not exploit other people, the environment, or future generations" (O'Brien, 2008, p. 7). Forging beyond that sustainable happiness, O'Brien (2008) went so far as to link joy to the culture of childhood itself, stating that "Perhaps the cultural integrity that children are accessing [in active transportation/walking to school] is the culture of childhood. A more venturesome view would be to see this as accessing a culture of joy" (p. 101).

Evolution of Young People as Planners

Young people under the age of 18 are typically between a quarter and a third of a city's population in the US. Still, scholars like Ragan (2013) comment that "youth have not been seen as a demographic important enough to engage with . . . and they are not a focus for governments or funding agencies." As discussed earlier in this chapter, urban planners typically do not recognize young people and public schools as critical stakeholders in their cities or value their potential to provide insightful local knowledge to inform practices and strategies for planning cities.

Conventional Understanding of Young People in Planning Discourse

The canon of city planning, those works taught in universities to prepare practitioners and academics alike, largely does not consider the role or potential of young people. For example, in *Cities of Tomorrow* (Hall, 2002), one might expect discussion of the group of individuals who will lead our cities in the future, the young people of today. While Hall lamented that young people are "often almost ignored and largely rejected by their contemporaries" (p. 2), he goes on to do largely the same thing. For example, in his chapter titled "Cities of Imagination," Hall makes no reference to young people, the very group whose imaginations are largely unbounded.

Even when city planning texts do acknowledge the needs of young people, they rarely incorporate young people into the actual processes of planning. In the most recent edition of *Contemporary Urban Planning*, John Levy (2016) mentioned consideration of routes to school for street safety, the differing infrastructure impacts on children and seniors, and the potential long-term benefits of visiting elementary-aged students in classrooms. These suggestions are not new to the field. Nearly sixty decades earlier, leading to her push for "eyes on the street," Jane Jacobs (1961) drew on real life examples, and her own child's experience, to explain that "children in cities need a variety of places in which to play and learn" and "an unspecialized outdoor home base from which to play, hang around in, and to help form their notions of the world" (p. 80). Although these texts have demonstrated an understanding of the presence of young people in a city and some consideration of their observed needs, the authors have neglected to include how young people themselves could impact the city planning process. Imagine the increased understanding attained by directly asking for young people's views on planning as part of a rigorous planning process that elevates them as legitimate participants with unique perspectives and expertise and prepares them to function in that capacity.

Movement Forward

Planning scholars and advocates for more democratic and inclusive participation planted seeds decades ago for making room to include young people. Arnstein (1969) put forward one of the most influential models of democratic public participation, arguing that genuine "participation" requires the redistribution of power. In putting forth the "Ladder of Participation," she asserted that citizen participation is citizen power. Without the reallocation of power, seen as both money and decision making, participation simply "allows the powerholders to claim that all sides were considered, but makes it possible for only some of those sides to benefit. It maintains the status quo" (Arnstein, 1969, p. 216). As important today as it was in 1969, she recognized the need for inclusion of residents of all races and socio-economic statuses in any meaningful participation.

Thirty years later, Hart (1997) customized Arnstein's "Ladder of Participation" for those aspiring to authentically engage young people in community building and action projects. Hart constructed several "rungs" on the ladder to help people move beyond manipulation and tokenism to meaningful, substantive collaboration between youth and adults. His aspirational rung was youth-led "activities in which decision-making is shared between youth and adults working as equal partners" (p. 45). In subsequent years he has modified his "ladder" to reflect and address the asymmetrical power relations between adults and youth (Hart, 2008). Hart and others now strive to continue to equalize the energy between young people and adults while cultivating respect for the different qualities and capabilities that each brings to the table.

Hart and many other geographers, sociologists, landscape architects, and planners have worked at the intersection between their respective disciplines to advocate for youth engagement in city design and policy development. Their work and Hart's ladder metaphor have inspired architects, planners, educators, and others working on city planning projects with children and youth. However, for the most part, young people's insights have not been consistently adopted, integrated, or codified into planning practice within the university pipeline or city administrations.

Hart's work has also informed, and was informed by, global efforts to position young people as critical to cities. One of the most significant models is the Child Friendly Cities Initiative (CFCI), led by the United Nations International Children's Emergency Fund (UNICEF). CFCI supports municipal governments in realizing the rights of children at the local level using the United Nations Convention of the Rights of the Child (UNCRC) (United Nations, 1989). It extends social justice principles that evolved from public engagement to include the rights of children and youth, including the right of young people to participate in planning and local decision-making. Since its inception in 1996, CFCI has been adopted in over 3,000 municipalities across more than 40 countries, impacting an estimated 30 million children and young people. Those cities have committed to become official Child Friendly Cities, ensuring "the voices, needs, priorities and rights of children are an integral part of public policies, programmes and decisions" (*What Is a Child-Friendly City?*, n.d.).

David Driskell's (2002) *Creating Better Cities with Children and Youth: A Manual for Participation* further built on the theoretical underpinnings about young people's participation formulated by Hart and others, while focusing more on a practical application of those theories. His book demonstrated how critically important it is for children and youth to engage with adult policymakers to influence and inform decisions that profoundly affect the quality of everyone's lives. It showed how access to young people's knowledge – both intuitive and based on their lived experience – can be a powerful lever for change. In arguing passionately that the fresh perspectives of youth "may be exactly what is needed to see clearly into the realm of new possibilities," he declared, "It is my strong conviction that tapping into young people's ideas and reflections is essential to improving our cities" (Driskell, 2002, p. 13). Driskell went on to co-found Growing Up Boulder (GUB) in 2009, while serving as the Executive Director of Planning, Housing and Sustainability for the City of Boulder, CO. GUB is now an established program of the University of Colorado, Boulder (*About Us*, 2015).

Driskell (2002) laid the groundwork for Victoria Derr et al.'s (2018) meticulously detailed and substantive *Placemaking with Children and Youth: Participatory Practices for Planning Sustainable Communities*. This comprehensive handbook expanded upon the theory and practice articulated in both Hart and Driskell's works, making the clear case that young people are experts about their own neighborhoods and communities. Designed as a guide for adults, it illuminated a range of ways in which adults can be allies and help young people develop their ideas and build their capacity to respectfully engage with adults and systems in ways that engender fruitful results. Around the same time, Bishop and Corkery's (2017) *Designing Cities with Children and Young People: Beyond Playgrounds and Skate Parks* brought an international and interdisciplinary perspective on how planners, designers, and policy makers can include children and youth in planning and design of the built, urban environment. This work bridged a scholarship, research, and practice gap by informing how young people can share their urban design insights with initiatives around the world.

As the topic of engaging children and youth in planning continues to grow in research and practice today, adoption of meaningful changes to support youth inclusion in planning remains sluggish in the field. In a review of 25 years of progress since the passage of the UNCRC, Lansdown (2014) warned, "Most children in the world continue to be denied a voice, and where progress has been made, it is often inconsistent and partial" (p. 176). He presented seven specific recommendations, including calls to professionalize engagement beyond isolated, project-based opportunities dependent on the sporadic goodwill of adults and short-term funding, innovative forms of authentic and shared accountability, and learning and building on important lessons from the past.

Pushing the Field Forward

More recently, in the *Journal of the American Planning Association*'s "Including Youth in the Ladder of Citizen Engagement," Botchwey et al. (2019) outlined three case studies engaging youth directly in planning initiatives, including UC Berkeley's Y-PLAN initiative, and advocated for three new rungs in Hart's ladder of citizen engagement in planning. Those rungs – consent, advocacy, and incorporation – would sit just below partnership. In discussing Y-PLAN projects, the authors noted that "projects between 2003 and 2005 offered youth more power within planning processes, and they slowly expanded power to eventually approximate partnership" (Botchwey et al., 2019, p. 262). They concluded that "planners must listen when youth are exercising the right to express themselves. Youth have much to teach planning practitioners about their neighborhoods and play spaces" (Botchwey et al., 2019, p. 268). Young people offer a wealth of knowledge and much potential to improve our cities, but only when they are at the table and planners are prepared to hear what is being communicated and act on what they hear. The Y-PLAN methodology and practice continue to grow and deepen. The critical importance of authentic engagement of low-income BIPOC youth is a central aspect of this work, as illustrated in the Part II case studies.

Two recent articles shared this assertion and warned of potential obstacles and pitfalls to avoid. First, Clay and Turner (2021) offered critical insight into the subtle ways "adult allies" all too often co-opt youth activist agendas, in essence using young people to support and buttress their own work and perspectives, rather than enabling youth to assert their own visions and priorities. Additionally, Mansfield et al. (2021) conducted an extensive literature review of 87 articles examining what is unknown about the barriers and enablers of young people's participation in planning. Most importantly, these authors argued for the need for deeper analysis of institutional impacts, particularly those that impact the most vulnerable and marginalized populations and settings. Mansfield et al. (2021) concluded that "Excluding the most vulnerable of scenarios misses the opportunity to understand the impact of participation on children's vulnerability in extreme situations . . . and ignores the perpetuation of the vulnerability of children through continued exclusion" (p. 13).

This book recognizes and builds on such research and professional practices of the growing number of youths in planning programs across the US and globally. Adding to that existing body of work, this book presents in-depth discussions of nine Y-PLAN case studies engaging young people in resilience, housing, and transportation planning projects. Of critical importance, the majority of Y-PLAN students are low-income, BIPOC, and attend Title I schools, which by definition have high percentages of children from low-income families (Title I, Part A Program, 2018). In other words, they are the "most vulnerable" students whom Mansfield et al. (2021) feared are too often excluded. Accessing students directly through their public school classrooms, during the school day, provides for the most equitable sampling of the community, as public education is the only remaining institution that is charged to reach all young people, including those from historically marginalized populations. Moreover, planning scholars have argued "repositioning public schools as neighborhood-based anchor institutions advances efforts to use community development as a mechanism to empower residents and augment community control in the urban revitalization process" (Patterson & Silverman, 2014, p. xv). In this way, positioning low-income BIPOC youth to engage with community and city leaders within their own classrooms reaches students more equitably and leverages the untapped potential of public schools in improving entire communities.

While recognizing the growing body of research and literature on youth engagement in city planning and policy-making, for the most part youth participation in city planning remains disconnected from research in the field of education. The UC Berkeley Y-PLAN initiative seeks to support that connection by engaging directly with education research and building upon progressive education theories and research. Y-PLAN is grounded in "Communities of Practice" (CoP), a critical social theory that bridges the typically siloed fields of city planning and education (McKoy & Vincent, 2005). As defined by Jean Lave and Etienne Wenger (1991), communities of practice are groups of people who share a concern or a passion for something they do, a shared practice, and learn how to do it better as they interact regularly. The concept of a CoP relies upon the notion that learning is human nature, it is inherently social and participatory, and that educational activities must engage people as learning communities to achieve a larger impact. According to Wenger (1998), "building complex social relationships around meaningful activities requires genuine practices in which taking charge of learning becomes the enterprise of a community" (p. 272). Through the Y-PLAN methodology (as described in Chapter 3), young people and their educators, planners, leaders, and policymakers work together to form an intergenerational CoP as seen in Figure 1.1. Across the country and around

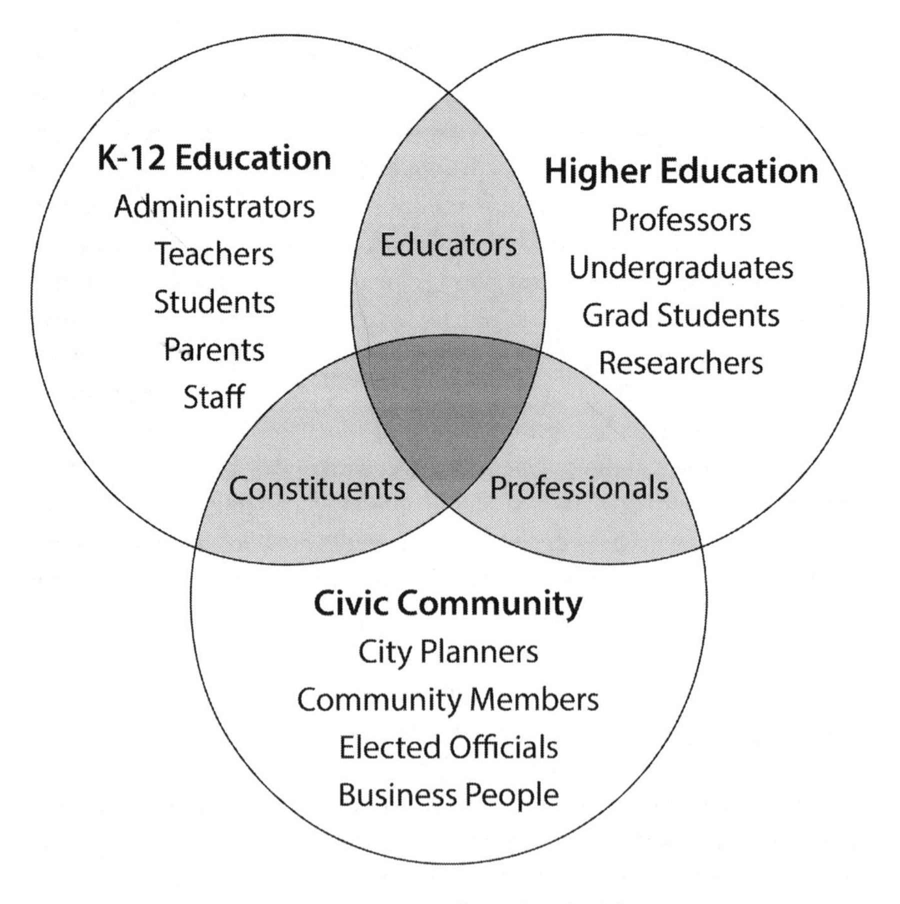

Figure 1.1 Community of Practice: Participants.
Source: UC Berkeley Center for Cities and Schools.

the globe, Y-PLAN participants conduct projects in the context of their own local communities, bridging gaps between cities and schools and across the sociocultural divides of age, race, socio-economic status, and educational attainment.

Through civic learning experiences in public school classrooms, students have addressed a range of issues such as housing insecurity, displacement, transportation access, economic development, and community resilience. Y-PLAN is distinguished from other programs working to engage youth in city planning by a set of core conditions. These conditions, include partnering young people with an authentic civic client, maintaining a social justice and equity focus, keeping the projects place-based, implementing a school-based curriculum, and adhering to a rigorous 5-step research methodology. Chapter 3 will discuss each of these conditions in greater detail.

As so many civic leaders have said, engaging young people brings a fresh perspective and vision for everyone at the planning table. Planning scholars have also recognized the importance and challenges of visioning in city planning (Gaffikin & Sterrett, 2006; Shipley, 2002). Considering planning for the future of a city-region's growing complexity and scale, Neuman and Hull (2009) recognized that "if we cannot imagine, then we cannot manage" (p. 782). Ache (2017) built on that sentiment, stating that "if actors are incapable to develop an imagination, or as is suggested . . . a vision or an idea, they will not be able to manage the growing urban complexity" (Ache, 2017, p. 1). The opportunity presented by these statements is to meet the challenge to increase visioning within planning for cities. Who better to advance the work and vision of planning cities for more justice and joy than the very young people from our most marginalized and high need communities, with the most at stake. Who better to bring "this sense of possibility . . . and seeing what is not yet there, instead of focusing on what is given" (Ache, 2017, p. 3).

Structure of this Book

This book presents the power and promise of engaging low-income and BIPOC young people and the public schools they attend in planning just and joyful cities. Part I, starts in Chapter 2 by building on the literature presented here with a review of research centering youth and community participation in city planning processes and literature on youth agency. This leads to the development of a theory of change for planning just and joyful cities for and with young people, where everyone learns to work as intergenerational communities of practice toward the transformation of our cities. Chapter 3, digs deeper into how this theory is activated on one model, UC Berkeley's Y-PLAN initiative. Through this lens of change and development, the authors examine how civic leaders and city planners can work with teachers and community members to learn from and with children and youth about how their neighborhoods, transit systems, and schools are, and are not, working for them. As will be shown, the key is to ensure that young people come to planning processes not as window dressing, but as genuine agents of change who work with policymakers to present new ideas for their future, supported by solid data and other evidence.

Part II presents research and practice concerning youth in city planning from multiple perspectives and within three core fields of professional planning practice and policy: resilience, housing, and transportation. While young people are essential contributors to each of those sectors, Part II shows that the input of professional planners and young people differs, and this difference refines the discourse on housing, deepens it within transportation, and serves to redefine resilience entirely. Each chapter reviews current literature, describes what happens when young people are added into the planning mix, and enhances this understanding using case studies from UC Berkeley's Y-PLAN initiative. Each begins with a vignette to center youth voices and show the range of ways young people directly inform this discourse and planning initiatives.

In Chapter 4, we find that when considering resilience, young people call for planners and civic leaders to take immediate and equitable action with respect to climate change now to preserve our future. In planning for resilience, our young people begin by turning the discussion on its head, redefining the very concept itself. Echoing the sentiments heard in classrooms from New York to Oakland, one young planner from the Tohoku region of Japan declared, "We are strong and can rise above challenging circumstances. We *are* resilience." In redefining resilience, these young people flip the script on what resilience can pragmatically mean – instead of objects that are built, young people view their school communities as untapped assets that can provide critical social infrastructure in the face of natural disasters and sea level rise, if they are given adequate support and resources.

In Chapter 5, we observe how, while working on questions related to housing, young people support many of the policies that professionals are

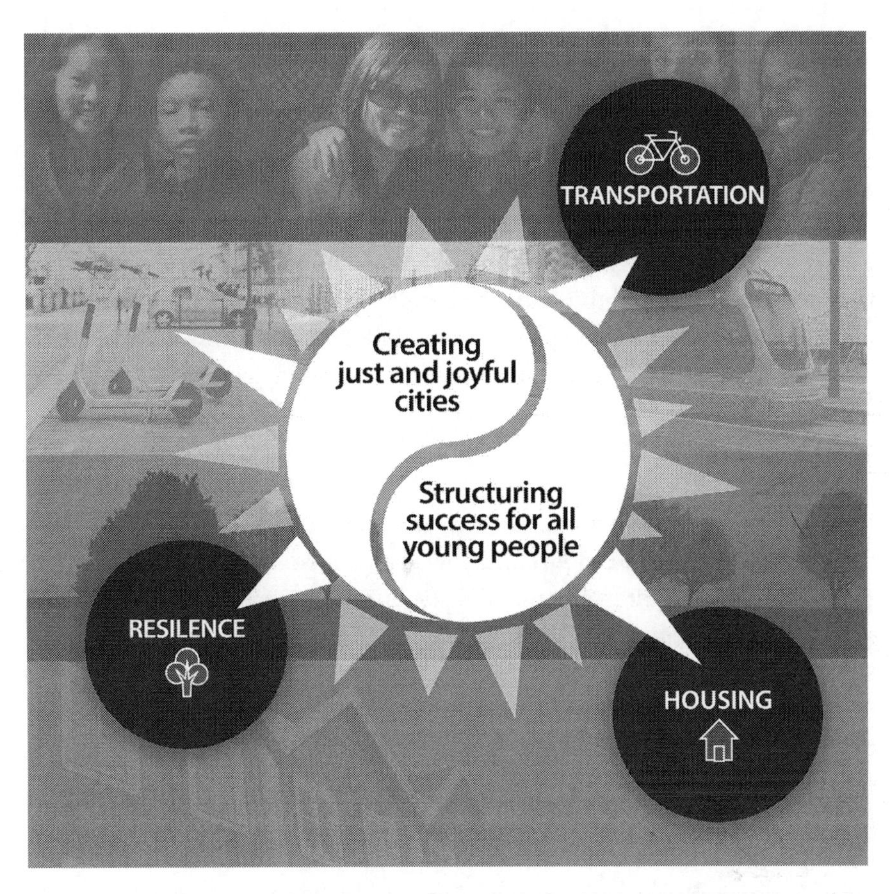

Figure 1.2 Elements and Goals of a Just and Joyful City: Resilience, Housing, and Transportation.

Source: UC Berkeley Center for Cities and Schools.

advancing, showing how young people's experience of housing is not dissimilar to that of adults. Their experiences add nuance within the existing discourse, and their insights often differ in more subtle, but critical ways. They call for more affordable, safe, comfortable housing for families and teachers located near schools, relevant amenities, and transit that prioritizes the needs of existing residents.

In contrast, in Chapter 6, we see that when young people are asked to grapple with transportation issues, it becomes clear that they navigate our transportation networks differently than adults. They have fewer choices in transportation modes and often have more financial and time constraints. As a result, young people's experiences differ categorically from those of adults. While their parents might navigate primarily by personal automobile, most low-income young people travel by foot, bike, scooter, skateboard, city bus, and increasingly shared mobility systems to school, home, work, and leisure activities. They often do so without the safety net of a credit card or sometimes a cell phone, and as a result, they understand and navigate the transportation networks entirely differently than the adults around them. Young people recommend new technologies and alternatives to foster greater independence and provide them with safe, reliable, and equitable access to opportunities within their schools, cities, and region.

Despite these differing approaches, what is clear across youth engagement in city planning projects in widely diverse locations is that young people reject that these three sectors are separate – instead, they see them as interconnected and interdependent. Their proposals include changes needed across all three simultaneously, affirming efforts to move toward just and joyful cities. In Chapter 4, the Japanese youth leveraged their experiences in the aftermath of the 2011 Great East Japan Earthquake to support a resilience plan in Oakland, California. Meanwhile, in Chapter 5, students from East Palo Alto, one of the few remaining low-income communities in Silicon Valley, tasked with addressing housing displacement, reject the notion of building in an environmentally sensitive area, despite their urgent call for increasing the housing stock. Finally, in Chapter 6, we view how, when conducting a transportation project, students from Oakland offer transit-oriented development recommendations from parklets to housing to community development spaces and public safety improvements. Just as bridges between our cities and our schools can facilitate the improvement of each institution, young planners approach their projects with a comprehensive and intersectional vision for just and joyful cities.

Part III of this book calls upon planners and policymakers today to recognize that we will never realize our highest aspirations until we incorporate the power and promise of young people, their schools, and educators into the process of planning. Chapter 7, titled "The Essentials," presents the "Six Essentials for Planning Just and Joyful Cities," a foundation to guide the city planning field forward. The "Essentials" involve prioritizing the need for young people's safety and stability, as all members of an intergenerational community of practice develop mutual understanding with one another, sharing and listening across institutional boundaries and silos. Over time, trust and relationships grow as participants cultivate genuine connections, engaging not just with one age group in school, but recognizing the power of all ages to contribute valuable insights and ideas for cities' growth and development. In the process, professionals increasingly share their skills and tools, developing a shared sense of responsibility with young people as they continue to professionalize partnerships between adults and youth. As the partnerships look to the future, they bridge gaps between disparate networks, discourses, and perspectives, and begin to recognize the powerful roles that connectivity and social networks hold for people of all ages. Finally, Chapter 8 reviews how decades of research and inspiring practices around the globe demonstrate the urgency of diversifying our pipeline of planners to include young people, while expanding the capacity of planners and reimagining the field today. It is painful to envision the costs of *not* bringing these insightful voices to the table.

Imagine what could happen if we worked together to build strong and lasting relationships between community leaders and the low-income BIPOC youth living in the cities they are planning. Imagine what might happen if we tapped into the millions of young people across the country and the world and unleashed their ideas and inspiration throughout our urbanizing city centers. Imagine if young people felt empowered to use their personal experiences and fresh insights to improve their neighborhoods and cities. Imagine where communities could be if we prepared future leaders to know, through their own experience, the power of working with young people to generate a shared vision of what makes a city just and joyful.

Imagined together, the future will be brighter for us all.

Notes

1 Youth and adult representatives from the following cities attended the 2014 UC Berkeley National Youth Planning Summit: Dallas, Detroit, New York (Bronx, Manhattan, and Queens), New Orleans, Oakland, Berkeley, San Francisco, Washington DC. Presentation boards of global Y-PLAN initiatives from Japan, Mali, Burkina Faso, Cote d'Ivoire, Niger, and Mauritania were also featured.

2 There are many differing definitions of what ages are considered to refer to children, youth, and young people. This book refers to "children" as birth to 11 years (largely elementary school), "youth" as 12–18, and "young people" as a more inclusive term reflective of all ages under 18.

References

About Us. (2015). Growing Up Boulder. www.growingupboulder.org/about-us.html

Ache, P. (2017). Vision Making in Large Urban Settings: Unleashing Anticipation? In R. Poli (Ed.), *Handbook of Anticipation: Theoretical and Applied Aspects of the Use of Future in Decision Making* (pp. 1–21). Springer International Publishing. https://doi.org/10.1007/978-3-319-31737-3_43-1

Arnstein, S. R. (1969). A Ladder of Citizen Participation. *Journal of the American Institute of Planners*, *35*(4), 216–224. https://doi.org/10.1080/01944366908977225

Ballas, D. (2013). What Makes a "Happy City"? *Cities*, *32*, S39–S50. https://doi.org/10.1016/j.cities.2013.04.009

Bishop, K., & Corkery, L. (Eds.). (2017). *Designing Cities with Children and Young People: Beyond Playgrounds and Skate Parks* (1st ed.). Routledge.

Blackwell, A. G. (2015, October 23). The Case for All in Cities. *The Nature of Cities*. https://www.thenatureofcities.com/2015/10/23/the-case-for-all-in-cities/

Botchwey, N. D., Johnson, N., O'Connell, L. K., & Kim, A. J. (2019). Including Youth in the Ladder of Citizen Participation: Adding Rungs of Consent, Advocacy, and Incorporation. *Journal of the American Planning Association*, *85*(3), 255–270. https://doi.org/10.1080/01944363.2019.1616319

Clay, K. L., & Turner, D. C., I. I. I. (2021). "Maybe You Should Try It This Way Instead": Youth Activism Amid Managerialist Subterfuge. *American Educational Research Journal*, *58*(2), 386–419. https://doi.org/10.3102/0002831221993476

Cloutier, S., & Pfeiffer, D. (2015). Sustainability Through Happiness: A Framework for Sustainable Development. *Sustainable Development*, *23*(5), 317–327. https://doi.org/10.1002/sd.1593

Connolly, J., & Steil, J. (2009). Introduction: Finding Justice in the City. In *Searching for the Just City: Debates in Urban Theory and Practice*. Routledge.

Derr, V., Chawla, L., & Mintzer, M. (2018). *Placemaking with Children and Youth: Participatory Practices for Planning Sustainable Communities*. New Village Press.

Design for the Just City. (2018). Design for the Just City. www.designforthejustcity.org/about

Driskell, D. (2002). *Creating Better Cities with Children and Youth: A Manual for Participation, 1st Edition (Paperback) – Routledge*. Routledge.

Fainstein, S. S. (2010). *The Just City*. Cornell University Press. www.jstor.org/stable/10.7591/j.ctt7zhwt

Gaffikin, F., & Sterrett, K. (2006). New Visions for Old Cities: The Role of Visioning in Planning. *Planning Theory & Practice*, *7*(2), 159–178. https://doi.org/10.1080/14649350600673070

Griffin, T., Cohen, A., & Maddox, D. (2015, October 19). *The Just City Essays: 26 Visions for Urban Equity, Inclusivity and Opportunity*. https://nextcity.org/features/view/just-city-essys-toni-griffin-theaster-gates-angela-glover-blackwell

Hall, P. (2002). *Cities of Tomorrow: An Intellectual History of Urban Planning and Design Since 1880* (3rd ed.). Blackwell Publishing.

Hart, R. A. (1997). *Children's Participation: The Theory and Practice of Involving Young Citizens in Community Development and Environmental Care*. Routledge. www.routledge.com/Childrens-Participation-The-Theory-and-Practice-of-Involving-Young-Citizens/Hart/p/book/9781853833229

Hart, R. A. (2008). Stepping Back from "The Ladder": Reflections on a Model of Participatory Work with Children. In A. Reid, B. B. Jensen, J. Nikel, & V. Simovska (Eds.), *Participation and Learning: Perspectives on Education and the Environment, Health and Sustainability* (pp. 19–31). Springer Netherlands. https://doi.org/10.1007/978-1-4020-6416-6_2

Jacobs, J. (1961). *The Death and Life of Great American Cities*. Random House.

Lansdown, G. (2014). 25 Years of UNCRC: Lessons Learned in Children's Participation. *Canadian Journal of Children's Rights/Revue Canadienne Des Droits Des Enfants, 1*(1). https://doi.org/10.22215/cjcr.v1i1.12

Lave, J., & Wenger, E. (1991). *Situated Learning: Legitimate Peripheral Participation* (1st ed.). Cambridge University Press.

Levy, J. (2016). *Contemporary Urban Planning* (11th revised ed.). Routledge. www.routledge.com/Contemporary-Urban-Planning-11th-Edition/Levy/p/book/9781138666382

Mansfield, R. G., Batagol, B., & Raven, R. (2021). "Critical Agents of Change?": Opportunities and Limits to Children's Participation in Urban Planning. *Journal of Planning Literature*, 0885412220988645. https://doi.org/10.1177/0885412220988645

Marcuse, P., Connolly, J., Novy, J., Olivo, I., Potter, C., & Steil, J. (Eds.). (2009). *Searching for the Just City: Debates in Urban Theory and Practice* (1st ed.). Routledge.

McKoy, D., & Vincent, J. (2005). The Center for Cities & Schools: Connecting Research and Policy Agendas. *Berkeley Planning Journal, 18*(1). https://escholarship.org/uc/item/1n55g80x

Negrete, V. (2011, July 7). *The Just City*. Planetizen – Urban Planning News, Jobs, and Education. www.planetizen.com/node/50215

Neuman, M., & Hull, A. (2009). The Futures of the City Region. *Regional Studies, 43*(6), 777–787. https://doi.org/10.1080/00343400903037511

O'Brien, C. (2005). Planning for Sustainable Happiness: Harmonizing Our Internal and External Landscapes. *Undefined*. /paper/Planning-for-Sustainable-Happiness%3A-Harmonizing-Our-O%27brien/076ed43b37b65cc8f55914ef3fb6578e4126c427

O'Brien, C. (2008). Sustainable Happiness: How Happiness Studies Can Contribute to a More Sustainable Future. *Canadian Psychology/Psychologie Canadienne, 49*(4), 289–295. https://doi.org/10.1037/a0013235

Patterson, K. L., & Silverman, R. M. (Eds.). (2014). *Schools and Urban Revitalization: Rethinking Institutions and Community Development* (Vol. 1). Routledge.

Ragan, D. (2013). *Cities of Youth: Cities of Prosperity*. UN Habitat. https://unhabitat.org/books/cities-of-youth-cities-of-prosperity/

Shipley, R. (2002). Visioning in Planning: Is the Practice Based on Sound Theory? *Environment and Planning A: Economy and Space, 34*(1), 7–22. https://doi.org/10.1068/a3461

Strawn, B. D. (2020). Contextual, Embodied and Clinical Joy. *The Journal of Positive Psychology, 15*(1), 63–66. https://doi.org/10.1080/17439760.2019.1685573

Title I, Part A Program. (2018, November 7). [Program Home Page]. US Department of Education (ED). https://www2.ed.gov/programs/titleiparta/index.html

United Nations. (1989). *Convention on the Rights of the Child (UNCRC)*. https://www.ohchr.org/en/professionalinterest/pages/crc.aspx

Walljasper, J. (2004, October 31). *Cities of Joy*. www.pps.org/article/november2004joy-2

Wenger, E. (1998). *Communities of Practice: Learning, Meaning, and Identity*. Cambridge University Press.

What Is a Child-friendly City? (n.d.). UNICEF: Child Friendly Cities Initiative. Retrieved March 7, 2021, from https://childfriendlycities.org/what-is-a-child-friendly-city/

youth agency
CoP = (intergenerational) Communities of Practice
Community Participation

Professionalizing partnerships

UC Berkeley Y-Plan Iniatative

Tenents: joy & justice

Envisioning > managing

2 Theory of Change

- Looking at affordable housing and displacement = the civic issue used to explain theory in this chapter

Introduction

> In my own words, affordable housing means houses that fit people's salaries. What I mean when I say that they fit people's salary is that they don't have to pay more than they can earn at work. These houses can be an opportunity for people that don't have enough money to pay the rent.

The clarity and precision of this definition, offered by eighth-grader Liliana[1] during the final rehearsal for her Y-PLAN (Youth-Plan, Learn, Act, Now) presentation, prompted her classmates, teacher, and facilitator to encourage her to speak first during the next day's final digital roundtable. One year earlier, as a recent immigrant, Liliana had participated in her class's Y-PLAN project completely in Spanish, the only language she spoke at the time. She had contributed to her team's poster, advocating "*educar a la comunidad para que dejan de contaminar la tierra ya que eso daña a la atmósfera y nadie sabe si con este daño lleguemos a vivir hasta el 2050*" [educate the community so that they stop polluting the Earth since that damages the atmosphere and nobody knows if with this damage we will live until 2050]. Despite her passion for the project, she had watched silently as her team presented. Now, one year later, Liliana proudly accepted the opportunity to present first. In one year, she had developed not only the language skills to engage fully in a project in her second language, but also the confidence to lead it, by presenting to professionals from across the state through video conferencing technology.

DOI: 10.4324/9781003141778-3

Image 2.1 At the UC Berkeley Regional Youth Planning Summit in 2019, students from Escuela Popular present their bilingual proposals for housing and transportation to civic leaders.

Source: Robinson Kuntz.

This forum took place in May, 2020 in San Jose, California. At the time, the world was in what we would later learn to be just the beginning stages of the global COVID-19 pandemic. Schools were shuttered and replaced with hastily-designed and executed "distance learning" formats for the final months of the 2019–2020 academic year. School attendance plummeted across the country, and teachers struggled to connect with students, especially those who did not have access to suddenly essential computers, Wi-Fi, and sufficient space at home to carry out and complete their studies. While the pandemic impacted everyone, it did so inequitably, exacerbating existing crises, such as the lack of affordable housing, displacement, the digital divide, racism, and homelessness. These issues were the subject of the Y-PLAN project for Liliana and her class of young scholars from Escuela Popular, a public school in San Jose populated by immigrant students whose families have immigrated from Mexico and Central America. Many of them had experienced these crises personally.

Despite the low attendance nationwide through the initial shelter-in-place orders, this project enjoyed nearly full student participation throughout its duration. The final digital roundtable brought local leaders, university scholars, and regional planners from across California together to hear the Escuela Popular students' recommendations. Through the course of the project, these young people gained access to professional planners and academics and to the tools of their trades. They used these tools as they conducted and analyzed surveys and interviews in both English and Spanish. As part of a site mapping tour in the final days before the state locked down for COVID-19, the students navigated their city, viewing it through the lens of housing access and affordability. Having persisted in mastering the new online world, Liliana set the tone for the students' presentation. She made abstract concepts, such as housing affordability, personal and relatable, and her classmates followed suit. During the roundtable, these middle schoolers – through their oral and visual presentations – modeled the critical importance of cultivating relationships in the effort to transform and stabilize communities facing housing displacement. Their suggestions featured realizable short-term goals, such as bringing tenants and landlords together to engage in dialogue over a meal, promoting mutual understanding. They also proposed longer term visions, such as creating community gardens designed around central barbecue areas with picnic tables to encourage gathering. Their presentations reminded the adults of the power of interpersonal connections across divisions of age, race, and socioeconomic status. As the video call concluded, their school director thanked the students for "giving us this moment of inspiration [and] offering a new way of thinking. We often pit landlords and tenants against each other, and maybe we should stop and do something different if we want different results."

All too often, well-intentioned adults, including city planners, regard youth engagement and input as nice but not necessary and integral to the process of change. As young planners generate a wide range of innovative proposals drawing from both their lived experience and emerging knowledge of city planning professional practices, they demonstrate that the insights of diverse youth are, in fact, essential. In doing so, they disrupt stereotypes and assumptions about how young people learn, how they access and experience resilience, how they navigate their cities, and how they and their families sustain and transform their communities. After reviewing literature that affirms the need to embed young people and public school practitioners in city planning now, this chapter dives deeper into analysis and conclusions drawn from planning for and with young people. It offers an alternative to traditional methods of public participation in planning that

> . . . do not achieve genuine participation in planning or other decisions; . . . satisfy members of the public that they are being heard; . . . improve the decisions that agencies and public officials make; [nor] incorporate a broad spectrum of the public.
>
> (Innes & Booher, 2004, p. 419)

Instead, it replaces these methods that "often antagonize the members of the public who do try to work with them" and "pit citizens against each other" (Innes & Booher, 2004, p. 419) with a theory of change striving to build more just and joyful cities for and with young people.

Displacement: Past and Present

Just as segregation in schools has historically mirrored that of our cities, impacts of displacement devastate not only our low-income communities but also their schools. Displacement in this context refers to circumstances in which households and families are driven out of their communities or are unable to relocate into a neighborhood that was "previously accessible to them because of conditions beyond their control" (*Resources | Urban Displacement Project*, 2021). While it is widely accepted that school demographics are an inevitable result of the racial composition of neighborhood attendance areas, Rothstein (2017) contends that the true link is more iterative. In the era of Separate but Equal, by "placing the only schools that served African American children in designated African American neighborhoods and providing no transportation for Black students who lived elsewhere," Black families were compelled to seek housing there, thus creating and reinforcing neighborhood segregation (p. 132). In this way, opening, closing, or relocating schools legally restricted to serving Black or white children became a pervasive method for city and regional governments to segregate housing and neighborhoods.

These historical trends have alarming implications amidst today's landscape of school closures. Public school enrollment numbers are declining in many gentrifying cities due to both a decrease in families in general and higher rates of private school attendance among the wealthier, increasingly white families, who now populate many formerly low-income, Black, Indigenous, People of Color (BIPOC) communities. Pearman (2019) found that "schools located in gentrified neighborhoods nationwide now serve around

32,000 fewer students than comparable schools located in non-gentrified areas, even if these two sets of schools served similar numbers of students before gentrification began" (p. 209). When enrollment numbers decline, cities have too many schools to serve their student population, and school closures follow.

The complex mix of land-use decisions and assessing what is economically efficient is another key determinant. Bierbaum (2018) argued that in making decisions about facilities, schools assume the role of planners. In doing so, they legitimize decisions about school closures and their racially disparate impacts, and they become "deeply engaged in the racialized and politicized making and unmaking of places" (p. 2). Bierbaum demonstrated that when school districts act like technocratic city planners, choosing schools for closure based on land use priorities, rather than the protection of community networks, city dwellers lose social anchors. Even when families whose children once attended the now-closed schools are free to select among "better" schools without legal racial restrictions, they are forced to choose between two forms of disruption: traveling (sometimes very far) to a new school that may or may not provide a welcoming environment for them or leaving their home and moving to a new community altogether.

It is clear, then, that an infusion of equity and empathy into planning processes is crucial for addressing the challenges in our cities and nowhere is it more critical than in battling the surge of displacement that is destabilizing low-income BIPOC communities. Left unabated, the current trajectory of displacement across the United States will continue to decimate longstanding, robust communities in our cities as well as our schools. Interrupting this trend and stabilizing these communities require a concerted, collaborative process of developing and reinforcing social networks, fostering a sense of belonging in individuals, and creating equitable access to opportunity across boundaries of race, class, and age. As evidenced in the literature cited in the following, activating all potential agents of change is essential for the future of our cities.

To empower residents to see themselves as agents of change, and to set in motion the process by which they can act as change agents, there is a need to cultivate relationships centered on trust and mutual understanding between residents and civic leaders over time. Engagement cannot be simply the act of inviting residents to a meeting without providing adequate background information and training. "Having a meeting" is nothing more than offering an "information session" and is not building an authentic process of mutual engagement. Instead, equitable and impactful engagement requires all partners to spend time together to see and experience local spaces and places through each other's eyes. Ensuring such equitable access to opportunity for residents – of all ages – throughout our communities and schools is key to successfully planning just and joyful cities in the future.

In Communities

Driven by racist policies and laws such as redlining that created vast chasms in the intergenerational accumulation of wealth in the United States (Cohen-Cole, 2010), centuries of *de jure* segregation have created deeply segregated communities within our cities and suburbs. Many BIPOC communities have been intentionally designed with inadequate services and amenities, substandard access to jobs, low-quality schools, and high concentrations of poverty. As an influx of wealth in urban centers drives up today's housing costs, a disproportionate number of people living in these communities are once again being forced out of their homes. As Rothstein (2017) noted, "revitalization does generally occur when a neighborhood becomes attractive to the middle class, but all too often the gentrification that follows does not include strict enforcement of inclusionary zoning principles" (p. 211) What does this mean? When a percentage of new housing fails to include a sufficient supply of low-income apartment units, "it gradually drives the African American poor out of their now-upgraded neighborhoods and into newly segregated inner-ring suburbs" (Rothstein, 2017, p. 211).

Unfortunately, as Karen Chapple (2015) noted, even when long-term residents can avoid displacement, "proximity is not solving the problem for either the concentrated urban or suburban poor; even with opportunity available, the poor cannot access it without family and institutional support systems" (Chapple, 2015, p. 281). That is, without social support systems, residents find it extremely difficult to navigate and protect against the opacity of housing development. These individuals are not typically part of formal city planning processes and so cannot access the language, tools, or ability to inform the process or take advantage of new opportunities that may result from the new development.

Reversing historic racial and economic trauma requires actions equal in deliberate intentionality to those that created the inequality in the first place. While Rothstein posited that "ending *de jure* segregation of housing requires undoing past actions that may seem irreversible," he offered suggestions for how direct local action among community members can forge change. For example, if Black tenants and homeowners are reluctant to integrate in part because of an "expectation of hostility (from subtly hostile neighbors, from police who follow their sons home), then community welcoming committees that, among other actions insist upon appropriate police training, could be useful" (Rothstein, 2017, p. 204). While this approach would need to be implemented in concert with an array of legal and political approaches to begin to rectify conditions that have been centuries in the making, it acknowledges the potential impact of social ties that transcend race, income, social class, and educational attainment.

Both Rothstein (2017) and Chapple (2015) underscore that developing social networks, and the social inclusion they foster, is a critical component of closing the opportunity and access gap, facilitating engagement with services, amenities, and jobs once they exist in a desegregated community. It is important to note that deep social networks already thrive in many of the communities currently facing the high levels of displacement that threaten their very existence. However, the social networks capable of engendering full utilization of community services must reach across differences in race, social class, and education levels to represent all stakeholders in a diverse community and provide all of them with open access to navigate each other. Unfortunately, that crossover simply does not happen without a strong support system to facilitate that integrative movement.

We can see an example of this process in Kruks-Wisner's (2018) research on how and when everyday citizens in India engage public officials in the pursuit of social welfare. She found that in India, the greatest factor in predicting which citizens demonstrated a greater sense of agency than others (measured by demanding the equitable distribution of services they deserved) was the extent of their "social and spatial exposure." She asserted that the extent of their exposure beyond their neighborhood, both socially and physically, mattered more than all other factors including education, caste, and gender. She noted, "More porous boundaries increased citizens' exposure to information and narratives about the state, as well as to the potential linkages to public officials and agencies" (p. 19). In other words, the depth of their social networks beyond those within their neighborhoods made all the difference in what they expected from their civic leaders. Isabel Wilkerson's (2020) *Caste* demonstrates how India's context is particularly relevant to that of the United States for these purposes. She explained that "as if operating from the same instruction manual translated to fit their distinctive cultures," both countries maintain "social hierarchies and abide great chasms between the highest and the lowest in their respective lands" through laws, protocols, terror, and force (p. 74).

Unfortunately, such boundaries prove challenging to overcome throughout the world, including the US, making broad and deep social networks difficult to cultivate. While Chapple (2015) identified "social seams," like grocery stores and parks as holding the potential to help stabilize mixed-income neighborhoods by facilitating interaction between diverse residents, she found such interactions often lacked the depth needed to garner enough familiarity to develop into robust social networks. Chapple (2015) found one factor above all else increased the likelihood of meaningful, extended, and in-depth interactions when they do occur: "the presence of children" (p. 133). Adults are often more open and can make themselves more available to engage with other adults in a less antagonistic way when children are in the mix. Perhaps feeling compelled to model "good behavior," adults often slow down, listen to different voices like children and youth, and step out of their traditional means of interacting or working. Thus, young people possess a dynamic potential to facilitate different relationships among community stakeholders and bridge social gaps. This simple recognition identifies the potential that young people wield to spark the development of social networks that can lead to, among other things, the retention of a community's residents, and along with them its history, identity, and heart.

In Schools

Despite the power of young people to bridge gaps and catalyze networks essential for our communities' prosperity, rarely are they actively engaged toward this end. In many ways, schools appear well-situated to support young residents in their development of the necessary social networks and to connect them to institutions and resources that could lead to greater access to opportunities. In fact, Noguera and Syeed (2020) concluded that "education may be our best and only resource for devising strategies to create a more just and sustainable world" (p. 214). However, if schools do not support students in exercising their power to participate in decisions related to their schools, there can be unintended consequences.

Posey-Maddox (2014) broadened the concept of "school gentrification" beyond a "simple increase in the number of middle-class children in city schools that have historically served higher numbers of poor and working-class students" (p. 12). She proposed including three additional components: "material/economic upgrades in a school, such as an increase in parent-teacher organization funds; the exclusion or marginalization of low-income students and families; and changes in school culture and climate" (p. 13). Through that lens, she revealed the limitations of relying on even "well-meaning" middle-class parents alone to drive or sustain high-quality, diverse, and integrated public schools (p. 145). In a case study of Morningside Elementary School[2] in Northern California, Posey-Maddox demonstrated the efficacy and power of white middle-class social networks and the power these parents have to transform schools as well as neighborhoods. Just like working-class families being displaced from their communities, this parent initiative unintentionally forced low-income and Black families from the school.

Despite attempts to build collaborative relationships between Black and white families through efforts like inclusive parent planning meetings, the white parents showed no real interest in power-sharing or making decisions differently. White, middle-class families' choices and priorities always dominated meetings and discussions. While "bringing about inclusive and equitable reform in urban education requires building relationships within and across school walls and expanding our notions of community," the author concluded that "constant and vigilant efforts to build relationships across the fault lines of race and class are key" (Posey-Maddox, 2014, pp. 158–159). Posey-Maddox's findings showed how hard it is to transcend social boundaries defined by race and class, yet how necessary it is for meaningful and equitable education reform.

Such insights are also affirmed in the *New York Times* (2020) podcast "Nice White Parents," which examined a similar situation at the School of International Studies in Brooklyn, New York. In both cases, white middle-class parents stated goals of increasing diversity and improving the social and academic development of the schools. In neither case were parents able to form the true social networks necessary to foster change and successfully resist displacement in and outside of schools, even within the confines of a school community that publicly recognized the importance of equity, at least rhetorically. Instead, the studies emphasized the challenges of overcoming deeply entrenched and racialized social and structural boundaries, which is necessary to increase their access to better educational options.

Notably, neither Morningside nor the School for International Studies directly engaged students as participants in their school reform processes. Despite the rising awareness of the importance of youth voices in school reform measures to improve school quality academic development (Mitra, 2018) and their unique social power and position, students are largely excluded from the dialogue.

Social Networks in Cities and Schools

As much as city planners, policy experts, and civic leaders can speak to descriptive statistics, they cannot speak to the lived experience of individuals and families currently grappling with an inability to secure adequate housing. The distance between professional and personal discourses is just too great. Residents, particularly those who are young, live in low-income communities, or identify as BIPOC, have those lived experiences and sensibilities often absent from planning discussions. Injecting those voices into processes that consider the connections between schools and cities might concurrently contribute innovative solutions and support the development of the very social networks needed to bolster it.

As evidenced in both the history of community segregation and school gentrification, good intentions are not enough to level a deeply unequal playing field. Instead, there is a great need for the disparate discourses of diverse constituents involved in community and school gentrification to interact, recognize reciprocal impacts, and engage in a dialectical conversation in order to address the different manifestations of this shared problem together. Booher and Innes (2002) spoke to the potential power of such a convergence when they explained that in the information age, "network power," which emerges when "diverse participants in a network focus on a common task and develop shared meanings and common heuristics that guide their actions," is what works most effectively (p. 225). They outlined three core conditions for network power to significantly emerge: diverse agents, interdependence, and authentic dialogue (p. 226), all of which would be present in collaborative planning with diverse stakeholders at the intersection of cities and schools. When these conditions are met, Booher and Innes (2002) found that "a central outcome in the generation of network power is that participants in dialogue build a sense of shared identity as part of a system or community, and perhaps a changed identity of their own in the process" (p. 231). This potential for identity transformation amplifies the power and importance of cultivating such networks.

Accordingly, within the realm of school improvement for the most disadvantaged students, Noguera (2004) found that "strategies that attempt to develop the social capital of parents and to cultivate the civic capacity of impoverished communities may be the most important steps that can be taken to further educational reform" (p. 2162). Potential strategies he outlined for developing social capital of parents included parental organizing, effective information sharing about rights and responsibilities, technical assistance, translation services, and childcare. In cultivating civic capacity of impoverished communities, his recommendations included community mentors and tutors, internships and career academies, and professional development (Noguera, 2004). By fostering authentic dialogue among diverse, interconnected stakeholders, these strategies both stand poised to contribute much needed community and parent insight into planning processes and cultivate the social networks needed for sustainable changes.

Meanwhile, in exploring the effects of the physical distance to schools and other amenities on parental involvement in their children's learning, which disproportionately impact parents from low-income communities, Makarewicz (2018) found a need for "planning interventions and investments that will improve parents' life contexts for engaging with their children's learning" (p. 13). In response, she posed that planners have several such tools at their disposal, including providing places for parents to meet, designing outdoor gathering spaces to foster informal interactions, co-locating amenities in low-income neighborhoods, and providing discounts to fees for cultural facilities. She noted that "the necessary planning interventions should be identified through participatory planning processes with parents and their children" (p. 13), and suggested involving low-income parents directly in neighborhood and transportation planning processes in order to learn from their experiences while cultivating social networks. Taken together, the recommendations of Booher and Innes (2002), Noguera (2004), and Makarewicz (2018) offer a glimpse of a system that could benefit from the contributions of all stakeholders while forging the networks that would sustain the impact into the future.

While involving parents from low-income communities in this way adds yet another competing demand on their already limited time, their children might be perfectly situated to offer much needed perspectives, insights, and potential solutions to address the most vexing challenges in the future. As Osnes (2018) noted:

> What is needed is community buy-in so that real individuals integrate those policies and plans into action in their daily lives and the lives of their communities. . . . Especially when youth-led, it infuses joy and creativity into the entire process. It could be that this inclusion of joy is possibly the most sustaining ingredient in ensuring continued engagement by a larger constituency, because we will always return to something time and again if it makes us feel good.
>
> (p. 199)

The infusion of the heart and soul of our cities and schools that can come from young people, along with their potential to spark the longer, deeper conversations as identified by Chapple (2015), provides a natural opportunity to cultivate meaningful relationships. As those relationships persist over time, they converge to form social networks transcending race, class, income, and education, illuminating the mechanisms by which such networks can benefit everyone involved, including the young people capable of reaching across historic boundaries without inhibitions. The city planners and civic leaders who take the time to develop trust learn to listen to young people's voices, their parents, their neighbors, and eventually, their communities. Such networks might finally cross the stubborn, exclusionary historical divides, and stabilize struggling communities, preserving their historical identities in the face of displacement. Perhaps a new understanding of a truly inclusive community could thus emerge.

This confluence of research points to the need for and potential power of deep, meaningful, and diverse social networks capable of closing gaps in access to opportunity and fortifying communities and schools against the displacement of people, of history, of culture, of identity. Across their separate discourses, these researchers agree not only that such social networks are essential, but also that they have thus far been stubbornly elusive. They have shown the deep and often seemingly impenetrable "fault lines" that exist in communities and schools between low-income BIPOC communities and largely middle-class and white urban planners and local decision-makers. They show how long-standing segregation in schools, communities, and cities is sustained through both socio-political acts and physically enforced separation.

As we shift to a sharper focus on student agency, new opportunities emerge regarding the roles young people can play as they develop new solutions to overcome deep divides in our cities and schools. Perhaps schools and their classrooms could become the needed social seams that Chapple (2015) and Rothstein (2017) invoke, facilitating the social bonds and institutional supports required to address gentrification and displacement in our communities – and our schools.

Planning Just and Joyful Cities With(in) Public Schools

Despite a decline in public investment and community confidence in our public schools, they remain uniquely and powerfully situated to shape American society. Patterson and Silverman (2014) discussed the critical role of public schools as bridging institutions, as they "are uniquely positioned at the neighborhood level and relatively accessible to neighborhood residents. In distressed urban neighborhoods, public schools remain one of the primary links between inner-city residents and the broader society," (p. xv). Public schools are the only US institution charged to serve all members of our society, regardless of race, class, income, or gender, between the ages of 5 and 16. The positioning of schools as focal points for communities offers an enormous opportunity to reach across historically persistent divides and access young people equitably.

While public schools in the United States have all too often mirrored and reproduced social inequalities, schools and the young people who occupy them nonetheless have the potential to reshape the larger communities in which they live. In doing so, they have the capacity to address the most vexing challenges of our time. As John Dewey (1916) long ago explained and Paulo Freire (2000) later reinforced, when schools critically engage young people in authentic work, inquiry, and problem solving, students develop a sense of agency and interrupt existing power hierarchies. Given access to this approach, young people can begin to resist the displacement that threatens to dismantle their own communities. In turn, schools can become places of critical thought and agency development, empowering students to envision and precipitate change. Exactly how to make this approach take place poses a great challenge to equity-minded educators, another key participant in the CoP utilized in Y-PLAN projects.

Situated Learning

Within our public school classrooms, there is often untapped potential to engage students in authentic learning processes beyond the hypothetical and theoretical. Social learning theories such as Situated Learning offer important insights supporting this approach and are central to the argument of this book. In their seminal work, Lave and Wenger (1991) departed from researchers who conventionally based contemporary education on the assumption that learning is something that individuals do on their own, something that has "a beginning and an end; that it is best separated from the rest of our activities; and that it is the result of teaching" (Wenger, 1998, p. 3).

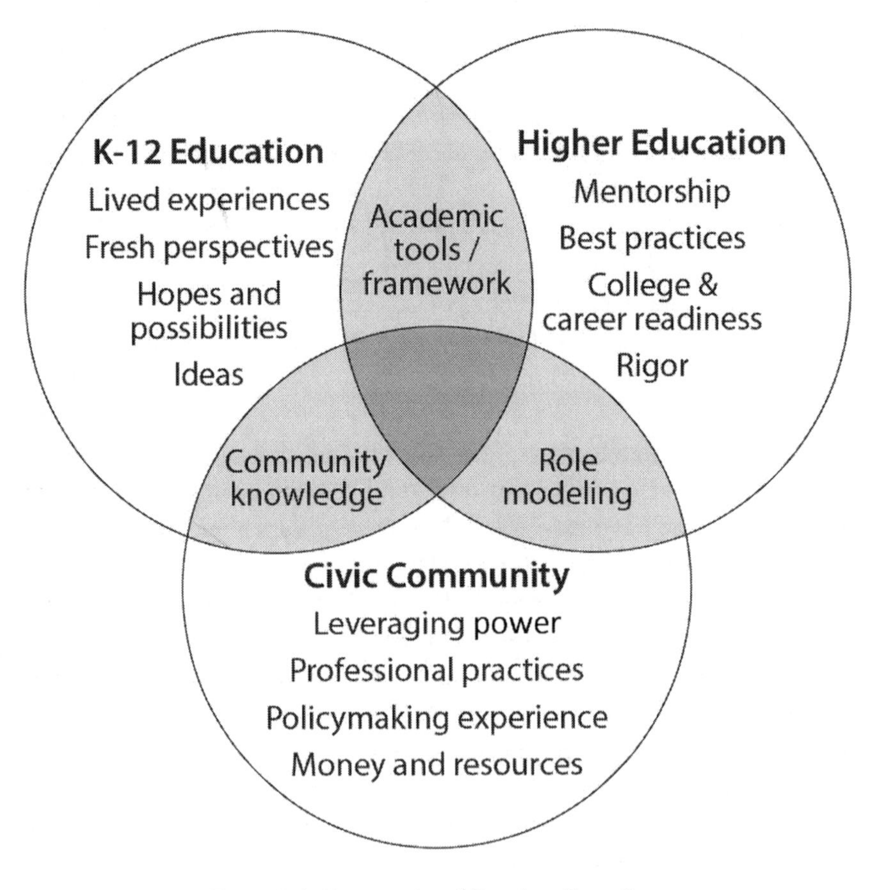

Figure 2.1 Community of Practice: Expertise.

Source: UC Berkeley Center for Cities and Schools.

Instead, following the work of Vygotsky (1978), they proposed that learning is social and observable in a person's changing participation in sociocultural activities over time. From this perspective, learning becomes a process  of engagement in a "community of practice" defined as a group of people who share a craft, profession, or set of activities (Lave &Wenger, 1991; Wenger, 1998). Central to this theory is that no one person is an "expert." It honors that each participant is a valuable, "legitimate," member of a community of practice. Each brings important insight and different expertise from lived experience to mentorship to an understanding of how to leverage power.

The theoretical focus on situated learning in a community of practice relies upon the notion that learning is human nature, that it is social and participatory and that education must engage learning communities to have a larger impact on promoting individuals' transformative participation in communities of practice. As such, Wenger (1998) argued "building complex social relationships around meaningful activities requires genuine practices in which taking charge of learning becomes the enterprise of a community" (p. 272). Today, a growing range of stakeholders, scholars, and disciplines discuss, employ, and document communities of practice (McKoy et al., 2019).

Civic Learning

One especially meaningful way to cultivate communities of practice with young people and city leaders together is around authentic civic learning. Here students engage with issues that relate directly to their own homes and communities. Civic learning is "a process through which young people develop the knowledge, skills, and commitments to interact effectively with fellow community members to address shared problems" ("Leveraging Equity and Access in Democratic Education (LEADE)," 2017). The importance of such participation in community life as a cornerstone of democracy has been discussed extensively since John Dewey's (1916) work. In this way, elevating civic learning emerges as an element that is crucial to the success of our nation.

For a deeply effective community of practice to exist around civic learning, it is essential that young people regularly access and engage with city leaders in authentic, meaningful work with pragmatic consequences beyond their classroom in their own communities. In the frame of civic learning then,

young people and their work must matter, inside and outside the classroom. Opportunities for such authentic civic learnings require adequate and effective preparation so that students can fully contribute. Participating in a community of practice around civic learning offers young people an opportunity to actualize their unique potential to bridge historically established societal divides

and to cultivate diverse social networks that reach across those divides.

Working within the constraints of the public school environment is, however, challenging. These ever-present constraints include: ever-changing class schedules, student absences, high teacher turnover, school closures, and, during the COVID-19 pandemic, the shift to distance learning. However, engaging with students during the public school day is a powerful and potent opportunity to extend access equitably to all young people, so that all students have the opportunity, time, and guidance to draw upon their lived experience while developing their capacity to use professional planning tools, vocabulary, and knowledge to contribute to positive change in our cities. Engaging young people in our public schools can and should be an essential component of equitable city planning.

Planning Just and Joyful Cities with Young People

To date, however, collaborating with local schools and integrating the lived experiences of young people are two critical missing pieces within most city planning efforts. Our younger children and youth bring much-needed ingenuity, out-of-the-box critical thinking, and hope to the table. The engagement of young people across cities and ages is vital for future generations – and cities themselves – to survive and prosper. Moreover, young people are themselves hungry to be part of the solution to the problems they see around them. They know that they have the most to lose and gain, as they will be the ones to navigate the challenges of our cities in the future. Young people who identify as BIPOC or who grow up in low-income neighborhoods disproportionately live on the frontlines of discrimination, displacement, and environmental degradation, due to both natural and human-made factors. Through their honesty and their vulnerability, our children and youth embody the authenticity to bring people together, building bridges across differences in socioeconomic status, race, age, and more. When we experience the power that is unleashed when we engage the creativity and passion of our young people, we begin to feel how painful it is to envision the high cost of *not* bringing these insightful voices to the table to be active participants in planning our collective future.

Incorporating young people into city planning, even within public schools, poses several challenges. After all, minors are rarely considered significant players in formal processes of governance. They do not have voting rights, are not property owners or significant taxpayers, and are not typically invited to the conference table – instead, powerful adults in proximity to them are assumed to represent their interests. As such, young people are rarely recognized as legitimate stakeholders in planning. However, given the right tools and structural support, young people can become powerful contributors to collaborative decision-making concerning schools and cities. Supporting the development of student agency, by recognizing the necessary conditions for it and creating those conditions for young people in the public institutions charged with educating them, can precipitate a major shift in outcomes for our youth and our cities.

Development of Agency

Anindya Kundu (2020) offered some key insights as to the important role young people can play to more directly increase their own agency. By examining the lives and trajectories of fifty individuals who ultimately developed a strong sense of agency, he showed that a combination of social and cultural supports, together with a willingness to tackle structures underlying inequality, cultivate an "inherent sense of agency" capable of helping to stabilize communities. Kundu (2020) contended that harnessing such agency can counter deeply rooted inequalities in our educational system yet "one of the first distinctions to make regarding agency is that it is more contextual than a person simply taking action" (p. 34). Kundu asserted that agency grows "out of this central premise: students' educational attitudes, goals, and achievements are malleable products of their experiences and social interactions, and these particular contexts, which are also shaped by cultural norms, enable students' continued development" (p. 33).

In his research on promoting the sense of agency, Kundu (2020) has described agency in four parts. First, Kundu argues "agency gives humans greater influence over their fates and external determinants, though different situations leave different amounts of space for exercising one's free will" (p. 34). In this way, he acknowledged that expressions of agency are context-specific, not a fixed or predetermined set of actions in a particular environment or circumstances. Instead, agency can come from a wide range of social and physical conditions connected to one's community – and school – revealing the wide range of opportunities for students to develop agency within our schools. Second, Kundu viewed agency in terms of "resistive actions" that can be reflected through individual and, perhaps more importantly, collective action – such as, boycotts and other forms of civil disobedience. Third, for Kundu, agency requires choice-making and deliberate action related to one's goals, extending actions to more directly affect or participate in the *process of social change*, leading to improved social and economic positions.

Finally, Kundu (2020) built on Paulo Freire's (2000) seminal work originally published in 1970, arguing that agency also requires that a person fundamentally believes that they themselves can change their situation through critical reflection on the broader structural forces present in their life:

> By reflecting critically on their social positions, students can increase their self-efficacy and realistically learn how to break free from their limited situations. . . . Students, guided by teachers, learn to see where they are, subject to broader structural forces in their lives.
>
> (Kundu, 2020, p. 36)

One of the most significant contributions of Kundu's research is the recognition of schools as essential places enabling all students, regardless of their backgrounds, to improve their opportunity. Kundu explicitly included social structures beyond school walls, such as housing and healthcare, as very real and important factors structuring success. He recognized that collective actions and interactions among diverse people in a community contribute to student agency and the belief and reality that they have the power to effect change (Kundu, 2020). Young people have visions and ideas about how to address today's challenges, including both natural and man-made disasters, and they want to be a part of problem-solving processes both within and beyond their schools and communities.

Conditions and Indicators of Agency for Young People

Imagine what could happen if students could draw on robust social and professional networks, sufficient to grant them access to information, public officials, agencies, and places of power to develop authentic relationships and trust across traditional barriers of race, class, and place. What if young people had the opportunity and space to navigate the city as full-fledged stakeholders within a powerful network and to contribute in crafting its future? Imagine the potential if students of all ages had the ability to transform those people, places, policies, and processes to help their cities and schools better meet the needs of their diverse residents.

Meanwhile, imagine if concurrently the same process enabled city planners to directly **access** the lived experiences of the residents they serve. What if they had the opportunity to learn how to **navigate** their unique and often unwieldy public schools – the largest public institutions in their cities? Finally, what if planning professionals were able to work *for* and *with* young planners to leverage their expertise and lived experience in order to **transform** city systems to favorably impact all city communities and populations, particularly people of lower income and/or those who identify as BIPOC. To Noguera and Syeed (2020), achieving transformation requires tapping "into

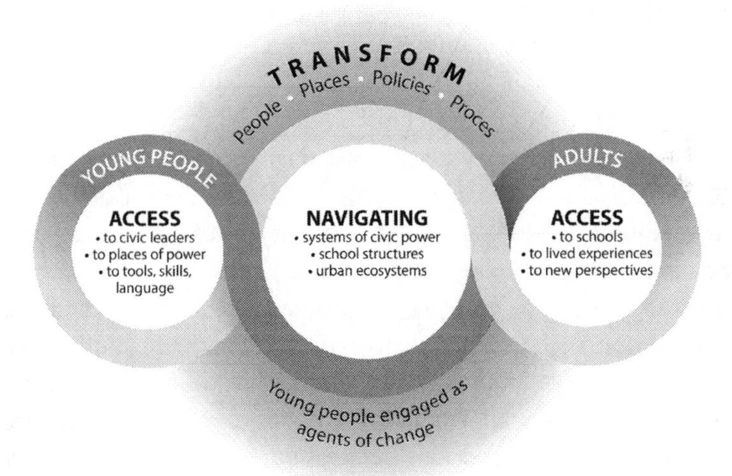

Theory of Change
Planning Cities for Justice and Joy

Figure 2.2 Theory of Change.
Source: UC Berkeley Center for Cities and Schools.

the ability of children to use their imagination to solve problems, to apply what they have learned to address real-life challenges, and to think critically and creatively about their place in the world" (p. 213). Together all participants in this process would gain a new and essential understanding of what it means to plan a truly inclusive, joyful, and just city.

These three critical conditions of agency – access, navigate and transform – form our conceptual framework for understanding how we can address and change the course of the displacement of low-income families from their communities and schools and ameliorate the harm these forces inflict on young people. Young people and civic leaders, deeply engaged in this process, can work together to plan just and joyful communities throughout our nation.

Conclusion

Today, our cities across the nation and globe have been brought to their knees. This is particularly true in California, as young people and communities face not only COVID-19, economic hardship, and racial injustice, but also historic and deadly wildfires and resulting dangerous air quality. Literally and figuratively, young people and their families are often struggling to breathe. Despite these unparalleled challenges, students of all ages are working in supportive communities of practice to step up with a powerful sense of agency. In doing so, they are proving the need to "Forget the old adage that children are to be seen, not heard. . . . The blending of generations holds the capacity to shape our world" (Wood, 2019). They are showing that by working in partnership with the adults charged with planning our cities, they can meet these challenges with equanimity, creativity, and hope.

Many social justice and youth development leaders believe that public schools as an institution, with their awful history of racist and discriminatory practices, are too permeated with societal biases to do "real and impactful" work with young people. They see schools as too often reproducing social inequalities and unjust economic and racialized policies. Similarly, city planners and policymakers fear schools are too rigid and impenetrable to enable the formation of solid, trusting, and sustainable partnerships between themselves and students. But to the contrary, school staff and their young scholars, when given the opportunity, are motivated to model power-sharing and collaboration, which are necessary to resist the devastating levels of displacement (and other civic issues) in our cities.

In this book, we reveal how young people in our schools can cultivate this sense of agency to leverage their untapped power and to rebuild our cities as places of welcome and opportunity for all. There has never been a more important time for young people to play a direct, visible role in calling for change, in and outside of school and within cities. Given the opportunities, skills, and knowledge to learn how to access social systems of power and navigate new ways of thinking about, planning, and managing cities, they become active participants in transforming the very definition of city planning to more fully honor local conditions and the socio-political needs and concerns of a diverse populace.

Notes

1 Names of all young people are pseudonyms.

2 The author's pseudonym for the school.

References

Bierbaum, A. H. (2018). School Closures and the Contested Unmaking of Philadelphia's Neighborhoods. *Journal of Planning Education and Research*, 0739456X1878501. https://doi.org/10.1177/0739456X18785018

Booher, D. E., & Innes, J. E. (2002). Network Power in Collaborative Planning. *Journal of Planning Education and Research*, *21*(3), 221–236. https://doi.org/10.1177/0739456X0202100301

Chapple, K. (2015). *Planning Sustainable Cities and Regions: Towards More Equitable Development*. Routledge.

Cohen-Cole, E. (2010). Redlining. In *The New Palgrave Dictionary of Economics* (Vol. 4). Palgrave Macmillan. https://ideas.repec.org/h/pal/dofeco/v4year2010doi3840.html

Dewey, J. (1916). *Democracy and Education*. Dover Publications.

Freire, P. (2000). *Pedagogy of the oppressed* (30th anniversary ed.). Bloomsbury.

Innes, J. E., & Booher, D. E. (2004). Reframing Public Participation: Strategies for the 21st Century. *Planning Theory & Practice*, *5*(4), 419–436. https://doi.org/10.1080/1464935042000293170

Introducing "Nice White Parents," a New Podcast from Serial Productions. (2020, July 30). The New York Times Company. www.nytco.com/press/introducing-nice-white-parents-a-new-podcast-from-serial-productions/

Kruks-Wisner, G. (2018). *Claiming the State: Active Citizenship and Social Welfare in Rural India*. Cambridge University Press.

Kundu, A. (2020). *The Power of Student Agency: Looking Beyond Grit to Close the Opportunity Gap*. Teachers College Press.

Lave, J., & Wenger, E. (1991). *Situated Learning: Legitimate Peripheral Participation* (1st ed.). Cambridge University Press.

Leveraging Equity and Access in Democratic Education (LEADE). (2017, November 28). UCLA Center X. https://centerx.gseis.ucla.edu/leade/

Makarewicz, C. (2018). Supporting Parent Engagement in Children's Learning through Neighborhood Development and Improvements to Accessibility. *Journal of Planning Education and Research*, 0739456X1880403. https://doi.org/10.1177/0739456X18804036

McKoy, D., Eppley, A., & Buss, S. (2019, October 19). *The Critical Role for Young People and Schools in Resiliency Planning*. Federal Reserve Bank of San Francisco. www.frbsf.org/community-development/publications/community-development-investment-review/2019/october/the-critical-role-for-young-people-and-schools-in-resiliency-planning/

Mitra, D. (2018). Student Voice in Secondary Schools: The Possibility for Deeper Change. *Journal of Educational Administration*, *56*(5), 473–487.

Noguera, P. A. (2004). Racial Isolation, Poverty, and the Limits of Local Control in Oakland. *Teachers College Record*, *106*(11), 2146–2170. https://doi.org/10.1111/j.1467-9620.2004.00431.x

Noguera, P. A., & Syeed, E. (2020). *City Schools and the American Dream 2: The Enduring Promise of Public Education* (Kindle iOS version). Teachers College Press.

Osnes, B. (2018). Youth Shine in Performance for Resilience. *Theatre Topics*, *28*(3), 191–202. https://doi.org/10.1353/tt.2018.0043

Patterson, K. L., & Silverman, R. M. (Eds.). (2014). *Schools and Urban Revitalization: Rethinking Institutions and Community Development* (Vol. 1). Routledge.

Pearman, F. A. (2019). Gentrification, Geography, and the Declining Enrollment of Neighborhood Schools. *Urban Education*, *55*(2), 183–215. https://doi.org/10.1177/0042085919884342

Posey-Maddox, L. (2014). *When Middle-Class Parents Choose Urban Schools*. University of Chicago Press.

Resources | Urban Displacement Project. (2021). Urban Displacement Project. www.urbandisplacement.org/resources#section-56

Rothstein, R. (2017). *The Color of Law: A Forgotten History of How Our Government Segregated America*. Liveright Publishing Corporation.

Vygotsky, L. S. (1978). *Mind in Society: The Development of Higher Psychological Processes*. Harvard University Press.

Wenger, E. (1998). *Communities of Practice: Learning, Meaning, and Identity*. Cambridge University Press.
Wilkerson, I. (2020). *Caste: The Origins of Our Discontents*. Random House.
Wood, S. (2019, April 26). *Y-Plan Ends with A-Z Guide From Youth in Improving S.F. Bay Area*. East Palo Alto, CA, Patch. https://patch.com/california/east-palo-alto/y-plan-ends-z-guide-youth-improving-s-f-bay-area

Affordable Housing
Displacement 7 Destabilization } civic issue
Agents of change
Trust and mutual understanding
Equitable and impactful engagement
Intentionality to combat historical racial & economic trauma
Critical component of healing is social inclusion (points to importance of community connection)
Sense of agency
Collaboration & shared power
Importance of social networks, diverse constituents, and authentic conversation
Public schools } public institutions
Aspects of agency
Mutually beneficial for planners & youth
Importance of intergenerational action
(CoP)

3 Activating the Theory

Introduction

Despite the heavy fog that obfuscated the panoramic skyline view from the 43rd floor of 4 World Trade Center on a crisp April morning in 2017, its grandeur remained. All eyes settled on the four high schoolers from Brooklyn's Williamsburg High School for Architecture and Design (WHSAD). These young planners represented more than 600 peers, the overwhelming majority of whom were Black, Indigenous, People of Color (BIPOC), from nearly 20 different NYC public schools. They came together to share their

Image 3.1 Photo – World Trade Center Roundtable – student panel.

Source: Ricardo Kuettel.

DOI: 10.4324/9781003141778-4

process, their outcomes, and the significance of their visions for the future, with leaders from all corners of our nation's largest city – from the NYC Chancellor's Office to New York City Housing Authority and Transportation Department. These powerful adult leaders came to listen, learn, and brainstorm paths forward with these young planners.

Professionally produced proposal boards for 18 projects adorned the room. They were designed by the young people, each group responding to their own civic client's project question, and to a range of planning issues from resilience to housing to transportation. The proposals called for more support staff and expanded library hours across NYC schools; the creation of a Merchants Association; a safety awareness campaign for pedestrians, bikers, and drivers; social media campaigns to increase awareness of teen dating abuse and healthy relationships; community gardens; and waste sorting stations. However, on that April morning, these young planners had visions for this Roundtable beyond unveiling these myriad project proposals. Above all else, they came to illuminate the processes that they and their peers undertook to guide them to such thoroughly researched and carefully analyzed conclusions.

Project by project, the young planners stepped to the podium to offer an overview of the first four steps in the Y-PLAN (Youth-Plan, Learn, Act, Now) research process, which connects students in public schools with civic clients seeking youth input in addressing authentic civic issues. One young planner began by describing the experience of her peers at Urban Action Academy High School, during Step 1: Start Up. She described meeting with her civic client, the Mayor's Office to Combat Domestic Violence (MOCDV). Their project question was *What elements of a social media campaign would increase youth participation in relationship abuse prevention?* The next young planner introduced Step 2: Making Sense of the City. He shared stories of mind mapping the school grounds, conducting a site analysis of the surrounding Bushwick neighborhood, and methods for collecting and analyzing data. A third young planner presented Step 3: Into Action, which includes translating data analysis, brainstorming solutions, and developing proposals. She described how students engaged in a design charrette to generate their visions for change: making models, creating drawings, outlining policies, and creating professional proposal boards. The fourth student showcased Step 4: Going Public. He shared highlights from two Y-PLAN NYC Summits where hundreds of students convened to present their proposals to each other, their civic partners, and to community leaders. Finally, their teachers shared their plans for Step 5: Looking Forward,

Image 3.2 Student leaders representing high schools throughout New York City meet with powerful civic leaders on the 43rd floor of the World Trade Center for a Roundtable where they share how they engaged in the five step Y-PLAN process to develop proposals for their clients.

Source: Ricardo Kuettel.

Looking Back. These plans for the students included drafting policy proposals, writing internship essays, corresponding with civic clients, and crafting action plans for the future.

As the young planners and teachers concluded their presentations, adults and youths launched into a communal brainstorming session focused on the optimal future involvement for each stakeholder in the room. The NYC Housing Authority group shared their view of the urgent need for youth insights into their "Next Generation NYCHA" strategic plan, focusing on recycling, crime, and healthy food access. A representative from the NYC

Office of Sustainability suggested engaging multiple schools on the same project to garner more diverse input, an idea that the Brooklyn Borough President's Office would implement with great success during the following academic year. School superintendents from throughout the city discussed ongoing mentorships, work-based learning, and employment opportunities for students. The representative from the City's Department of Transportation offered to share Vision Zero Initiative[1] geocoded pedestrian and bicycle safety data for young people to examine, allowing for fresh perspectives on the data while helping students develop work-based skills and prepare for internships.

At the end of the conversation, the students reiterated how meaningful it was for them to collaborate with professionals to address challenges they share as a community today and in the future. One young planner asserted, "As many times as I've heard 'you are the future. You're the reason why we're powering up the city,' if adults don't support us, it's not going to work. Top powers and youth combined will make the city better."

This powerful Roundtable dramatized the ways in which our public school systems can encourage students to interrupt, rather than reproduce, destructive or unjust patterns and systems in our society. As Noguera and Syeed (2020) described, school "transformation calls for us to recognize the obstacles facing children and the communities where they reside and then rethink the model of schooling entirely so that these community institutions can become more responsive to the needs of children, particularly those who are most disadvantaged" (p. 213). In doing so, our schools can play a pivotal role in helping young people develop a sense of agency, thereby equipping them with the college, career, and civic readiness skills they need now and in the future. As these NYC students demonstrated, one way to do so is by re-envisioning classroom learning as an intergenerational community of practice, with the potential to catalyze identity transformation and a true sense of agency.

A University-Led Approach to Youth Engagement: The Y-PLAN Initiative

In 2000, the UC Berkeley Department of City and Regional Planning launched a course engaging students from various disciplines in the Y-PLAN process, and it has continued to offer it every spring. Within the framework of this studio, university students have partnered with hundreds of K–12 classrooms, city planners, and civic leaders to form intergenerational communities of practice using the Y-PLAN methodology to engage in authentic city planning projects. Reflective of typical planning studios, the Y-PLAN course project is determined by an authentic client, a city planner or civic leader, and features a compelling question for students to answer and the potential for the participating client to utilize the findings and recommendations. Over the last twenty years, the Y-PLAN studio has developed into an award-winning, interdisciplinary course also embedded within UC Berkeley's Graduate School of Education, and has brought over 500 undergraduate and graduate students into the heart of planning for cities with and for young people.[2] Central to this studio, students have had the opportunity to work as "mentors" in K–12 classrooms, collaborating with teachers across multiple subjects to guide students through the five step Y-PLAN "Roadmap to Change" process, as described in detail below.

The insights learned from the early years of this course led to the founding of the UC Berkeley Center for Cities and Schools (CC+S) in 2004, an action research center hosted at the UC Berkeley Institute of Urban and Regional Development and co-sponsored by the Departments of City and Regional Planning and Education. Founded by Deborah L. McKoy, in partnership with planning scholar Jeffrey Vincent, CC+S launched with the mission to strengthen the connection between cities, schools, and young residents by enhancing professional recognition, conducting research, and cultivating interdisciplinary communities of practice. Y-PLAN has always been and remains today the heartbeat of the CC+S, keeping research and policy work focused on the needs and everyday life of young people.

Since its inception in 2004, Y-PLAN has reached more than 10,000 young people across the US and internationally, as will be illustrated in the Part II case studies. To ensure any public schools could adapt and implement the Y-PLAN "Roadmap to Change," CC+S developed models and curricula aligned to all major national and state educational standards and current pedagogical teaching models. Concurrently, committed to a local, community-based approach, CC+S focused on building the capacity of local cities and schools to collaborate and foster independence from the university. What began as a discrete, four-week volunteer project in a single high school classroom in West Oakland, California (McKoy & Vincent, 2007) grew to reach dozens of cities across the United States and over ten countries. While the processes deepened and its reach expanded, Y-PLAN's steadfast commitment to working with students from communities that are the furthest from opportunity has never wavered. Collaborating with teachers directly within the core curriculum in some of the hardest-to-reach public school classrooms, students work in teams to construct proposals to respond to their community's most vexing challenges. Through Y-PLAN, students across the academic trajectory plan to learn while learning to plan. In the process, their impact on city leaders, planning processes, policies, and built environments has rippled through cities and communities across the nation and around the globe.[3]

At its heart, Y-PLAN is a participatory planning and civic learning strategy and methodology that brings together the fields of city planning and education. It bridges the gaps between our cities and our schools by leveraging communities of practice and civic learning (McKoy & Vincent, 2007). This process builds social connections and deepens relationships between civic leaders and young people. It features meaningful, authentic engagement with substantive challenges, such as creating more equitable housing and transportation. Foundational methods include primary source data collection and exposure to professional best practices as well as validation of the lived experiences of diverse populations. As recognized by each member of a community of practice, the work is a shared goal, the enterprise of a community (Wenger, 1998). Integral to this process is that no one person stands out as the expert. Rather, all participants contribute important insights in their unique areas of expertise. Such collective work and shared practice lead to the development of better products together, benefiting everyone.

The Double Bottom Line: Adults and Young People Learn From and With Each Other

In capturing its dual outcomes for young people and adults, the Y-PLAN "Roadmap to Change" employs a double bottom line approach, captured in the following two key principles. As its first principle, Y-PLAN builds the capacity of young people to learn and utilize professional best practices as they collect and contribute data and insights from their daily lived experiences to the planning and policy making process. In so doing, they develop college, career, and community readiness skills. Through this process, students also develop their capacity to be agents of change for themselves and their communities. As its second principle, Y-PLAN engages adult professionals and civic leaders who participate in authentic planning processes with young people in order to develop their capacity to respect and value youth insights. The process leads to plans, policies, and designs for healthier, more sustainable, and equitable communities for everyone.

Y-PLAN civic and community partners evolve as they begin to see their city through young people's eyes and recognize the importance of daylighting the nuanced ways in which young people navigate the built environment, from home to school to work and beyond. Places and policies begin to shift as civic partners incorporate youth data, insights, and recommendations to make cities more family- and child-friendly. Processes within city planning improve as their systems become more reflective of and responsive to the diverse concerns and needs of residents. When adopted by those in power, young people's recommendations change the processes used to implement civic change and have the potential to make cities more accessible and livable for everyone.

As Y-PLAN prepares entire classes of K–12 students to address authentic civic problems posed to them by city leaders, education in the classroom begins to break away from conventional hierarchical pedagogies. Reflecting its roots in a top-ranked public research university, Y-PLAN offers the tools and encourages students to engage in the rigorous academic research process. Students investigate timely and relevant questions, conduct primary and secondary source research, formulate sophisticated proposals for change, and present them to established professionals, civic leaders, and experts in the field. As a result, adults genuinely partner with young people in joint activity, thus elevating academic rigor throughout the process.

Aligning to Schools and Core Curriculum

For equity purposes, it can be beneficial to house youth planning processes and experiences within the public school classrooms during the regular school day. While accessing youth through schools is internationally regarded as an easier way to reach out to and include young people in civic processes (Lansdown, 2014), city planners in many US cities often complain about the isolated nature of schools today. Even when cities want to partner with public schools, it is challenging to do so on a more than *ad hoc* basis, because of rigid schedules and privacy protection policies. However, Y-PLAN's collaboration with schools has shown that embedding planning and engagement processes in the core curriculum, aligned with

Common Core and Next Generation Science Standards (NGSS), makes it possible. Moreover, working in the public school classroom can dramatically increase numbers of diverse, historically marginalized students who have an opportunity to participate, not just those students affluent enough to have access to after-school activities.

Many youth planning initiatives such as Y-PLAN and others are also integrated into another educational strategy called community schools. Using public schools as hubs, community schools are considered both a place and a set of partnerships between children, youth, families, and communities, with each bringing a range of resources to support a whole child approach to academic development (*What Is a Community School?*, n.d.). Numbering over 5,000 across the US (McDaniels, 2018), community schools offer an integrated approach for cities to support academics, health and social services, youth and community development.

City planning and academic curricular alignment can amplify the depth, rigor, and richness of virtually every subject matter or course. Almost half of Y-PLAN classes have been in STEAM (science, technology, engineering, art, and math) classes, with academic rigor reflected in Y-PLAN's alignment with NGSS, which articulates for students the relevance of science, technology, engineering, and mathematics for everyday life (*Next Generation Science Standards*, 2021). The other half of Y-PLAN projects have been split about roughly evenly between the social sciences and humanities.

At the high school level, Y-PLAN is also frequently framed within school districts' College and Career Readiness goals and frameworks, particularly aligning with career pathway school reform strategies increasingly known as Linked Learning. Warner and Caspary (2017) reported, "Linked Learning strives to provide all students – regardless of race, socioeconomic status, gender, prior academic achievement, or special learning needs – with equitable access to and opportunities for full participation in a variety of high-quality career-themed pathways." As school districts implement Y-PLAN across many diverse career pathways, from Information Technology to Culinary Arts to Environmental Sciences, the interdisciplinary nature of city planning as a profession is thus communicated to hundreds of young planners. Ultimately, the Y-PLAN method prepares young people to participate in partnership with city planners and civic leaders to build more equitable and livable communities. In doing so, the Y-PLAN process allows the field to more easily increase the transparency and accessibility of urban planning to all (Coghlan & Brydon-Miller, 2014).

Centering the generative potential of adults and young people working together as intergenerational communities of practice, particularly within the context of the traditional school day, supports young people to be active in shaping our schools, neighborhoods, and cities. In the process, these young people begin to identify themselves with a new sense of agency, as planners. They recognize this field as a place with great potential for transforming the environments in which they live, work, and learn.

Quality Framework for Shared Impact

After twenty years of facilitating Y-PLAN, best practices for producing high-quality, impactful outcomes in city planning have emerged. To date, hundreds of Y-PLAN projects have been conducted following the five-step process showcased by the students at the World Trade Center Roundtable in New York highlighted at the beginning of this chapter. Outcomes have included development of student agency, cultivation of networks, transformational planning proposals, implemented city policies, and transformed urban environments. The impact of Y-PLAN projects is directly correlated with the extent to which they incorporate a balance of the lived experiences of students and their communities and the professional practices of city planning. When students tap into their personal experiences living, learning, working, socializing, and moving within their cities as well as the experiences of their peers, families, and neighbors, they develop proposals rooted in their own realities – the social realities of urban living. Meanwhile, the infusion of professional knowledge and practice into young people's perspectives equips them with the cutting-edge skills, language, and conceptual tools of planners, thus preparing them to conduct authentic research and produce informed proposals. The students' fusion of their lived experiences with the planners' professional tools and practices challenges the adult participants to consider the holistic needs of the communities they serve, creating the potential for the transformation of the city planning field.

Based on two decades of experience, CC+S developed an equity-driven Quality Framework for Shared Impact to provide guidance for students, educators, and planning practitioners to create just and joyful cities together. Considered in concert with lessons and data from other Y-PLAN projects, this Quality Framework for Shared Impact situates projects to balance the two key factors of lived experience and professional practice.

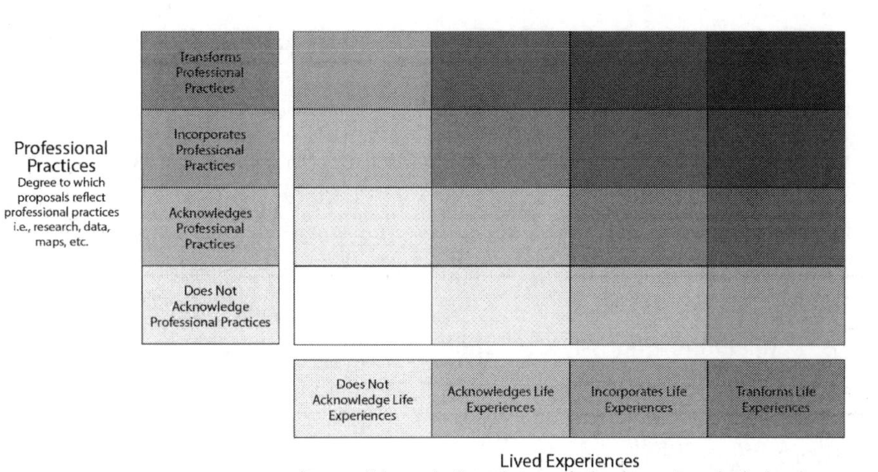

Figure 3.1 Quality Framework for Shared Impact.

Source: UC Berkeley Center for Cities and Schools.

In the framework, both drivers of quality – *lived experience* and *professional practice* – are considered on a scale of 1–4, with one being the least impactful and four the most impactful. From this analysis, it unequivocally emerges that high-quality planning proposals developed while engaging young people require strength in *both* dimensions. The less a proposal incorporates the lived experiences of all community members, especially those who are marginalized, the less impactful are the outcomes. Similarly, when a proposal does not incorporate best practices and tools used by planning professionals, the young people's recommendations are less readily implementable. When lived experience and professional practice are actualized in tandem, the results are potent: the proposals are heartfelt, sound, and actionable.

To foster thoughtful innovation, rigorous critical thinking, and actionable proposals, the most effective methodologies for youth engagement must facilitate specific moments of collaboration and knowledge-sharing between young people and adults. From that essential blend of the personal and the political, the heart and the data, youth and practice, a new kind of network begins to form, one that transcends traditional divisions of age, race, educational attainment, and social class. Young people and professionals begin to understand that they can and must learn from each other.

A Five Step, School-Based Methodology Built on City Planning Fundamentals

Against the backdrop of the Quality Framework for Shared Impact, Y-PLAN's "Roadmap to Change" reflects core participatory planning fundamentals. It emphasizes community engagement through participation in knowledge generation and collective action that lead to empowerment. All students engage in a multi-disciplinary process of inquiry throughout the "Roadmap" as they brainstorm possible solutions to authentic city challenges and validate and test their theories using best planning best practices.

Step 1: Start Up

As with many participatory city planning processes involving communities in strategic and management processes (Coghlan & Brydon-Miller, 2014), a Y-PLAN project begins with Step 1: Start Up. Here, young planners gain a better understanding of the project question, their role in the city, and how

Y-PLAN Roadmap to Change

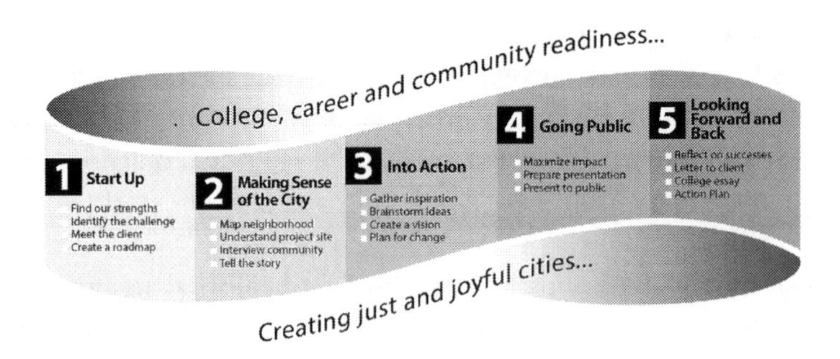

Youth - Plan, Learn, Act, Now

Figure 3.2 Y-PLAN Roadmap to Change.

Source: UC Berkeley Center for Cities and Schools.

this project impacts their lives. They identify the unique strengths they and each of their classmates bring to the table. They also start to articulate some of the changes they would like to see in the city.

During Step 1, the students and their civic client meet and start to learn about each other. Civic clients are city or community leaders who want the insights of young people to help them tackle challenges they are working on, such as how to increase transit ridership, or how to more equitably house the city's residents. At this stage, civic clients introduce the challenge, framed as a project question to the students. This question supports the client's work on a current project and asks for young people to develop proposals and recommendations that the client has the power to act upon or implement.

In the Start Up step, students, civic clients, and teachers begin to build a community of practice, with the goal of implementing positive changes in their city. It is important to note that this is not the time to start to ask or invite young people to share ideas and "input" as young people. Like any professional planner or graduate student, they need and expect to be given the time to learn more about the work context and to conduct research that can then lead to informed, thoughtful recommendations.

Beginning in Step 1, the rigorous inquiry process of Y-PLAN prompts everyone to step back and ask why things are the way they are. It is likely that students will challenge city planners with questions, such as *Why do conditions differ so dramatically across our city? Why are power plants, dumps, freeways, and overcrowded housing prevalent in some neighborhoods and not others? Will changes "for the better" result in displacement of those of us who can't afford to live here anymore?* When adults genuinely acknowledge and internalize those very real, raw, and valid concerns, everyone can start to explore their impact.

To illuminate Step 1 in the Y-PLAN process, at the World Trade Center Roundtable, the young planner from Brooklyn showcased her school's client, the Mayor's Office to Combat Domestic Violence (MOCDV). Noting the need for messaging and campaigns directed specifically to the needs and experiences of teens, the MOCDV representatives posed the question, *"What are the elements of a social media campaign that would increase youth/school participation in relationship abuse prevention?"* The clients also requested that students conduct research and generate proposals for posters, taglines, hashtags, and phrases to reach out to young people and encourage healthy relationships.

Image 3.3 To launch Y-PLAN in Step 1, Start Up, students meet their client and learn about their project question. Here, in Brooklyn, NY, students meet with the Director of the Mayor's Office to Combat Domestic Violence to discuss how to reduce violence in teen relationships.

Source: UC Berkeley Center for Cities and Schools.

The civic leaders pitched their project question by leading a two-day Healthy Relationship Workshop for three classes of students, all of them majority male. Students listened critically and thoughtfully during the sessions. Many immediately saw the need for this work and reflected on the importance of addressing the domestic violence in their own homes or schools. Some students pushed back on the premise of the project. One young man said, "Women are not equal in a relationship because I am a man and men created women in the Bible," and another claimed, "I would kill her if she left [a marriage], and that's a fact." MOCDV representatives were undeterred. They encouraged the students to set aside their biases, delve into their research, and engage with the campaign in a meaningful way. They reiterated that they genuinely needed student input and recognized this as an opportunity to model the egalitarian, respectful healthy relationship behaviors they were charged with promoting. With that, the members of this intergenerational community of practice began to understand their different perspectives as well as their shared mission. They were ready to move together into the Step 2 on the "Roadmap to Change."

Step 2: Making Sense of the City

In Step 2: Making Sense of the City, students leave the confines of their classroom. They begin to navigate their city, map their site, and explore the concept of "place" in their neighborhood. They look through a new lens at places they travel through every day. They analyze the strengths, weaknesses, opportunities, and threats (SWOT) of their site in an exercise known to planners and others as a SWOT analysis. They also design, distribute, and analyze surveys of community residents, and conduct interviews with key stakeholders. The students use professional city planning tools to study and analyze the data they collect as well as their own lived experiences. During the Y-PLAN process, the city they know so well becomes a text for learning for everyone.

At the World Trade Center Roundtable, the student from Williamsburg High School of Architecture and Design described the way her peers approached Step 2 of the Y-PLAN process. They used critical research tools, such as mind mapping, site mapping, SWOT analysis, surveys, and interviews. Their mind maps reflected their memories of their respective neighborhoods, routes to school, and other places of import to them. One young woman drew her friend's house, saying that she spent all of her time there because her own home was adjacent to the freeway and plagued with constant noise and pollution. Another young man drew three blocks around his neighborhood, including a park and railroad tracks. He explained that the crime and violence around them made him feel unsafe walking there, especially at night since there were no lights. He added that the tracks created a barrier preventing him from accessing the nearby park.

The student at the World Trade Center Roundtable continued to explain to civic leaders how students in different schools built upon their mind maps by gathering more data on their site mapping tours. She shared how students from East Bushwick Campus High School for Public Service (EBC) worked with their Council Member's office on the project question: *"How can EBC students promote themes of inclusivity, diversity, and immigration across the Broadway Corridor through the DoT Arterventions project to improve safety?"* Their site mapping tour focused on a stretch of Broadway that many students walk along on their way to school. On the tour they looked at the site with fresh eyes, as they took photos, wrote field notes, and made notations on their maps: They observed cracked sidewalks, loose wires, broken lamp posts, poorly lit areas, and litter as well as places they could improve.

By the time these young planners returned to their classroom, their impression of the corridor, which they had earlier viewed with trepidation, began to emerge as one of possibility.

The young planner at the World Trade Center Roundtable also shared an example from The High School for Enterprise, Business, and Technology (EBT) to illuminate other aspects of the Making Sense of the City phase. For these students, the project question was: *"How can we support students in temporary housing so they can consistently attend and succeed in school?"* After creating mind maps, and going on site tours, the students composed their SWOT analysis. They analyzed the current conditions of the local library and how it might support students living in temporary housing. Their identified strengths featured the comfortable places to read, work, and study

Image 3.4 In Step 2, Making Sense of the City, students conduct a real-time site mapping walk at their project site. Here, students in Brooklyn, NY, collect data about the conditions they observe by taking photos, interviewing people, and making field notes on their maps.

Source: UC Berkeley Center for Cities and Schools.

as well as resources available to support students' personal and academic needs. The weaknesses they saw underscored the reality that the library was closed during prime times for students (lunch and after-school) and suffered from a severe shortage of adult resource people and up-to-date materials. Students saw opportunities to increase staffing and utilize existing spaces to host activities, such as social events, parent outreach meetings, homework sessions, and college prep activities. The main threats focused on the lack of staffing and the need for resources to support homeless students, in shelters and at school.

After students complete mapping and SWOT analyses, they bolster their research by conducting interviews and compiling surveys. The young planner at the World Trade Center Roundtable shared how the students from the Academy of Innovative Technology leveraged Google Forms to create and distribute surveys to peers. These students gathered data about how to maximize use of the library as a vibrant resource accessible to all students. She also shared how the students at Origins High School conducted interviews as part of their goal to reduce waste in the school cafeteria. To increase the impact of their research, they interviewed key stakeholders: Dean of Students, Principal and Assistant Principal, Head Custodian, and Head Chef. Students noted, "All stakeholders agree that food waste is a problem, but everyone has a different take on why it exists and what should be done." With this data in hand, students were ready and eager to move into action and develop their own proposals for change.

Step 3: Into Action

In Step 3: Into Action, students' visions, recommendations, and proposals take shape. Teams of students and adults gather all primary and secondary source research. They go on virtual or real-time urban inspiration tours to view best practices and exciting projects in their own city and around the world. Students then participate in a process known to designers, architects, and planners as a "charrette," an intensive brainstorming session in which participants translate their insights, knowledge, and experiences into their visions for change. After their charette, students consider the constraints of their visions and weigh the costs – in terms of money, resources, or other feasibility concerns – with the relative benefits or potential for impact of each. They meet with local and global experts to ask questions and receive feedback on their ideas during "desk crits." By the culmination of Step 3,

Image 3.5 During Step 3, Into Action, students work in teams to analyze the data they collected about the opportunities and constraints of their site. Here NYC team members are incorporating data as they generate proposals responding to their project question.

Source: UC Berkeley Center for Cities and Schools.

student teams have created a set of short- and long-term recommendations that together cohesively address the project question posed to them by their civic client.

To highlight the Into Action step in the Y-PLAN process, the third student at the World Trade Center Roundtable contrasted the charrette processes at different high schools. For example, after completing their research, students at The High School for Enterprise, Business, and Technology moved into a charrette to explore and imagine new youth-centered ideas to support students in temporary housing at their school. They suspended judgment and rapidly brainstormed proposals based on the information gathered during the SWOT analysis and urban inspiration tour. Students broke into their research groups and their teacher distributed large pieces of paper, colorful markers, and post-its. Students then dove into a more in-depth brainstorming session where they utilized these materials to vision ideas within three categories: Academic Support, Social and Emotional Support, and Parent Outreach. By the end of the process, students in the Academic Support group proposed several recommendations: transportation options for students traveling far from shelters; extended after-school library hours; additional library support staff; and online make-up options for students who are chronically absent. The Social and Emotional Supports team recommended reading positive inspirational quotes at the beginning of every day; structuring peer support and mentorship; hosting family game nights; and supporting students to feel more comfortable speaking out and asking for help. Finally, the Parent Outreach group suggested addressing parents directly; creating a support program for them; and hosting fundraisers and donation boxes at school to support families in need.

Meanwhile, students at Urban Action Academy used a different approach for their charette as they generated proposals and created products for the Mayor's campaign to prevent domestic violence and teen relationship abuse. Throughout Step 2, the students had considered everything from the experiences of students at their school to characters in Toni Morrison's *The Bluest Eye*, which they studied as part of their English Language Arts core curriculum. When it was time for Step 3 and the charrette process, the teacher was impressed, and almost overwhelmed, with the totality and diversity of the evidence they had collected: surveys, interviews, poems, literary responses, artwork, site maps, and workshop notes. In response, the teacher embarked upon a unique approach. She pushed the desks to the periphery where they would remain throughout the week and placed all the artifacts on the floor in the center of the room. For the first day, the students added their notes, ideas, and artifacts to the mix. The following day, they began to categorize the artifacts. Finally, on the third day, they selected groups of artifacts to guide their brainstorming for proposal development. In the end, their proposal for a "Teens 2 Teens" campaign emerged. The mission of "Teens 2 Teens" was to gain the attention of the NYC youth community about dating abuse and to educate young people about healthy and unhealthy relationships. They launched the *#LetThemKnow* hashtag to encourage teens to speak out and build a culture of dating based upon trust, equality, safety, and respect. They proposed promoting *#LetThemKnow* on social media and created a YouTube video to encourage teens to share their stories on social media platforms. These students also proposed a "Teens 2 Teens" webpage for teens to post testimonials and learn about dating abuse. They also proposed a teen task force to run the social media profiles for "Teens 2 Teens" utilizing the hashtag to gather content for the website and to spread the word to high schools throughout NYC.

Step 4: Going Public

Step 4: Going Public is often the most visible and exciting phase of the Y-PLAN experience for students, teachers, and civic leaders. It is finally time for students to share their proposals in a public arena with their civic clients and stakeholders. Students work together to create slide decks, professional presentation boards, models, and written briefs. Often, students partner with arts and music classes to develop creative presentations, such as dramatic skits, raps, videos, and poetry. They learn public speaking techniques and

Image 3.6 In Step 4, Going Public, student teams present to clients, civic leaders, parents, and peers in City Hall, Council Chambers, or other important civic settings. Here, students from Brooklyn step up to the podium to share proposal boards, narrate digital slideshows, and field questions from the panel about their vision for change.

Source: Benjamin Deibert.

prepare for oral, visual, and digital presentations. This part of the process takes students into an important civic setting: in the Council Chambers or City Hall, around a conference table with civic leaders, on stage in a college campus auditorium, or in a virtual Zoom roundtable. In these settings, the student teams share their proposals for urban transformation with their client, parents, civic leaders, educators from other schools and districts, and peers. Some teams make modest recommendations for how to incrementally improve a community or city. Others offer grand visions for how to enact structural and systemic changes in various sectors. Together, they create a tapestry of young people's visions for a more equitable and just future for everyone.

Returning to the World Trade Center Roundtable, the final young planner stepped forward to describe how Step 4: Going Public was on display at a Digital Apps Forum held by Grover Cleveland High School students the previous year. At that Forum, students presented their work to their clients. NYC Department of Education's Chancellor Carmen Fariña was in attendance

Image 3.7 Students eagerly share the digital apps they designed with NYC Department of Education's Chancellor Carmen Fariña. The apps were designed to enable people with different ages and abilities to navigate and access public spaces safely.

Source: Andrew Woodbridge NYC DOE.

with great interest, and ABC 7 News covered the event. Students showcased the suite of digital apps they developed and released in response to their Council Member's challenge to create accessible digital tours of their neighborhood. At the forum, they presented their apps, each offering a solution to the multiple challenges facing residents of all ages. Their apps had the added benefit of being downloadable in the Google Play store – a rare real time outcome atypical for planning projects.

As part of Step 4, the day before the World Trade Center Roundtable, 150 people had gathered at another Y-PLAN NYC Summit on Long Island University's Brooklyn campus to showcase the power of this step in the Y-PLAN process. There, students from sixteen NYC public high schools made a series of public presentations to teachers, dozens of civic clients, and education and community leaders. During a poster session, students proudly showcased the proposal boards they created in response to their respective civic client's project questions. These professionally crafted displays explicated their research process and vividly showcased their policy and design recommendations.

Adult allies circulated through the exhibition, engaging with students and offering critical feedback and written reviews. The entire group then gathered for a formal PowerPoint session. Student leaders from the various projects presented a more in-depth rendering of their respective teams' work to a panel of academics, policy directors, educators, Y-PLAN alumni, and civic clients. After each presentation, the panelists asked the students follow-up questions and offered critical feedback, assessing the content, the research process, and the students' professional presentation skills. The event encapsulated the potency of the Going Public component of the Y-PLAN process. Civic leaders and stakeholders with an investment in the student work, and the power to take action on their recommendations, reviewed their proposals with deep interest. Students publicly showcased the skills and knowledge they had developed during the Y-PLAN process while also centering their voices about their everyday life in the city. According to one student planner, "presenting was the greatest struggle and the best part because it wasn't just in our heads anymore, it was in the world."

Step 5: Looking Forward, Looking Back

Step 5: Looking Forward, Looking Back is often the most transformative component of Y-PLAN's "Roadmap to Change." It gives students and clients alike the space to reflect upon their experience and plan the next steps for their proposals, their city, and themselves. During this part of the process, students' sense of agency and their identity as civic actors emerges, as they reflect upon their personal growth during this process and future options that have opened up. Y-PLAN's "Roadmap to Change" guides students to leverage this experience as they craft college essays or internship applications. John Dewey is often credited with the sentiment: "We do not learn from experience . . . we learn from reflecting on experience" (Dewey, 1916). In that vein, Y-PLAN student scholars also translate their presentation boards and presentation slides into policy briefs that they submit to their clients. In response, civic leaders often write letters back to the students detailing the impact of the young planners' insights and proposals on their practice, policies, places, and processes. Individually, the students identify actions they would like to pursue. Collectively, with their teams or whole classes, they enumerate the next steps needed to implement their recommendations, identifying action items for each other, and for their civic partners as well.

Often most surprising to the adult partners – and what is most important to the young planners – is that during this process they were being listened to, respected, and taken seriously. It is all too common for adults to short-change young people and write off their input, believing that youth seek only instant gratification. The Y-PLAN process demonstrates that this is not the case among its young participants. Young people seek respect and the recognition that their ideas and visions for the future are considered with the gravitas they deserve. Some of the most contentious and impactful conversations between young people and adults in NYC were about the next steps. Students wanted to know what was going to happen next and how their ideas were going to be used – or not. It is always inspiring when students' ideas are immediately actionable. It is equally important for the adult participants to make transparent to them the often invisible process of city planning can be slow and replete with challenges. Not every proposal gets implemented.

Learning that changing one's physical and social environment and city planning takes time. Generating imaginative ideas, such as those presented at the World Trade Center Roundtable and other Y-PLAN public presentations, is an essential part of being genuine stakeholders and agents of change in one's city. The nine in-depth case studies in Part II describe how a wide range students' input can be utilized and impactful in short- and long-term city planning processes. Sometimes, proposals and recommendations are adopted quickly into formal plans and policies. Other times, recommended changes to the built environment will only be implemented many years later.

By the end of Step 5, students and adults in the community of practice alike are transformed, personally and professionally, and the seeds are planted for city transformation, both physical and political. As Grover Cleveland teacher Mr. Woodbridge explained at the Digital App Forum discussed earlier, the goal is "to prepare them for college and a career. They are doing the same things adults do." Chancellor Fariña encouraged the students to work hard to turn their passion for technology into an enterprise or career they love while commending them for the impact they are already having on their community. "Think about what you do after you leave high school and think about as you get to college how you make sure that this becomes possibly a job for you in the future," Fariña told the students. "The other thing I am happy to be here today is I didn't know this park existed. Now I will need to use your app to really come back and really appreciate it more" (Giudice, 2016).

Conclusion

The high school students at the World Trade Center Roundtable beautifully described how the Y-PLAN research and visioning process was actualized in one year through multiple projects throughout New York City. For over twenty years, this same process has engaged participants and places across a wide range of ages, demographics, places, and settings – from post-Katrina New Orleans to earthquake prone Oakland; from a charter middle school in Washington, DC to an after-school program in Detroit; from first graders to adult workforce development extension classes; and from China to West Africa to Japan. Y-PLAN projects that follow the "Roadmap to Change" described earlier have shaped participants and places across a wide range of ages, demographics, places, and settings.

Part II focuses upon three critical city planning themes: Resilience, Housing, and Transportation. Each chapter sets the stage through literature and practice and then offers a vignette, three in-depth case studies, and dozens of examples of how young people and adult planners collaborate using the Y-PLAN methodology to make change in cities across the country and around the globe.

While the details of each project's implementation adapt to meet the needs of diverse contexts, each case study reflects three core conditions from the theory of change for planning just and joyful cities for and with young people, as introduced in Chapter 2. First, students gain access to professionals and tools from both the private and public sectors, and those leaders simultaneously gain access to the lived experiences of the youth living in diverse communities. Over time, youth prove to be powerful leaders, agents of change navigating complex housing, transportation, and environmental policies, volumes of data and civic systems, and people and places of power in diverse professional settings. Adult participants concurrently learn to navigate their cities and schools through the eyes of young, diverse residents, often developing enduring relationships across distinct and decisive social networks. Working collectively, all members of these intergenerational communities of practice begin to transform themselves and the systems in their communities, never losing sight of their local context and commitment to the critical needs and complexities of their home.

Notes

1 Vision Zero is a strategy first implemented in Sweden, and now also increasingly across the USA and globe, to eliminate all traffic fatalities and severe injuries, while increasing safe, healthy, equitable mobility for all residents. To learn more visit https://visionzeronetwork.org/.

2 This course is also funded as part of a statewide University of California initiative, University-Community Links (UC Links), supporting a network of university and community partners, working closely together to sustain after-school and in-school programs that extend access to quality educational resources and activities that support the academic preparedness and college readiness of P-12 youth from underserved California communities.

3 The UC Berkeley Y-PLAN program website hosts a database of over 250 Y-PLAN projects searchable by sector, city, and school. To learn more visit http://y-plan.berkeley.edu/in-action.

References

Coghlan, D., & Brydon-Miller, M. (2014). *The SAGE Encyclopedia of Action Research*. SAGE Publications Ltd. https://doi.org/10.4135/9781446294406

Dewey, J. (1916). *Democracy and Education*. Dover Publications.

Giudice, A. (2016, January 7). Ridgewood Students Unveil Community Apps for Forest Park. *QNS.Com*. https://qns.com/2016/01/ridgewood-students-unveil-community-app-for-forest-park/

Lansdown, G. (2014). 25 Years of UNCRC: Lessons Learned in Children's Participation. *Canadian Journal of Children's Rights/Revue Canadienne Des Droits Des Enfants, 1*(1). https://doi.org/10.22215/cjcr.v1i1.12

McDaniels, A. (2018, August 22). *Building Community Schools Systems*. Center for American Progress. www.americanprogress.org/issues/education-k-12/reports/2018/08/22/454977/building-community-schools-systems/

McKoy, D. L., & Vincent, J. M. (2007). Engaging Schools in Urban Revitalization: The Y-PLAN (Youth-Plan, Learn, Act, Now!). *Journal of Planning Education and Research, 26*(4), 389–403. https://doi.org/10.1177/0739456X06298817

Next Generation Science Standards. (2021). www.nextgenscience.org/

Noguera, P. A., & Syeed, E. (2020). *City Schools and the American Dream 2: The Enduring Promise of Public Education* (Kindle iOS version). Teachers College Press.

Warner, M., & Caspary, K. (2017). *Access & Equity in Linked Learning: A Report on Pathway Access and Academic Outcomes for Traditionally Underserved Students*. SRI International.

Wenger, E. (1998). *Communities of Practice: Learning, Meaning, and Identity*. Cambridge University Press.

What is a Community School? (n.d.). Coalition for Community Schools. Retrieved March 31, 2021, from www.communityschools.org/aboutschools/what_is_a_community_school.aspx

PART II

Young Planners in Action

pivotal role of schools
but must rethink school model →
Intergenerational CoP

4 Spotlight on Resilience

Introduction

"I can start," Luis[1] said, interrupting the momentary silence that was often typical of the large video conference calls that had become prevalent over the preceding nine months of the COVID-19 pandemic.

"Okay, Luis," Dr. Moore responded. "I appreciate your enthusiasm, but you are not a student in this class, so I'm going to ask one of my students to begin." The calm in the veteran teacher's voice conveyed a sense of control to the adults who were participating (a bit uncertainly) on the call. They ranged in their experience with high school students from seasoned teachers to city planners who had not spoken with teenagers since they were teens themselves.

At Dr. Moore's request, Luis clicked his keyboard to mute his voice, and other voices entered in seamlessly. It was the morning of December 9, 2020, just a few days after the Bay Area had returned to the strictest of stay-at-home orders due to the COVID-19 pandemic. These young planners were presenting the culmination of their fall semester's work, sharing their recommendations for safe, equitable school reopening with their client, California's Capitol Collaborative on Race & Equity (CCORE), and others. Their project title – "Your Life Matters" – filled the center of the shared screen. The UC Berkeley Y-PLAN (Youth-Plan, Learn, Act, Now) coordinator clicked through their recommendations on their project website, which had been compiled by two classes of Kennedy High School's Information Technology Academy (Kennedy) seniors. More than fifty state and local leaders, from the West Contra Costa Unified School District Superintendent to the California Governor's Strategic Growth Council and Office of Planning and Research were online,

DOI: 10.4324/9781003141778-6

eager to hear the students' voices. Two-thirds of the young planners were Latinx, with the remaining third split about evenly among students identifying as Black, Asian, or multiracial, and they all lived in the low-income community surrounding their school in Richmond, CA. They had spent the fall navigating the tumultuous shift to distance learning during the 2020 global COVID-19 pandemic. In doing so, they leveraged their new virtual context, conducting primary and secondary source research and crafting proposals, to address growing racial inequalities in their education. They did this via Zoom, with students connecting under harsh conditions, in their cramped bedrooms and often competing with siblings for physical, audio, and internet space, or as we learned on the call, sometimes from the sites of their full-time jobs.

Teams of students met online and mapped their school and community. They analyzed the strengths, weaknesses, opportunities, and threats (SWOT), and gathered inspiration by learning about best practices. They conducted surveys in English and Spanish, gathering nearly 500 responses from their community. The students brainstormed in break-out rooms to propose recommendations based upon their research. They created a website to showcase their proposals calling for integrated approaches to address the conditions they wanted to change.[2] On December 9th, they presented the results of all of their hard work, using their developing planning skills to share their unique insights and diligently acquired knowledge with their clients and with others in the audience. As magnified during the pandemic, these students dramatically demonstrated the power of resilience, stepping into their role as planning experts in their own right to shed light on daily life in their community.

For over two hours, two classes of young people sequentially unmuted their microphones to offer glimpses into their own realities to the convened adults, all professionals or city representatives responsible for planning the seemingly unplannable. As each of the groups shared their findings, their project titles filled everyone's computer screens: "A Look Inside Our Community," "Sharing our Strength," "People being People," "Equalizers," "Equity in Education: Welcome." Some students presented in English, others in Spanish, with translation provided for the English-only adults, and in many cases they presented over a cacophony of background noise. By the end of the session, nearly 60 students had shared the insights they had developed through this rigorous, three-month research process.

The final group's proposal titled "Our Home Within Our Community" particularly resonated with many attendees. These young planners advocated passionately and eloquently that there was a need for both physical and mental health support for teachers and students, by showing the audience just how much has been lost as school doors shuttered across our country. They called for supportive homerooms, advisors, and proper ventilation systems, explaining that Kennedy does not have windows in classrooms and that ventilation is critical to student and staff safety, especially during the pandemic. During their presentation, Dr. Moore sent a message over the chat to the nearly 100 participants on the line that underscored the need for this work: "Luis just explained to me that he is in my class. He just hadn't joined before today because he hasn't had access to the internet." This lack of access had already been theoretically known by the adults in attendance, but this student, who managed to join this critical Zoom class despite the obstacles to his participation, made it heartbreakingly real. It gave an anonymous societal problem a name and a voice.

While far from perfect as focal points for planning and change, schools as community institutions provide more than academics and peer socialization. Many North Americans learned about the key role of our public schools in childhood nutrition at the start of the pandemic in Spring 2020, reinforcing the vitality of schools in community support. However, that is not the only invisible role schools play that has been affected due to school closures. As students sheltered in place, our young people lost a building – a physical place – that has provided stability, escape, and support for them – all critical dimensions of a resilient environment. Despite that loss, the youth planners from Kennedy adapted. In a time when everyone was pressed to their limits, these young planners offered more than an example of successful schooling during a historic crisis. They demonstrated their desire and ability to help us see and hear each other more fully, to infuse justice and joy into our cities, and in doing so, to redefine how we see resilient communities now and in the future.

Setting the Stage Through Literature and Practice

Resilience is a core concept in city planning with origins in ecosystems, engineering, and disaster preparedness. In considering how resilience in our cities impacts our schools and young people – and how resilience in our schools and young people impact our cities – we focus first on three domains of the resilience literature: urban, community, and educational resilience. From their earliest conceptions by C. S. Holling (1973) nearly fifty years ago, these domains interact with and inform each other, while also informing many other types of resilience, such as ecological, social-ecological, disaster, and engineering resilience. We follow with practical examples of bringing young people into the resilience planning mix and dive into three powerful case studies illustrating the opportunities and challenges of engaging young people in the resilience planning process.

Resilience is difficult to define and prior to now, conversations and discussions about resilience have not largely considered young people and public schools. Yet as we strive to define, contextualize, and develop systems of resilience through conceptions like urban resilience, community resilience, and socio-ecological resilience, we have found that a vital piece of the puzzle has been missing: our schools and the students they serve (McKoy et al., 2019). In setting out to define urban resilience, Meerow et al. (2019) conducted an extensive literature review, uncovering 172 studies with 25 distinct definitions that varied significantly across critically important categories, from the term "urban" itself, to the concept of equilibrium, to the timescale needed for action. After identifying six conceptual tensions that a complete definition should address, the scholars defined urban resilience as the ability of an urban system "to maintain or rapidly return to desired functions in the face of a disturbance, to adapt to change, and to quickly transform systems that limit current or future adaptive capacity" (p. 39). This definition is notably similar to the formulation put forth contemporaneously by Davidson et al. (2016), which defined "evolutionary urban resilience" as "the ability of an urban system or city to respond to the new requirements imposed by internal and external shocks or change processes by learning, adapting, reorganizing, and transforming its subsystems to take advantage of new opportunities" (p. 6). Both definitions consider the city as an ecosystem and allow for resilience to be demonstrated as an informed return to the original state, an adaptation to it, or a transformation to an improved one.

The concept of community resilience is similarly complex. Davidson et al. (2016) explained that community resilience draws from both psychological resilience, which considers an individual's capacity to deal with adversity or change, and disaster resilience, examining how systems respond to disasters. They defined community resilience as the "capacity of the social system to work toward a common objective" (p. 4) and noted that it "considers both system characteristics that support change and the processes through which agency can be created and enacted so as to retain a community's core structures and processes" (p. 5). What distinguishes community resilience from urban resilience is that community resilience considers people's agency and their ability to effect change. It also values the elements of people's culture which must be preserved for a community system to sustain resilience. Additionally, the complementary field of climate adaptation, which considers adjustments in groups as well as institutional behaviors that can reduce society's vulnerability to climate change, can be extended to this concept of community resilience. Smit and Wandel (2006) noted that what they called "practical adaptation initiatives," (or the capacity of a given community to adapt) elevated the unique conditions that matter to its residents and the lived experience of community members. At the time of their publication, Smit and Wandel acknowledged these were still not common within adaptation research or in the world of climate change.

Some researchers are digging deeper into specific dimensions of community resilience, such as social networks and connection. Klinenberg (2013) pointed to a strong correlation between social cohesion and community resilience capable of gleaning new insight into the importance of a robust social infrastructure. In communities impacted by natural disasters, from hurricanes to heatwaves to storm surges, people's connections to each other clearly contribute to both individual and collective resilience. As such, solutions developed to safeguard our cities most effectively cannot seek solely to mitigate the impacts of disasters in their aftermath but must also seek to develop and strengthen social networks in both ordinary times and those of prosperity (Klinenberg, 2013).

Meanwhile, growing critiques have challenged the very concept of resilience as a positive construct for all communities. For example, Baker (2019), cautioned, "if system resilience, rather than system transformation, becomes the focus of energy policy, we will miss an important opportunity to foster lasting justice" (p. 6). She asserted that not everyone, particularly not low-income communities of color, "bounce back" from climate change events in ways that are better for them and their communities. For that reason, she argued for "a disruption of the normative underpinnings of resilience . . . that exacerbate conditions of vulnerability in low-income communities and communities of color" (p. 6). Baker proposed an entirely new framing to be used all together: anti-resilience, which "explicitly utilizes an anti-racist and anti-oppression frame and creates an opening for policy approaches that aim for greater inclusion of people of color and low-income communities in the renewable energy transition" (p. 9).

Even while pushing beyond urban resilience to consider the unique needs of people and the connections between them, community resilience, practical adaptation, and even anti-resilience initiatives still miss a key piece of the resilience equation: our schools and the young people who attend them. The discourse of educational and school resilience has grown simultaneously yet separately. Embedded in this parallel domain are key community understandings that can begin to bridge the gap and forge a more comprehensive notion of community resilience, one that positions young people and schools at its core.

Educational resilience is commonly defined in the educational domain as "the heightened likelihood of success in school and other life accomplishments despite environmental adversities brought about by early traits, conditions, and experiences" (Wang et al., 1994, p. 46), focusing on the individual learner and drawing significantly from psychological constructions. However, in examining the resilience of learners, studies have shown that the classroom and school environments have an impact. For example, in a study from the University of Malta entitled "Resilience for All," Carmel Cefai (2007) identified "caring and nurturing relationships between students and teachers," positive relationships among peers, and engagement in meaningful work as essential in developing resilience in students. Cefai (2007) ultimately concluded that "classrooms are more likely to operate as protective and competence-enhancing contexts for their students, including those at risk, when they function as caring, inclusive, and prosocial, and learning-centered communities" (p. 130), thus identifying community within the classroom as critical for the resilience of students.

In their "Review of Research on Educational Resilience," Waxman et al. (2003) extended the importance of community for resilience from the classroom to the wider school context. They identified students' sense of belonging to the school, support from teachers, and connections beyond the school into the community as factors that facilitate resiliency among at-risk students. They found that deep relationships are even more of a driving factor for successful development than individual programmatic approaches (Waxman et al., 2003). They concluded that to develop resilient students, we must cultivate a caring classroom community and nurture relationships within the school, thereby creating a resilient climate and culture throughout the school and beyond – into the city itself.

Krasny et al. (2009) sought to "address the gap in the literature bridging education at the university and secondary level with resilience thinking." They examine the value of social and situated learning, including a community of practice, in three cases: one at a university in Sweden, one at a university in the US, and one at an American high school after-school program. They found recursive relationships among the educational programs and their larger social-ecological systems. The authors suggested that education and society are mutually transforming in an ongoing process and concluded that their work is an initial step in bringing individual notions of learning together with systems perspectives of resilience (Krasny et al., 2009). Their work served as an initial foray into the gap between education and resilience literature.

The work of engaging young people into resilience planning has begun to bridge this gap. Case study action research, as described in this chapter, finds in fact that perhaps one of the greatest contributions young people bring to the field of resilience is their resistance to being put into a box. While scholars addressing the disparate domains of resilience define it on their terms, for their purposes, through their own specific professional bents, young people go beyond such boundaries. Young planners often see resilience broadly as a community able to thrive in the face of adversity, as evidenced by the Kennedy students in the opening vignette. They also view it through a more personal lens, driven by their own lived experience. When invited to collaborate with professional planners and policy makers, students analyze the depth of the challenges before them, from housing to healthy food access, from waterfront accessibility to carbon emissions, from poverty to urban violence and gentrification. Given a platform, students speak of the important role of home, of connection to place, and of social ties that make up their communities. In conversations about resilience, whether as it applies to themselves as individuals, to their schools or their communities, or to their region, young people resist stereotypes and convenient classifications.

As long as the conception of young people's resilience remains distant and distinct from that of our cities, the two will not mutually benefit from the light each can shine on the other. Fully actualized resilience planning will require the convergence of these conceptions. Such a convergence would necessitate a shift in the relationship between young people and those with power in the cities. This shift can be realized by forging intergenerational communities of practice, as described in Part I, Chapter 2, and critically examining equity concerns embedded in the existing understanding of resilience.

Embedding schools and young people, especially those who identify as low-income BIPOC into the fabric of the resilience discussion and planning efforts at a local and/or systemic level, benefits young people and everyone. It also allows for fruitful collaboration and mutual growth with adults and professionals, as they strive to solve some of the most vexing challenges of our time.

Bringing Together Young People and Resilience Planning

The engagement of young people in the process of resilience planning is an expanding area of cross-disciplinary study that may deepen the alignment between the city and school policies and practice. A range of approaches, from social media and digital technologies to arts and theatre, have been employed to effectively inspire young people to take action toward a more resilient future, especially in regard to promoting community support for climate change related issues.

Current research has also called on city leaders to recognize children and youth not as passive victims of disasters, but as important stakeholders and core players in future advocacy efforts (Treichel, 2020, p. 26). In a review of adaptation research and practice literature focusing on how child-centered responses to climate change can contribute to building the resilience of households and communities, Treichel (2020) stated, "It is timely to consider how to more effectively include children in climate change adaptation action more broadly, and the consequences for them and their communities" (p. 26). Similarly, Lee et al. (2020) recognized that countries vary widely in their attempts to engage young people in climate change planning overall and identified several different methods, from digital technology to creative arts to educational programming, that show promise in increasing such engagement.

Traditionally, education research has situated climate resilience within the science curriculum. However, Rousell and Cutter-Mackenzie-Knowles (2019) asserted that to achieve maximum potential, we need to broaden our view of the concept to include disciplines beyond science and environmental education classrooms. They challenge educational researchers to dare to expand the discourse past climate change knowledge itself and to engage "directly with children and young people themselves in genuinely collaborative, imaginative and creative ways through the emerging transdisciplinary field of climate change education" (p. 203). A Siegner and Stapert (2020) study evaluated a climate change curriculum implemented through an integrated social studies and language arts framework. As they explored the connection between information and social action as part of the curriculum, they found that an "action/solutions focus can be strengthened by better incorporating authentic and meaningful student climate action projects in the local community" (p. 523). Busch et al. (2019), however, have found scientific knowledge of climate change to be a weak predictor of climate action. Instead, they identified social norms and efficacy as the strongest direct predictors of such behavior.

If climate education truly endeavors to encourage action, it must expand its view beyond conventional structures of education and begin to target improving individual efficacy and adjusting social norms in collaboration with young people. In one such expansion beyond environmental education, Napawan et al. (2017) has called on climate resilience planners to use social media to engage young people, leveraging digital technology as a tool to encourage youth to evaluate their built environment.

Arts and creative expression are another avenue to involve young people in resilience planning. Fletcher et al. (2016) conducted a multi-site arts-based youth engagement research project called Youth Creating Disaster Recovery and Resilience (YCDR2). This Canadian-United States applied research initiative was aimed at learning from and with youth ages 13–22 about their disaster experiences. The project used creative and arts-based methods to engage youth in participatory workshops in their disaster-affected communities amid ongoing recovery efforts. The process revealed specific and often overlooked needs for youth-friendly spaces, processes, and opportunities, as well as the creative responses and adaptations of young people who have lived through disasters. Young people throughout the world have demonstrated their capacity and desire to help their community during and after a disaster, as well to support young people in other communities who have experienced a disaster, and they demonstrated their creativity and passion for linking thoughtful planning and action throughout the process. Their final products are showcased on the project website[3] and were presented at the Children & Youth Forum at the United Nations World Conference on Disaster Risk Reduction in Sendai, Japan in 2015.

Osnes (2018) has also framed the role of artistic performance to engage young people in youth-led community engagement for resilience planning. As part of the 100 Resilient Cities global initiative and based on her work at the University of Colorado, Boulder, Osnes designed a unique theatrical performance called *Shine* that has been performed by local youth in eight different communities from 2015 to 2017 from Boulder, Colorado, to New York City, New York, to Tuba City, Arizona, within the Navajo Nation. This performance sought to center local knowledge and weave climate science and artistic expression into storytelling focused on the interrelationship among energy, humanity, and climate. This powerful, artistic work was featured in the City of Boulder Resilience Strategy, as an exemplary way to involve people in conversations around resiliency (Weber et al., 2004, as cited in Osnes, 2018, p. 192; Guibert, 2016, as cited in Osnes, 2018, p. 198).

A series of papers has also called for educators' support of more active youth participation in resilience and climate change planning and action. Sanson et al. (2019) called on professionals in child development to listen more carefully to young people's voices and to provide new opportunities for active engagement, with a special focus on engaging the highest-need children and youth in the process of envisioning alternative futures, since they are the young people most often overlooked in planning for climate change. As an example, Sanson et al. (2019) pointed to the recent worldwide increase in school strikes for climate action, where young people are expressing their deep concerns about their future and their determination to prevent future environmental catastrophe. They further urged that adults must begin to act now to support the climate action charge that young people are voicing.

Derr et al. (2018) built upon this work in their research and analysis of three cities in three nations (again all participants in the Rockefeller 100 Resilient Cities initiative) – Boulder, Colorado; Mexico City, Mexico; and Thessaloniki, Greece – that integrated children and youth into resilience planning with mixed results. They acknowledged the integration of children and youth into these processes is challenging but possible and found that children and youth can lend valuable perspectives and help shape priorities for resilience strategies at multiple stages of the process. In mapping and research, for example, young people can identify community assets and vulnerabilities and can contribute to processes where local knowledge is valued (Derr et al., 2018, p. 23). However, they also found that bringing these youth engagement projects to the level of full implementation has been problematic, a finding that underscores the need from the beginning to include adults with the power to implement young people's visions in the process of putting good ideas into action.

Additional authors in the field have offered a range of factors that support resilience planning engagement with children and youth, with a particular focus on the importance of fostering young people's agency. The Sendai Framework for Disaster Risk Reduction (United Nations, 2015) viewed children as agents of change whose participation in disaster risk reduction should be supported). Additionally, Sanson et al. (2019) identified a range of ground-breaking legal cases, where young people have claimed their own agency and taken things into their own hands. They are doing so by using the courts to try to force governments into action on the climate crisis. In 2018, the Colombian Supreme Court ruled in favor of 25 youth plaintiffs, arguing that deforestation in the Amazon threatened their rights to a healthy environment (Dejustica, 2018). In August 2018, 15-year-old Greta Thunberg famously led a school strike demanding the Swedish government to take more serious action to address climate change. She galvanized many young people into action: an estimated 1.4 million children and youth in 1,400 cities in 110 countries took part in a global strike in March 2019 (Carrington, 2019, as cited in Sanson et al., 2019, p. 204).

While challenges persist, there has been a great deal of progress over the past decade in substantiating why young people and their schools need to be active participants in resilience planning. A United Nations Department of Economic and Social Affairs newsletter (2018) declared the urgency of investing in youth today to prepare for current and future adoption of sustainability measures. The publication stressed the need to impart awareness and a sense of environmental stewardship at a young age. All of the earlier-cited research and examples call for initiatives that move past simply listening to young people in the community and governmental settings. They have advocated for giving young people opportunities to engage deeply in civic society overall (Hart, 2008). In response to Hart's and others' calls for substantive and institutional participation among young people in our cities, the following section showcases three case studies of young planners in action from UC Berkeley's Y-PLAN initiative.

UC Berkeley Y-PLAN Case Studies

Aligned with Y-PLAN's Theory of Change described in Part I, the following case studies represent three (out of more than 50) projects explicitly related to environmental resilience facilitated by UC Berkeley over the past two decades.[4] Projects have grown along with the field, beginning with community garden design projects, expanding to sustainable housing, transportation, and public space initiatives, and more recently evolving into climate action plans to tackle sea level rise, community resilience, and the role of school facilities as community emergency hubs. The case studies include: disaster planning and recovery in Tohoku, Japan, climate action planning in Richmond CA, and improving resilience to sea level rise in San Rafael, CA. Each case study includes an analysis of how it demonstrated the key aspects of youth engagement work: access, navigation, and transformation. These case studies also exemplify the youth planners' constant interest in finding ways to achieve both justice and joy in their communities. While these components emerged from the literature mentioned earlier, through their activities in their own communities, students have used the Y-PLAN process over time to deepen their engagement and facilitate significant changes in their own communities.

Tohoku, Japan: Sharing Knowledge Forged From Disaster

Why Plan for Tohoku, Japan

On March 11, 2011, a magnitude 9.0 earthquake struck in the Pacific Ocean off the northeast coast of the Tohoku region of Japan. The Great East Japan Earthquake, as it is now called, triggered a massive tsunami that flooded more than 200 square miles of coastal land. Waves were estimated to be as high as 38 meters, the height of a 12-story building. The government estimated 20,000 people were dead or missing and close to 500,000 people were forced to evacuate (Reid, 2019). Furthermore, a nuclear power plant meltdown in the Fukushima prefecture triggered a nuclear emergency. The economic loss from the earthquake, tsunami, and nuclear disaster is estimated at $360 billion (Reid, 2019). Though Japan is known as a leader in disaster preparedness, the 2011 Tohoku earthquake caused overwhelming damage and inspired a global humanitarian response. As Otani (2016) explained, "The memory of the devastation caused by the Great Earthquake still lingers in our minds. It seems like only yesterday. However, when we think back, we remember not just the difficulties but the resilience of the people from Tohoku."

From 2012 to 2019, one thousand high school students from the coastal and rural communities of Tohoku, Japan came to UC Berkeley – typically in cohorts of 100[5] – to participate in the annual three-week Y-PLAN youth leadership studio sponsored by the United States Japan Council through a global program called TOMODACHI. Building upon the strength and hope of young people who hailed from the three prefectures most impacted by the disaster – Iwate, Fukushima, and Miyagi, this intensive experience also helped them cultivate new leadership skills as they developed powerful plans and visions for the future.

Young people were especially impacted by the earthquake and tsunami. As survivors, nearly all students in the studio knew someone who had died or remained missing. They witnessed the prolonged aftermath of the disaster as their communities attempted to recover socially and physically. Despite progress, residents even now, ten years later, still see visible evidence of destruction across their towns: a disaggregated built environment, social networks in disarray, and residents still suffering from Post-Traumatic Stress Disorder (PTSD). Like their elders, young people know the fear, pain, and uncertainty of social and physical disorder. They also know what is safe, what nourishes people, what helps them survive, and most importantly, what is needed in the future.

Each year, the students' first challenge was to respond to tough, authentic problems facing civic leaders and residents in Oakland, Berkeley, and Richmond, CA, from climate change to homelessness to economic development and degraded public space. As they met these challenges, the students brought all they learned about resilience from their experience in Tohoku to inform their recommendations for communities half a world away.

In 2016, on the fifth anniversary of the tragedy, Oakland's Chief Resilience Officer (CRO)[6] framed a question for the students. The CRO recognized the power of this opportunity to learn from and with Japanese youth. Studying Oakland's Howard Terminal, an underutilized massive, mothballed deep-water shipping dock in the Port of Oakland, the students from Tohoku grappled with issues related to disaster preparedness and community revitalization. Their project question was *How can Oakland build a healthy, equitable, and resilient community to meet environmental, economic, and social challenges such as climate change, sea level rise, earthquakes, drought, and fire?* This question created the context for an authentic and mature cultural exchange between the City of Oakland and Japanese youth. The CRO and other civic partners genuinely wanted and needed the students' unique perspectives and knowledge about how to meet big challenges, based upon their experience surviving a far-reaching environmental crisis and living in its aftermath.

This challenge was also extraordinarily relevant to these young people. They were about 10 years old when the earthquake and tsunami struck, and while they could remember it vividly, they also had enough critical distance to reflect meaningfully upon it. For five years, they lived through the long-term repercussions of destruction and nuclear meltdown. They knew in very graphic and visceral ways what it means for a community to rebuild in the wake of a disaster of this magnitude. They held a unique perspective and level of expertise on many of the issues related to emergency preparedness, resilience, and the quest to revitalize and enable residents to thrive.

Intergenerational Community of Practice

The students' study of the Oakland waterfront around the Howard Terminal site underscored the importance of authentic civic participation when the issues impact multiple stakeholders. This project exposed students to a wide range of people and urban conditions. As they met community leaders and toured low-income Oakland neighborhoods, students confronted deep urban problems that US communities face, including industrial areas visibly impacted by decades of racist planning, policies, and investment priorities. When observing and analyzing the city, one group of students said they were "crying for Oakland" because of the homelessness, gentrification, environmental degradation, and torn social fabric they witnessed. Many aspects of Oakland's Howard Terminal site itself specifically resonated with the students. The waterfront location, the topography, and the industrial infrastructure mirrored conditions in coastal communities in Tohoku. Hence, they were highly motivated to share their knowledge and put their hearts and souls into offering recommendations for the City of Oakland to build resilience in a pragmatic and meaningful way.

Throughout this process, the Japanese students gained access to adult professionals – engineers, architects, educators, and planners who introduced them to the mechanisms of government and the technical aspects of city planning. Access to these adult leaders helped the students build their urban planning vocabulary and enhance their ability to strategically collect

Image 4.1 As part of their research about Oakland's waterfront and resilience preparedness, Japanese students interview local residents and businesspeople to collect data about their social and economic needs. Their instructional mentor from UC Berkeley helps translate and bridge the language gap.

Source: UC Berkeley Center for Cities and Schools.

and analyze data. This exposure enabled the young people to make higher-order connections as they developed their proposals and advocated for change. For example, as one team was generating proposals to revitalize the Oakland waterfront, they met with environmental activists and landscape architects who challenged them to incorporate more strategic interventions to respond to sea level rise. Having access to these professionals helped the students strengthen their proposals.

Meeting adult professionals, touring sites with civic leaders and learning about best practices around the world also taught the students to navigate systems of governance and community maintenance. From planners they learned how to apply technical tools and skills as they incorporated maps, models, and data into their visual presentations. From business professionals and civic leaders, they learned how to make a pitch, develop a cost/benefit analysis, and outline short-term and long-term strategies to reach goals. As a result, the young people learned to realistically strategize about how to successfully navigate these systems and realize their visions for change. Throughout, the students applied their knowledge of resilience from Tohoku as they grappled with and navigated through the systemic challenges facing Oakland.

Four teams generated proposals to transform the Howard Terminal site, each with a different focus for a more resilient city. One proposal featured promotion of tourism and alternative forms of transportation along the waterfront, linking the desolate site to the more vibrant, nearby Jack London Square. Another team focused on developing recreational hubs that could also function as disaster relief centers and food storage in times of emergency. Two proposals highlighted creative re-use of the shipping cranes and of the massive fuel storage tank on the site.

While their design and policy recommendations included acute "disaster response" strategies, the proposals also focused on long-term community building as a bulwark of Oakland's resilience – as strong social connections were critical to the students' experience and ability to recover back home. During the earthquake and tsunami – and in the aftermath – people with robust community ties were able to mobilize and help each other. In towns where people were isolated, more people were stranded, died, or were lost during the event, and they were more likely to suffer from PTSD or depression in the ensuing years. To the students, accessible public transportation systems, a thriving tourism industry, vibrant public spaces, and secure, permanent housing were important systemic changes needed to strengthen and build community resilience. These young planners drew on their own devastating experiences to help transform another community to protect it from such a fate, and along the way their own identities and sense of self began to shift, transforming them from student to expert, from victim to leader.

Analysis: Sustaining Influence and Impact

Each year of the Y-PLAN Tohoku initiative, after the students presented their proposals and recommendations in response to the question posed by their local clients, they then launched into the second part of the Y-PLAN Tohoku Studio. Young people applied all of the skills, attitudes, and pedagogical approaches they had learned to craft individual plans of action for their home communities. During this phase, the students were joined by Adult Allies, local community leaders from Tohoku whose primary goal was to expand the students' capacity to continue to develop and implement action when they returned to Japan. While in the Y-PLAN studio, these adult leaders also gained access to and learned to navigate the Y-PLAN methodology while engaging with and deepening their relationships with the students. Upon their return to Japan, they helped the students build a local community of practice, gain access to people with professional skills and tools, and navigate systems and places of governance, business, and education as they actualized their visions for change in Tohoku.

Students returned to Japan with a deeper understanding of how local actions can create global change. After the Y-PLAN experience, many made the important link between personal suffering and the large-scale systemic impacts of the earthquake and tsunami. They had become more educated about nuclear safety protocols and sustainable energy policy. For example, those from Fukushima were able to look critically at the systemic factors that led to the hydrogen explosions, release of radioactive contamination, and meltdown of the Daiichi nuclear power plant. To deal with fear and uncertainty in that whole region, young people have launched campaigns to raise awareness and educate the populace – and tourists – about the impacts of radiation. One student focused his action plans on the workers assigned to decontaminate the affected areas of the nuclear power plant. These workers

Image 4.2 After the students create their proposals, they meet with adult experts to conduct a cost-benefit evaluation of each component. They then incorporate this feedback, revise their proposals, and strengthen their Action Plans for their return to Japan.

Source: UC Berkeley Center for Cities and Schools.

were being stigmatized and treated like "untouchables" by the community. He aimed to eliminate discrimination and increase these workers' status by celebrating and honoring them for their service. Another group has worked to help consumers understand that produce grown in certain regions of Fukushima is safe and untouched by radiation. Some, inspired by both the trauma and their leadership aspirations, have gone on to become engineers, health professionals, and environmental activists.

Adult Allies continue to work with youth and local schools in Japan to build the future of the region. One educator, Kenichi Bamba, who directs the community organization Bridge to Fukushima, uses the Y-PLAN methodology to train dozens of teachers, and young people in and outside of classrooms. Together these communities of practice are building leadership and community development capacity for a resilient and sustainable Fukushima. Bamba's hope is that in the future the community can say how Fukushima has been able to change because of the disaster lessons, not despite them.

By surviving a devastating disaster, and by thriving in their day-to-day lives over many years in its aftermath, young planners who came to UC Berkeley from the many towns in the Tohoku region of Japan embody resilience. Through their lived experience, they intuitively know the importance of social infrastructure and community cohesion. They have the desire and ability to bring together people, places, and institutions to foster solidarity and support, a key asset young people bring into the resilience equation. As they develop additional skills and tools to expand and deepen their knowledge, they are enriching our collective understanding about resilience. In the process, they learn about the importance of long-range planning to change the status quo in deeply meaningful and sustainable ways. They recognize how small or isolated actions can build toward large, global impacts. Finally, working together and with new transformative experiences across continents, they become more resilient, community stewards ready to lead toward a more just and joyful future for all.

Richmond, CA: Tackling Climate Change and Public Health

Why Plan for Richmond?

Located 16 miles northeast of San Francisco across the Bay, the city of Richmond, CA, is best known for its role in the World War II home front effort.

During the early 1940s, tens of thousands of workers from all over the country streamed into the city, which housed the most productive shipbuilding operations of the era, to work in the wartime industry. Many were African American sharecroppers who came out of the South in response to the call for workers. The city's population exploded during those years, with the employees of 55 war-oriented businesses working around the clock.

At the end of the war, industrial production rapidly declined, and Richmond's population steadily decreased. The decline did not happen by accident. The men and women who had been productive workers during the war effort lost their livelihoods through racist and sexist business and employment practices as well as fiscal issues related to government subsidization of sprawl and legislative changes, like California's Proposition 13. Oil refining, shipping, warehousing, and distribution operations rose to prominence. Richmond's downtown business district began to decline in the early 1970s, as its major retailers either moved or closed. Some targeted redevelopments along the waterfront and in the northeastern part of the city transformed Richmond's geography as well as its economy – leading to some gentrification in these areas.

Throughout this history, Standard Oil – now called Chevron USA – has grown and remains the City's major industry and employer. In describing his city, one long-time Richmond resident and veteran educator explained that:

> We live in the shadow of Standard Oil and some of the best universities in the country, yet we are some of the poorest, highest crime areas in the San Francisco Bay Area. This is the ghetto. And we are trying to survive.

Bisected by a major freeway linking different parts of the Bay Area, Richmond is now an attractive corridor for new high-tech industrial, business parks, biotech, and commercial development. It is an ethnically diverse city, with a plurality of African American and Latinx families.

Within this context, in 2013, the Richmond City Manager's Office launched the City's process to develop the Richmond Climate Action Plan (CAP). The CAP came from directives in the City's 2030 General Plan to make the Energy and Climate Element actionable and it is a roadmap for how to reduce greenhouse gas emissions and prepare for the impacts of climate change on public health, infrastructure, ecosystems, and public spaces in the city. It emphasizes health equity and climate justice as important aspects of the document framework. A stipulation was included in the request for CAP proposals that the consultants must partner with young people to develop the final Climate Action Plan.

Intergenerational Community of Practice

The Richmond City Manager's office collaborated with the UC Berkeley Center for Cities and Schools in 2015 to utilize the Y-PLAN methodology to bring young people into the CAP planning process. Also involved were private sector and regional stakeholders, such as the Metropolitan Transportation Commission and the Bay Conservation and Development Commission. With several years of experience engaging youth in a range of Y-PLAN planning projects from affordable housing to transportation connectivity, Richmond High School (RHS) took on the CAP process, choosing to integrate it across four core classes (English, Social Studies, Health, and Government) in their Health Career Academy. During the spring of 2016, all 265 Health

Image 4.3 On their site mapping tour, students in Richmond, California assess the impacts of nearby oil refineries on the health and sustainability of their community.
Source: UC Berkeley Center for Cities and Schools.

Career Academy students, with guidance from UC Berkeley graduate and undergraduate student mentors, took on the research question: *How can youth-driven data and insights inform the development of the Richmond Climate Action Plan?*

Accessing professionals and mentors, along with professional tools and skills, bolstered the experience for the youth as they grappled with the challenges of offering input to the CAP. Within the school classrooms, the high school students engaged with college students, local adult leaders, and practicing professionals in a variety of fields. Some mentors came into the classroom and worked alongside with teens. Others served as guest speakers, sharing their work and constructive feedback for the students' project ideas. When the young people toured sites or learned about local resources, they did so in consultation with experts and professionals, giving the students access to information and insights about site-specific issues. The City Manager's CAP team periodically met with students, helping them link the theories they learned in the classroom to real life phenomena, from the science behind recycling to the health impacts of historic pollution on Richmond residents. The young people were equipped with the skills and vocabulary they needed to navigate and analyze their environments as planning professionals would, developing as both engaged residents and budding environmental planners. The collaboration provided the teens with opportunities to use these skills to offer substantive and meaningful input into the Climate Action Plan.

Within the hands-on, supportive, and well-structured curriculum of Y-PLAN, many students were excited about the opportunity to speak about their communities and present their ideas to civic leaders. Being able to recognize social issues, use professional tools to analyze and address an issue, and navigate the political landscape made the students more aware and informed about community issues from a variety of perspectives. Navigating their community to gather evidence provided the students with an opportunity to offer something tangible to their families, peers, and neighbors. As they observed local dynamics, conducted surveys, analyzed data, and researched the costs and benefits of their proposals, they saw people responding to their survey, looking at their data and referring to their insights and visions. Because the students often contextualized their proposals within existing realities, such as transportation accessibility, gentrification, homelessness, and violence, they validated the lived realities of people in the larger community.

The CAP experience provided multiple opportunities for the students to speak and represent their school and work. When the students went to City Hall to present their ideas to civic leaders from Richmond and the wider region, they found themselves respected by people of all ages in a professional setting. The students received feedback from the audience about the importance of their work. These experiences increased the students' feelings of pride in their capabilities and nurtured their sense of agency. They gained confidence that their voices mattered and that they could use their voices and the professional tools they learned, to navigate political systems and to inspire adults to listen.

Being able to play an effective role in making community change was empowering for both individual students and adults during the CAP process as well as in subsequent Y-PLAN initiatives in Richmond. Teachers reported the transformative experiences they witnessed among their students, noting that the students surprised and impressed them with their willingness and ability to overcome shyness and learning disabilities in order to present publicly, often for the first time, with confidence and success. One participant explained, "Y-PLAN allowed the students to go beyond themselves. It put the banquet in front of everyone and every student tried it. Some nibbled, some tasted, and some ate – but they all had something."

Meanwhile, participating in site visits, workshops, forums, and public events where professionals and youth worked collaboratively was also transformative for adults. Young people's challenges, identities, and behaviors helped the adults to better understand and empathize with the students' interests and lived experiences. For example, the youth had a much larger appetite to participate in sustainable practices than the adults had previously realized. They challenged some of the adults' preconceived notions that low-income communities did not value ecological practices such as composting, recycling, and repurposing. Some students argued that low-income communities lived more sustainably than higher income people. While perspectives differed, both groups came to understand they needed each other. Presenting in a high-level civic arena brought gravity and credibility to the students' work and impressed adults. Students gave inspiring speeches about the role of health, sustainability, and resilience in their lives, and they read their powerful personal statements which in turn led to more understanding and empathy from all those in attendance.

The CAP project also provided an opportunity for civic organizations to witness and appreciate the quality and value of student work. Civic organizations opened doors and took steps to offer students internships and other opportunities going forward. Some groups, such as Healthy Richmond, saw the value of adding "youth seats" on formal decision making, such as in their Community Advisory Committees.

Each adult who participated face to face with young people during this process developed increased cultural sensitivity and humility, while young people gained a better comprehension of, and respect for, the wisdom and experience it takes to navigate social, economic, and political systems, to pull the levers of power and make a change. Marking the formal launch of the CAP, students presented their findings and final recommendations in the chambers at Richmond City Hall to hundreds of parents, most of whom were Latinx, African American, and Asian, as well as city administrators, community organizations, and other stakeholders. Reflecting on the significance of this event, the City Manager noted, "We have learned so much from these young planners. They are changing our perspective and priorities for CAP."

Analysis: Sustaining Influence and Impact

The students' participation in the CAP process directly and indirectly catalyzed change within the public school system, city government, and the private sector. This process also enhanced the relationship between two key systems: public schools and city government. RHS's teachers were essential players in this process that extended well beyond the classroom. Teachers scaffolded the students' experience and positioned themselves as incubators of civic activism. As a result of the direct participation of young people, city representatives began to change locations for the CAP engagement process and they held follow-up meetings at RHS to build on this important connection to the students, their families, and the school at large. The city began to recognize that school facilities are a major feature of public infrastructure that can and should be a prime locus of climate policy implementation with the potential to be central to the city's overall sustainability and resilience policies. The city also helped RHS realize student recommendations for their campus by installing bike racks, water bottle filling stations, salad bars in the cafeteria, and 3-bin waste systems throughout the school. The physical changes at RHS became a model for how the city could support greater school-based resilience projects at other schools in Richmond.

This powerful case study of school-based planning exemplifies the power of young people's voices in shaping policy, particularly when young people are actively and authentically incorporated from the beginning of a project and their input is given weight and legitimacy. Collaboration with youth at RHS through Y-PLAN resulted in specific, tangible recommendations and policies that were included in the official CAP. Their contributions are highlighted throughout the CAP document and their "10 Top Personal Actions to Support our Climate Goals" is now featured prominently and permanently in the official CAP document, adopted in October 2016 (City of Richmond Climate Action Plan, 2016).

Throughout the Spring 2016 Y-PLAN Richmond process, the students shared their fine-grained insights about sustainability and resilience, arising from their keen, sensitive knowledge of local conditions. The young people understood these concepts as they related to their everyday lives because many had dealt with trauma, adversity, racism, and inequity throughout their whole lives. As the students brought their inner mettle into the mix, many posited that they and their families were the embodiment of resilience and sustainable living. The students' lived experience provided a moral compass for those civic leaders and CAP staff who did not live in the community or

Image 4.4 The students translate their proposals for a healthier, more sustainable and resilient city into policy briefs. Some proposals become realities, like the City of Richmond, CA incorporating student recommendations into the official 2016 Climate Action Plan.

Source: UC Berkeley Center for Cities and Schools.

experience the same conditions. Since most of these students were BIPOC from various backgrounds with a range of complex issues confronting them, they viewed the world from an intersectional perspective. Students linked social equity and environmental justice, and some articulated that a community or city cannot have one without the other. Informed by their lives in the Richmond community, these young people helped to broaden the definitions of resilience, sustainability, and health as they embedded local knowledge into Richmond's CAP and became recognized – by teachers, professional planners, and civic leaders alike – as leaders and stewards of the future.

San Rafael, CA: Fearless Creativity and Stewardship From our Youngest Planners

Why Plan for San Rafael?

The city of San Rafael in Marin County, California is projected to be severely impacted by sea level rise and flooding in coming years. The Union of Concerned Scientists (2018) projected that by the year 2045, San Rafael, especially the low-income Canal community, will be deeply impacted by climate-driven sea level rise. Over the next hundred years, a three-foot rise will push the San Francisco Bay into the Canal community and the low-lying business and industrial areas in nearby downtown San Rafael. These threats put thousands of low-income residents at risk of losing their homes, their neighborhoods, their livelihoods, and more.

Intergenerational Community of Practice

In 2018, the San Francisco Bay Area launched the Resilient by Design | Bay Area Challenge (RbD), a year-long collaborative design initiative bringing together 10 teams of residents and leaders, and national and international experts to focus on the future of the nine contiguous counties surrounding the San Francisco Bay. Sponsored by the Rockefeller Foundation as part of their previous Rebuild by Design competition and their 100 Resilient Cities initiative, each team was tasked with developing innovative community-based solutions to strengthen the region's resilience to sea level rise, severe storms, floods, and earthquakes.

Young people were also invited into the planning process to address this crisis of sea level rise, via the launch of the parallel Resilient by Design

Youth Challenge using the Y-PLAN methodology. This was an ambitious regional project that engaged more than 1,000 students across five Bay Area counties. Students in each participating school were paired with a team of professionals – planners, architects, engineers, landscape architects, and civic leaders – and shared their charge. In response to the unique conditions of their local Bay Area city or community, each youth team took on a research question related to resilience. While the professional teams engaged in the RbD Challenge focused on resilience in response to sea level rise and climate change, the Youth Challenge defined "resilience" in broader terms, with an emphasis on the local community's ability to survive and thrive in the face of physical, social, and economic adversity.

One of the RbD Youth Challenge teams was composed of forty-five fourth-grade students at Laurel Dell Elementary school in San Rafael who engaged with the issues and generated strategies to respond to rising seas within their classrooms. In a twelve-part series of intensive hands-on studio sessions, they worked side by side with architects, planners, engineers, landscape architects, and artists from UC Berkeley's Y-PLAN initiative, San Rafael's Youth in Arts, and the RbD "Bionic" team, one of the ten professional teams selected for the Challenge. The Bionic team and other adults from the RbD partner organizations had initial trepidations about introducing these big issues to such young students. When the Bionic team polled the San Rafael community, many adults said the issues associated with sea level rise were too overwhelming, too complicated, or too far in the future to be a priority for them. They feared that the topics of sea level rise and resilience might be too abstract and complex for young children to engage with in a meaningful way. They speculated that the long-term impacts might be hard for this age group to visualize, and hence might make it difficult for them to sustain interest. Lastly, they anticipated that because the projections about sea level rise are sometimes depressing and overwhelming, some children might even become scared.

Contrary to these expectations, when asked to join the RbD Youth Challenge, the fourth graders enlisted with vigor. They wanted to be engaged in authentic issues and were not daunted by real, thorny problems. When they gained access to the adult team members to generate proposals protecting local neighborhoods from sea level rise, many of the students fluidly demonstrated that they understood some of the dynamics of sea level rise and the threats it posed to their community. Many had already witnessed firsthand flooding, groundwater percolation, and storm surge in their neighborhoods. Some students living in the Canal lowlands described how the streets looked like rivers and took days to recede after flooding events and how, on multiple occasions during storm events and high tides, their parents had to wear high boots even to make it from their front door to the car. Others expressed deep interest and curiosity, asking questions like, *How old are we going to be when the water floods our streets?* and *How high will the water go?* Despite the seriousness of the topic, all of the students brought their own experiences into the collaboration with enthusiasm, optimism, and verve.

However, they needed access to information, expertise, and skills to understand the issues and to translate their experiences and emotions into proposals that would be respected by the wider community. With the help and input from a variety of adult resource people, they learned the science, as well as the social and political impacts of climate change. Architects showed them images of inspiring best practices from around the world. Case studies showing waterways and floating buildings in Amsterdam and Rotterdam vividly demonstrated how people live with water and rising seas. Landscape architects and engineers exposed them to the creative, protective strategies being implemented in New York City in the wake of Hurricane Sandy. Interactions with these professionals helped the students think realistically and substantively about how to buttress the city, while at the same time making it more livable. The children's eagerness to participate both humbled and energized the adults who knew, lived, or worked with them during this process.

Participating in the RbD Youth Challenge gave these young students access to information, people, places, and ideas beyond their immediate day-to-day realms. The adult professionals willingly and eagerly shared their skills and technical knowledge with the students. From adults, the students learned about the long-term, deep impacts of climate change. This exposure educated them about geography, science, history, and hydrology. Representatives from Marin County brought maps into the classroom to show the students sea level rise projections for the next 100 years. Engineers and landscape architects introduced them to technical strategies for dealing with flooding, groundwater percolation, and storm surges. The students were profoundly inspired when they learned about the various Resilient by Design adult teams' proposals for interventions at sites around the San Francisco Bay. In "desk crits," a one-on-one exchange prior to project completion, architects and civic leaders gave the children realistic assessments of their proposals. The students' understanding both surprised and delighted the Bionic team, and other professionals from the City of San Rafael, and the County of Marin.

The students not only had access and exposure to new information, people, and skills, the adults on the RbD team encouraged them to apply their newfound knowledge to navigate the larger San Rafael community to engage others. The adult mentors created pathways for the children to navigate through the political and social networks so they could match their desire, optimism, and creativity with the capacity to make a change. The adult mentors from UC Berkeley and partner organization, Youth in Arts, gave the students opportunities to publicly weigh in as organizers, innovators, and leaders in building community resiliency in anticipation of sea level rise, climate change, and other challenges.

The young students formed mutually beneficial, reciprocal relationships with adult professionals. The adults gained access to the lived experiences of

Image 4.5 During their charette, the fourth graders from Laurel Dell Elementary in San Rafael, California, built a scale model of the areas of the city most vulnerable to sea level rise. Their model included multiple strategies to protect the community while improving the quality of everyday life. Here, they present it at a press conference at the outdoor Flood Fair.

Source: UC Berkeley Center for Cities and Schools.

young people and families who were most likely to be negatively impacted by rising seas. It deepened the Bionic team's understanding of conditions on the ground and how climate change challenges are compounded by poverty, inadequate housing, and language and cultural barriers. Long-time bureaucrats and other adults were touched by the students' optimism, creativity, and enthusiasm. Many commented that the young students reminded them why they are doing the work they do. For example, after researchers from the Union of Concerned Scientists read an article about the fourth-grade students' work, they wrote a letter to the Y-PLAN team:

> We're delighted to learn about these students engaging, so fearlessly and creatively, with the problems posed by sea level rise. Several of us are mothers of children in that age group, we worry about the world we're leaving them, not to mention the strains our jobs put on them. As our lead author Dr. Kristy Dahl put it, "Sometimes when we think we need to shelter them from the enormity of this, we forget that they can give us a fresh, much-needed perspective." Reading about your work lifted our spirits.

In the end, both sides of the equation were strengthened, enriched, and inspired by the experience.

Analysis: Sustaining Influence and Impact

Taking on a "real world" challenge enabled the students to showcase their knowledge of community conditions and apply them to the future. They were imaginative, optimistic, and quite adept at generating realistic, yet inspirational strategies to respond and adapt to flooding and sea level rise. They used their creativity and love of art, beauty, and nature to envision positive strategies to meet the challenges impacting their neighborhood. For example, building upon the "best practices" they studied during their studio sessions, the fourth-grade students designed and built a model for a "floodable park" – a proposal to allow the canal adjacent to the park to safely overflow during storm events, but to be usable as a soccer field when waters receded. Their solutions also included lush living shorelines by the San Francisco Bay and delightful protective, boardwalks along the canal and San Rafael Creek.

Throughout the RbD Youth Challenge, students engaged with real, substantive issues and infused the discourse about resilience into their own discussions with fresh energy and perspective. Their participation energized many adults, engaged a diverse audience, and helped add credibility to the RbD Bionic team's work. Additionally, the youth challenged the adults. When youth participated in forums, they often asked questions like *Why haven't earlier generations slowed down global warming?*, *Why aren't electric cars more popular?*, and *Why are the homes in our neighborhood so weak that they will fall or flood during future storms?*

These young planners, along with many others throughout the San Francisco Bay Area, helped to re-define and expand the definition of resilience. Not only are they living lives that are the very definition of resilience, but

Image 4.6 Fourth-grade students built an interview kiosk, designed t-shirts, and displayed their climate change posters at the San Rafael Resilient by Design Flood Fair. Here, in the kiosk, they interview local leaders, parents, and children about community preparations for rising seas.

Source: UC Berkeley Center for Cities and Schools.

they are also augmenting and amplifying the "official" discourse. Many of the adults challenged themselves to listen more attentively and to respond to those *Whys?* with greater care and genuine concern. The students presented their work and engaged with stakeholders at various community forums, where they also impressed their families, teachers, and activists. In many ways, it was revolutionary for adults to consider that young people of this age were capable of engaging in a project of this magnitude.

When asked to engage in an authentic way with the challenges of resilience in these projects, young planners rise to the occasion and bring serious, fresh, and optimistic perspectives to the table. They want access to and opportunities to navigate real tools to analyze data, create models and maps, and provide leadership to help meet these challenges. For adults involved in the program, children and youth, even ones as young as the fourth graders at Laurel Dell Elementary, offer a bridge to the larger community in a way that is inspiring, heartfelt and personal. Engaging with real challenges activates children's sense of purpose and imbues them with a sense of pride and an investment in their own communities. When students are seriously and authentically engaged, transformation happens on many levels: within the individual students, within school classrooms, and within the political and social systems in the community at large. The RbD experience offered many students a varied set of tools to use to open the door to their creativity and leadership capabilities, while contributing to the common good of their community. Students' work was recognized and continued in a range of ways:

- For several years after the RbD Youth Challenge, the students' large model, their posters, and their proposals were on display at the Office of Economic Development and Innovation for the City of San Rafael, generating even more respect for their ideas.
- Future teams of students took on various components of the long-range planning of the San Rafael 2040 General Plan, working with the General Plan Steering Committee on different components of the plan such as Open Space, Accessibility, Diversity, and the Downtown Precise Plan. They met with professionals in their classrooms, developed models representing their recommendations, and made presentations to the Steering Committee.
- In Fall 2020, the input from Laurel Dell's third, fourth, and fifth grade students was incorporated in the San Rafael 2040 General Plan document – it

is now under review for approval by the City's Planning Commission, City Council, and other public agencies.
- Four students also wrote an Op-Ed piece about community development for the 2040 General Plan that was published in the local newspaper.

The sustained experience of engaging students in the civic arena and community planning process captured the attention of School Board Trustees, council members, city staff, and other civic leaders who requested that students be involved in other high-profile development projects in the city. One city official shared their perspective:

> Y-PLAN does this so well in making sure that our students are in front of elected officials and speaking in places that they would never be invited to. Our kids are our best investment. We need to make sure they have the tools to make decisions to change their trajectory and that of other students who look and sound like them.

Conclusion

Resilience is at the core of planning cities for and with young people, especially as it relates to community, policy, and place. When learning is understood as a result of everyone's participation within an intergenerational community of practice, fostering meaningful relationships between civic leaders and young people can create a more resilient city that works for all of its residents. All participants learn from each other's expertise and experience to create collective knowledge for the entire community's benefit (McKoy et al., 2019).

Throughout these case studies, when considering resilience, young people call for planners and civic leaders to take immediate and equitable action now to preserve our future. In planning for resilience, young planners begin by redefining the very concept itself. Echoing the sentiments heard in classrooms from New York to Oakland, one young planner from the Tohoku region of Japan declared, "We are strong and can rise above challenging circumstances. We *are* resilience." These case studies demonstrated how young planners flip the script on resilience, centering themselves and their school communities as untapped assets that can provide critical social and physical infrastructure in the face of natural disasters and sea level rise, if they are given adequate support and resources.

Engaging in the resilience planning process with young people reveals their desire to contribute to long-range planning. Contrary to popular belief, young people do not just live in the moment. Rather, they understand that the long-range plans of today will define the future that they will inherit, and believe they have a right to help shape. They would prefer to have a say now before it is too late. In shaping the future, due to their intimate knowledge of their communities, young people often look to leverage local action to create models that can be applied on a broader scale to effect global change. They are genuinely open to adapting solutions from elsewhere to fit their lives. In doing so, they start to realize they are not alone in their struggles, and that their solutions possess a generality that extend beyond their own communities to other localities throughout the world. Along these same lines, young people of all ages consistently elevate the importance of their own stewardship of their communities, both locally and as part of a global society. Their activism and leadership can catalyze the engagement of adults who may have previously seen themselves as being powerless or on the margins. Time and again, young planners focus themselves and their proposals on helping to develop the connections needed to drive community resilience.

Key to improving resilience in our cities, our young planners also challenge prevailing assumptions. They interrupt standard procedures and misconceptions in ways that yield new understandings of resilience and the natural environment. For these reasons, it is essential that planners begin to view children and youth's visions for resilience not simply as a nice thing to do, but as a necessary, integral part of the planning process, ultimately to be codified in local plans and policies, from a city's climate action plans to their general plans.

As disparate disciplines struggle to define the concept of resilience, our young people show that they already understand it with a clarity that has often been lost in the conversation at professional levels. Young people know what needs to be remediated in a very personal way, to feel safe, respected, and whole. Resilience, whether for an individual or across a system, requires stability; it requires understanding, relationships, and trust; it requires inclusion and responsibility; and it requires a connection. When presented with external definitions of resilience in youth and planning classrooms, the young members of this community of practice often persist in their own understanding. The key to resilience is found in them. They hold the missing piece of the puzzle we struggle to complete.

Notes

1 Names of all young people are pseudonyms.

2 Kennedy student website found here: https://sites.google.com/wccusd.net/ita-equity-yplan/home.

3 Youth Creating Disaster Recovery & Resilience (YCDR2) is a research project in Canada and the USA to connect young people who have been affected by disasters.

4 To see more examples of Y-PLAN work in specific sectors within planning, visit the UC Berkeley Y-PLAN website: https://y-plan.berkeley.edu/in-action.

5 The first year of the TOMODACHI program sent the largest cohort of 300 students. Thereafter the United States Japan Council (USJC), who runs the overall program, lowered the cohort size to 100 youth. While there are a number of diverse USJC programs, the Berkeley summer studio was one of the first created after the disaster in partnership and funding from a large Japanese telecom company, Softbank.

6 Oakland, California was selected by the Rockefeller Foundation to be one of 100 Resilient Cities designed to help cities around the world become more resilient to physical, social, and economic shocks and stresses. This formed a natural partnership with the Y-PLAN Youth Challenge.

References

Baker, S. H. (2019). Anti-Resilience: A Roadmap for Transformational Justice within the Energy System. *Harvard Civil Rights, 54.*

Busch, K. C., Ardoin, N., Gruehn, D., & Stevenson, K. (2019). Exploring a Theoretical Model of Climate Change Action for Youth. *International Journal of Science Education, 41*(17), 2389–2409. https://doi.org/10.1080/09500693.2019.1680903

Cefai, C. (2007). Resilience for All: A Study of Classrooms as Protective Contexts. *Emotional and Behavioural Difficulties, 12*(2), 119–134. https://doi.org/10.1080/13632750701315516

City of Richmond Climate Action Plan. (2016). www.ci.richmond.ca.us/DocumentCenter/View/40636/CAP-combined?bidId=

Davidson, J. L., Jacobson, C., Lyth, A., Dedekorkut-Howes, A., Baldwin, C. L., Ellison, J. C., Holbrook, N. J., Howes, M. J., Serrao-Neumann, S., Singh-Peterson, L., & Smith, T. F. (2016). Interrogating Resilience: Toward a Typology to Improve its Operationalization. *Ecology and Society, 21*(2), art27. https://doi.org/10.5751/ES-08450-210227

Dejustica. (2018). *Climate Change and Future Generations Lawsuit in Colombia: Key Excerpts from the Supreme Court's Decision*. https://www.dejusticia.org/en/climate-change-and-future-generations-lawsuit-in-colombia-key-excerpts-from-the-supreme-courts-decision/

Derr, V., Sitzoglou, M., Gülgönen, T., & Corona, Y. (2018). Integrating Children and Youth Participation into Resilience Planning: Lessons from Three Resilient Cities. *Canadian Journal of Children's Rights/Revue Canadienne Des Droits Des Enfants, 5*. https://doi.org/10.22215/cjcr.v5i1.1241

Fletcher, S., Cox, R. S., Scannell, L., Heykoop, C., Tobin-Gurley, J., & Peek, L. (2016). Youth Creating Disaster Recovery and Resilience: A Multi-Site Arts-Based Youth Engagement Research Project. *Children, Youth and Environments, 26*(1), 148–163. https://doi.org/10.7721/chilyoutenvi.26.1.0148

Hart, P. (2008). What Comes Before Participation? Searching for Meaning in Teachers' Constructions of Participatory Learning in Environmental Education. In A. Reid, B. B. Jensen, J. Nikel, & V. Simovska (Eds.), *Participation and Learning* (pp. 197–211). Springer Netherlands. https://doi.org/10.1007/978-1-4020-6416-6_12

Holling, C. S. (1973). Resilience and Stability of Ecological Systems. *Annual Review of Ecology and Systematics, 4*(1), 1–23. https://doi.org/10.1146/annurev.es.04.110173.000245

Klinenberg, E. (2013, January 7). Adaptation: How Can Cities Be "Climate-proofed"? *The New Yorker*. www.newyorker.com/magazine/2013/01/07/adaptation-eric-klinenberg

Krasny, M., Tidball, K., & Sriskandarajah, N. (2009). Education and Resilience: Social and Situated Learning among University and Secondary Students. *Ecology and Society, 14*(2). https://doi.org/10.5751/ES-03032-140238

Lee, K., Gjersoe, N., O'Neill, S., & Barnett, J. (2020). Youth Perceptions of Climate Change: A Narrative Synthesis. *WIREs Climate Change, 11*(3), e641. https://doi.org/10.1002/wcc.641

McKoy, D., Eppley, A., & Buss, S. (2019, October 19). *The Critical Role for Young People and Schools in Resiliency Planning*. Federal Reserve Bank of San Francisco. www.frbsf.org/community-development/publications/community-development-investment-review/2019/october/the-critical-role-for-young-people-and-schools-in-resiliency-planning/

Meerow, S., Pajouhesh, P., & Miller, T. R. (2019). Social Equity in Urban Resilience Planning. *Local Environment, 24*(9), 793–808. https://doi.org/10.1080/13549839.2019.1645103

Napawan, N. C., Simpson, S.-A., & Snyder, B. (2017). Engaging Youth in Climate Resilience Planning with Social Media: Lessons from #OurChangingClimate. *Urban Planning, 2*(4), 51–63. https://doi.org/10.17645/up.v2i4.1010

Osnes, B. (2018). Youth Shine in Performance for Resilience. *Theatre Topics, 28*(3), 191–202. https://doi.org/10.1353/tt.2018.0043

Otani, F. (2016, March 4). *TOMODACHI Generation: Fumiya Otani*. TOMODACHI Reception, Tokyo, Japan. http://usjapantomodachi.org/tomodachi-generation-fumiya-otani/

Reid, K. (2019, May 8). 2011 Japan Earthquake and Tsunami: Facts, FAQs, and How to Help. *World Vision*. www.worldvision.org/disaster-relief-news-stories/2011-japan-earthquake-and-tsunami-facts

Rousell, D., & Cutter-Mackenzie-Knowles, A. (2019). A Systematic Review of Climate Change Education: Giving Children and Young People a 'Voice' and a

'Hand' in Redressing Climate Change. *Children's Geographies, 18,* 1–18. https://doi.org/10.1080/14733285.2019.1614532

Sanson, A., Hoorn, J., & Burke, S. (2019). Responding to the Impacts of the Climate Crisis on Children and Youth. *Child Development Perspectives, 13.* https://doi.org/10.1111/cdep.12342

Siegner, A., & Stapert, N. (2020). Climate Change Education in the Humanities Classroom: A Case Study of the Lowell School Curriculum Pilot. *Environmental Education Research, 26*(4), 511–531. https://doi.org/10.1080/13504622.2019.1607258

Smit, B., & Wandel, J. (2006). Adaptation, Adaptive Capacity and Vulnerability. *Global Environmental Change, 16*(3), 282–292. https://doi.org/10.1016/j.gloenvcha.2006.03.008

Treichel. (2020, April). *Why Focus on Children: A Literature Review of Child-centred Climate Change Adaptation Approaches | Australian Disaster Resilience Knowledge Hub.* https://knowledge.aidr.org.au/resources/ajem-april-2020-why-focus-on-children-a-literature-review-of-child-centred-climate-change-adaptation-approaches/

Union of Concerned Scientists. (2018). *Underwater: Rising Seas, Chronic Floods, and the Implications for US Coastal Real Estate.* https://www.marincounty.org/-/media/files/departments/cd/slr/underwateranalysisfullreport.pdf?la=en

United Nations. (2015). *The Sendai Framework for Disaster Risk Reduction 2015–2030.* https://www.undrr.org/implementing-sendai-framework/what-sendai-framework

Wang, M. C., Haertel, G. D., & Walberg, H. J. (1994). Educational Resilience in Inner Cities. In *Educational Resilience in Inner-city America: Challenges and Prospects* (pp. 45–72). Lawrence Erlbaum Associates, Inc.

Waxman, H. C., Gray, J. P., & Padron, Y. N. (2003). *Review of Research on Educational Resilience.* https://escholarship.org/uc/item/7x695885

5 Spotlight on Housing

Introduction

On a rainy March afternoon in 2017, a group of high school students from East Palo Alto Phoenix Academy (EPAPA) stood with their professional partners, their civic clients, and their science teacher on the Baylands Trail overlooking the San Francisco Bay Area's tidal flats, just a few blocks from their high school in East Palo Alto, California. Recalling the students' earlier assertions about the dearth of housing in the community, one of their civic clients asked if they would want to see an affordable housing development along those expansive and tranquil tidal flats. One student, Juan,[1] assented and joked that he'd also like a soccer field, but another, Carlos, objected vehemently.

"What you got against a soccer field?" Juan defended. "Bro, so much already lives there. We can't steal that. They were there first. Taking that land would be doing to them what we feel like is unfairly being done to us."

These students on their field trip were pointing to the complex intersections between housing, environment, and identity. They want to see housing policies that do not just build affordable housing, but also preserve and celebrate cultural identity and recognize the joy of being in green environments. A short while later, the client asked the students if they considered themselves part of the San Francisco Bay Area. They looked at her like that was the most ridiculous question they had ever heard. "Of course we do," was the proud response. She asked if they would like to see those tidal flats change at all, to allow for new uses, including much-needed housing, and the students shook their heads to indicate no, but hesitated to identify their

DOI: 10.4324/9781003141778-7

reasoning, until Jessica, spoke up: "Because that's who we are. We're known for these flats. It's our identity."

They took the short walk back to EPAPA, which is a public charter school serving students from one of the few remaining low-income communities of color in the Silicon Valley region of the San Francisco Peninsula. On the way, they passed the elementary school that Jessica's younger siblings were attending. She pointed to the garden. "I remember when they were building that," she said, explaining that she went to that elementary school, too. She waved to the driver of a minivan parked outside the school. Then she turned back to the group, shyly admitting, "That's my mom."

Jessica's stories of deep place memory demonstrate how she and her family are ingrained in the fibers of this community. Unlike Jessica, her siblings in elementary school will not have the same opportunity to graduate from EPAPA; her class will be the last to enjoy that privilege before the high school is closed due to declining enrollment.[2] "It's really hard, living here" Jessica explained. She then told a story of having to move out of an apartment because the rent for the three-bedroom unit increased to $6,000 per month.

That tour had been unplanned. The client came to EPAPA to do some brainstorming work with students in their classroom as part of their shared Y-PLAN (Youth-Plan, Learn, Act, Now) project. When the adults admitted they had never visited the students' section of the Baylands, Jessica, Carlos, Juan, and their peers took it upon themselves to show them around. As part of that project, the students drew from their own lived experiences, and from the tools and practices shared by their clients, to generate their innovative solutions to the housing crisis and the ensuing displacement impacting their friends, neighbors, and themselves. In addition to proposing solutions that could tangibly help their communities, the undertaking was designed to aid the development of students' sense of agency that would drive their civic involvement for years to come. Near the midpoint of the project, Jessica shared,

> It feels important to us because they are asking *us*. I noticed students are waking up to how this is an actual conflict we have to face . . . they're directly talking to us, we're the ones to create change.

This chapter reviews research on housing policy, with direct implications for children and youth and then provides three in-depth case studies from the UC Berkeley Y-PLAN initiative to showcase the ways these housing-related initiatives prepare participants of all ages to access, navigate, and transform our cities and schools. When young people work directly with professional planners and engage in policy questions, they cultivate a new sense of agency and increasingly identify as planners themselves. Along the way, students push the policy conversations in housing planning. They question why small families and single, more well-to-do people often seek large spaces they do not fully utilize while larger, low-income families are relegated to overcrowded conditions in under-resourced neighborhoods. They call for higher density housing, land-use policies, and tenant protections to meet the needs of larger, multi-generational, and low-income families such as theirs. Through it all, students emphasize the importance of community. They know that housing is a tool that forms and protects strong social ties. The housing vision of our young people is focused on justice, buoyed by mutual respect, understanding, and the shared hope they seek to cultivate among all residents of a city. In their proposals and actions, they present a path toward fulfilling this vision.

Setting the Stage Through Literature and Practice

The housing crisis that those young planners from EPAPA are living with and working to interrupt is plaguing not only their city. It pervades their region, state, and beyond. Since taking office, California Governor Newsom has named the statewide housing crisis as a top priority of his administration, asserting that the "high price of housing and rent makes it almost impossible for many families to live in the communities where they work" (Office of Governor Gavin Newsom, 2019). As of June 2020, at least 1.2 million low-income renters in California do not have access to an affordable home (California Housing Partnership, 2016). Almost half of all moderate-income households in the state identify as cost-burdened, meaning they commit more than 30% of their household yearly income to housing costs alone.[3] The situation is more dire for low-income California households, 70% of which are cost-burdened, as are 90% of extremely low-income households (California Housing Partnership, 2016). These data points, while extreme, are not unique to California. Housing costs in several states have outpaced wages, resulting in similar experiences of unaffordability. According to the 2020 Out of Reach report, in the United States,

> the average minimum wage worker must work nearly 97 hours per week (more than two full time jobs) to afford a two bedroom rental home or 79 hours per week (almost exactly two full-time jobs) to afford a one-bedroom rental home at fair market rent.
>
> (*Out of Reach: The High Cost of Housing*, 2020, p. 2)

The housing crisis is especially acute for low-income Black, Indigenous, and People of Color (BIPOC) (*Out of Reach: The High Cost of Housing*, 2020, p. 7).

The needs of young people within housing policy have received global attention. Through the Child Friendly Cities Initiative (CFCI)[4] in Australia, Sherry (2017) has identified current trends in policy that ended up working against young people, since high density and master-planned developments have public space restrictions that are not youth- or family-friendly. She accordingly called for more child and youth-oriented play spaces and activities and revealed how some developers intentionally design high-density developments to exclude children and teens, such as noise restrictions and even development bylaws stating, "Children under 13 must be accompanied by an adult and supervised at all times while using any of the community facilities on the estate" (p. 133). Quite clearly, by design, such a development will not by itself yield a child-friendly city, nation, or world. Yet this study is especially interesting as it speaks to the reasons why planners need to recognize how youth input is not simply nice to have, but rather an integral aspect of fair and equitable housing development.

In a special edition of the International Journal of Housing Policy, Mackie (2016) presented and analyzed a collection of five research articles focused specifically on the housing needs and challenges facing young people globally. Article authors showed young people's experiences of housing is a contemporary global concern. They discussed a range of issues that youth increasingly face, ranging from lack of housing availability that limits their ability to leave their childhood home as they age into adulthood to the need for more suitable housing designs, such as private sector rental units as well as shared housing opportunities. While most of the research presented in this volume focused on Europe and East Asia, authors built on their insights to call for greater awareness globally of the political, economic, and cultural forces impacting young people's transition to independence.

While recognizing cultural differences concerning young people's independence (for example, young people in many Mediterranean countries generally leave the family home later than young people in Northern Europe), these authors argued that such issues are relevant beyond these borders as well. Finally, the volume's authors called attention to the need to focus on low-income young people, in particular, recognizing that middle-class households are more likely to live in more advantaged and owner-occupied housing, offering families far more stability than rental housing markets globally (Mackie, 2016).

Bringing Together Young People and Housing Planning

While researchers and politicians speak to the statistics documenting the housing crisis for far too many young people, they rarely speak of, or engage directly with, the lived experience of those young people currently grappling with the grim realities of inadequate housing. Engaging youth in their lived experience of housing instability could lead to stronger policies. This inadequacy of current policies and practices is most harsh in its impact for low-income families who have the fewest resources and, more often than not, lack positional power and control to address such challenges and change the status quo.

To counter this inequity, many community-based, housing planning programs designed to work for and with young people have emerged over the past decade. One important example is the Growing Up Boulder (GUB) initiative. GUB's vision is "to make Boulder an exemplary child- and youth-friendly city" and to do that, the program's organizers recognize young people as experts and provide them with access to many "opportunities for inclusion, influence, and deliberation on local issues that affect their lives" (*About Us*, 2015). They accomplish this through a wide range of partnerships and supporters including local officials, city planners, local businesses, university students, community organizations, and more. GUB prioritizes children and youth least likely to have their voices heard. GUB works to have 50% or greater of cohort spots filled by young people from the following backgrounds: immigrants, English Language Learners, low-income, ethnic minorities, first-generation college-bound students, and/or young people with disabilities (*About Us*, 2015).

One GUB project has grown into a well-documented case study, demonstrating the important role and perspective of young people in housing planning and development. As the city of Boulder started planning for its Comprehensive Housing Strategy, many residents were concerned about the future of housing density and ensuring that access to affordable housing would be possible for all residents. The GUB designers developed an outreach strategy to address the Comprehensive Housing Strategy's goals by focusing on density and affordability while also emphasizing young people's ideas for child-friendly neighborhood design (Derr & Kovács, 2017).

This study of young people's engagement in planning a city's future housing demonstrated how their involvement increased recognition, by the city government, of diverse needs within the city. This recognition included the integration of social and environmental sustainability into final recommendations for neighborhood planning. More specifically, this study demonstrated how young people's participation in planning brought important and underrepresented voices to a controversy regarding how to increase density within the city of Boulder during the early stages of their Comprehensive Housing Strategy (Derr & Kovács, 2017).

Similar to the GUB study, a recent study of youth experiencing housing instability and homelessness shows the importance of providing increased access to information, people, and places for housing-insecure youth. Opening access to these resources enables them to effectively participate in problem-solving and policy making processes aimed at improving housing policies and, ultimately, housing conditions. Importantly, Aviles and Grigalunas (2018) showed that while housing instability posed challenges for the positive development of youth, young people still possess the knowledge, strength, and resiliency necessary to navigate housing instability. Working closely with adults and learning to develop new relationships enabled young people to navigate critical challenges. In the process, youth participants shared their own experiences around the lack of affordable housing, jobs without sustainability and living wages, and poor resources in their communities, connecting their lived experiences to larger systemic issues contributing to Chicago's social inequality while also experiencing personal changes. Youth increased their social and community problem-solving and decision-making abilities. They also enhanced their capacity to advocate for just institutional practices and community well-being (Ginwright & James, 2002). Researchers have argued that it is imperative for the public to invest in young people's well-being via approaches that "center their voices, equip them with the knowledge, skills, and tools to better understand their social conditions while working collaboratively to develop transformative spaces and dynamics to combat the problems they face" (Aviles & Grigalunas, 2018, p. 236).

The UC Berkeley Center for Cities and Schools (CC+S) positions young people not only as essential stakeholders in housing policy but also as critical actors in planning future housing. This work started nearly three decades ago in partnership with the US Department of Housing and Urban Development (HUD). When HUD expanded its mixed-income housing policy in 1992 with the introduction of the HOPE VI initiative,[5] youth engagement was a priority in its community and supportive services division (McKoy et al., 2005). Over the next five years, more than 36 cities and 40 public housing developments participated in summer programming to engage youth in reimagining their futures in proposed mixed-income developments. As then Director of Public Housing Supportive Services Ronald Ashford noted, "This was remarkable. We had young people and adult professionals coming together to develop policy recommendations on how to make HOPE VI mixed-income communities work better for them and their families." Some recommendations from this national programming, such as increasing teen supportive services and counseling, mirror initiatives that have since become institutionalized at the municipal, county, and state levels. As Ashford described, they started to "ensure youth were at the planning table, identifying the need for critical needs such as more school counseling within the supportive services provided by Public Housing Authorities."

Building on the success of youth involvement in this national public housing initiative, UC Berkeley launched a university-community collaboration that brought university students into local high schools, to work together with their students (McKoy et al., 2005). The UC Berkeley Y-PLAN initiative grew out of this work. As described in detail in Chapter 3, Y-PLAN has since its inception centered the lived experiences and insights of young people, particularly those who are young, low-income, and/or BIPOC, by enabling them to work in direct partnership with the housing leadership and policy makers responsible for their housing. Each young participant is uniquely situated to offer valuable insights and potential solutions to the housing crisis facing so many communities around the US. Combining their lived experience of their community with data collected through the five-step Y-PLAN research process, they produce policy recommendations in dialogue and collaboration with civic leaders.

A wide spectrum of ideas and innovations have resulted from this youth-centered approach. For example, in terms of recreational spaces, youth wanted far more than the basketball courts that are generally installed in typical developments. Girls lobbied for tennis and volleyball courts; they challenged implicit binary gender stereotypes and the resulting exclusion by design engineered by planners and architects. Many youths wanted soothing water features, and quiet spaces to read or "be peaceful," in contrast to the usual generic structures and spaces based on stereotypical notions of what "kids" want. Other recommendations included the creation of spaces and programming to deepen the sense of community and to foster a college-going culture for students living in temporary housing (including special graduation ceremonies); the construction of laptop labs for homeless students; and accessory dwelling units (ADUs) for low-income families.

A Deeper Dive Into Youth Practice: Young People in Action Case Studies

Aligned with Y-PLAN's Theory of Change described in Part I, what follows are case studies representing three (out of more than 65) housing-related projects facilitated by the UC Berkeley Y-PLAN initiative over the past two decades, including an analysis of how each demonstrated the key aspects of youth engagement work: access, navigation, and transformation. From resisting displacement in Silicon Valley, CA, to designing mixed income housing in San Francisco's Bayview neighborhood, to supporting NYC students living in temporary housing, each case study exemplifies the youth planners' constant interest in finding ways to achieve both justice and joy in their communities. While these components emerged from the literature mentioned earlier, through their activities in their own communities, students have used the Y-PLAN process over time to deepen their engagement and facilitate significant changes in their own communities.

Silicon Valley: Resisting Displacement

Why Plan for Silicon Valley?

As communities in cities throughout the United States gentrify, the ensuing displacement is especially salient in the San Francisco Bay Area. On the peninsula just south of San Francisco sits Silicon Valley, the heart of the technology boom. High-paid workers from companies from Facebook, Apple, and Google to a steady stream of start-ups seek housing nearby to shorten their commutes, in the process driving up housing costs and overrunning low-income communities of color that have long thrived in the area. The few communities of color that remain, in East Palo Alto, Belle Haven, North Fair Oaks, and parts of Redwood City, are being increasingly threatened. One East Palo Alto teacher shared, "The gentrification that's happening in this neighborhood is real and you can see it every single day everywhere you look. It's an issue facing my students." As rents rise, low-income families are forced to relocate.

Intergenerational Community of Practice

When city planning was introduced to East Palo Alto Phoenix Academy (EPAPA), through Y-PLAN in the spring of 2018, the teacher was excited to engage students in her STEM (Science, Technology, Engineering, and Math) elective directly around issues of gentrification and displacement relevant to their daily lives. She explained that "actually being able to address it in class in a productive way, versus a 'this sucks, there's nothing we can do' type of way [is] really meaningful."

Throughout the spring, student scholars explored housing affordability through the lens of climate resilience. They partnered with planners, designers, and engineers from the Resilient by Design | Bay Area Challenge, researchers from UC Berkeley's Center for Community Innovation and the Urban Displacement Project, and professionals from Facebook, whose headquarters sit adjacent to their city limits. Along the way, students built a rapport with their clients, the Resilient by Design "Field Operations Team" and local city leaders, forming an intergenerational community of practice,

Image 5.1 During their site walk to observe the shoreline adjacent to their homes, the students from East Palo Alto, CA, reflect upon the fragile nature of their community as it faces the threats of displacement due to sea level rise and gentrification.

Source: Emmanuel Moran.

where students collaborated with civic leaders, design professionals, and community members. In doing so, these young planners gained access to civic, academic, and technology leaders, spaces, and tools. The professionals gained access to the realities of daily life for the primarily low-income, Latinx young residents from the communities they research, plan, work in, and serve.

During the project, Miguel, who according to his teacher sat silently in the back of most classrooms, wanted to make sure his story was heard in this context. He explained that his aunt and two cousins used to live with them, the three of them sharing a garage as their living space, until the cost of even that rent drove them out. He now lives in a space with three bedrooms that have been partitioned into smaller rooms. There is no kitchen or living room, just a hallway as a common space. He lives there with "fifteen or sixteen" people right now. He explained that he had a job last summer but spent everything he made buying food at McDonald's for the kids in the house. When his teacher offered to teach him to cook, he politely declined. It wouldn't help; his home has no kitchen, just a single hot plate.

Miguel's story powerfully demonstrates how working with young people makes visible needs and priorities which might not surface otherwise, from severe overcrowding to amenities others might take for granted, like access to a kitchen. Consider this in relation to the student-led tour of the Baylands that opened this chapter. On this tour, students remained steadfast in their desire to protect the environmental symbol of their community identity and refused to do to the creatures already living there "what we feel like is unfairly being done to us." Despite the depths of their personal experiences with the devastation inflicted on their community by a lack of affordable housing, students revealed that housing development is more complicated than just building homes. Their perspectives illustrated why it is so important to have young people's voices centered in these conversations. As one student said, "Y-PLAN gave me a platform to voice my opinion and use my voice to see change that I thought was necessary and could actually help my community in a positive way."

The students' initial semester's brainstorming charrette yielded a range of policy recommendations, including "right-sized" housing, policy supports, and community-building efforts. With Facebook, city governments, and a regional initiative all contributing to this project, it seems only logical that students identified public-private solutions to the housing crisis. First, students lobbied for right-sized housing through tiny houses on vacant land and similarly sized ADUs (to be built with public and corporate support) as well as smaller condos with support for low-income, local, first-time home buyers. Additionally, students designed a mixed-income apartment complex to draw together diverse residents who would share a common outdoor space. Their designs included "fancy studios for young, single tech employees," larger townhome-style units with direct outdoor access for families at the ground level, and additional affordable apartments above them. In their vision, the shared central courtyard would include something for everyone – a dog park, barbeque, playground, and a small soccer field – to encourage interaction between diverse residents. Parking would be on the outside of the buildings to keep the area safe for children and pets.

Students also called for policy supports, including strong rent control, anti-harassment laws, financing programs for low-income, local home buyers, home repair funds for the elderly, and even a pedestrian corridor development near housing. They noted that rent control is not effective if tenants are unaware of its existence, if they are too fearful of eviction, or if they are cautious for reasons of immigration status to question the landlord.

Interviews elicited story upon story of illegal rent increases, units in disrepair, and other shady landlord tactics going unchecked, and students cited such evidence to highlight the need for additional policy supports to protect the most vulnerable.

They also proposed ideas for the community to support and sustain itself, including community land trusts and mixed-use units with shared amenities, but the class' favorite idea was their Mexican-style *plazita*. The students selected a vacant lot, ideal for its central location, and designed a *plazita* to reflect the cultural background of the majority of the long-term residents of East Palo Alto. Reminiscent of ones found in Mexico, their *plazita* would provide an opportunity for residents to buy and sell local handmade goods and foods, share cultural activities, and stimulate the local economy. Meanwhile, they envisioned it as attracting the area's newer residents as well,

Image 5.2 High school students in East Palo Alto, CA, present models and boards featuring imaginative housing proposals to protect their vibrant, intergenerational community from the impacts of sea level rise as well as displacement due to gentrification in Silicon Valley.

Source: Kingmond Young.

thereby familiarizing them with the local culture and welcoming them into it.

This project continued past the school year, and the students' presented recommendations led to real changes for themselves and their communities. Fourteen students, including Miguel, Carlos, Juan, and Jessica received paid summer internships to research housing conditions in their community and this research sparked follow-up projects during the next academic year. As students recommended a variety of solutions to anchor community identity while protecting existing residents from displacement, they demonstrated a continuing desire to leverage what residents had noted as their neighborhood's strength: the people themselves.

One year later, by the time the final EPAPA graduating class departed for college, they had crafted policy briefs, slide decks, and StoryMaps, and had presented their proposals, insights, and experiences at youth summits and research symposia at UC Berkeley attended by hundreds of people, City Council meetings in East Palo Alto and Menlo Park both in person and over video conferencing during a pandemic, and in Facebook's own boardrooms on multiple occasions. They have been interviewed by several local news outlets, witnessed Facebook and local non-profits commit funds to implement their visions, attended fundraisers with regional and national leaders and politicians, and helped design and serve on a Y-PLAN Alumni Youth Leadership Council.

Along the way, this intergenerational community of practice has surpassed its original charge. This cadre of young people embark upon the next phase of their lives with a deep social network that includes the teachers, Housing Commissioners, Mayors, Facebook Vice Presidents, and US Congresswomen, paired with a renewed sense of agency to apply however they choose. Meanwhile, the participating adults are also inspired to approach their work through a new lens, and with renewed energy and humility. As expressed by one teacher, it was powerful to see students build confidence in their own ability to enact positive change through the process. She explained the way she was particularly struck by the change in Carlos:

> In the beginning, he was very critical, saying "This is gentrification, Facebook is causing these problems, I don't want to participate in this, who do you guys think you are," and then him really coming in on his own and saying actually "You're right. I want to have a voice in this because it's happening."

When one mayor apologized to the young people for the city's failure to provide adequate housing for their families, a student replied that he did not need to apologize, because at that time he had not yet realized the depth of the problem. Now that he does understand it, however, it is time for him to act. When the Mayor introduced those students to his city council a few months later, he explained to the civic leaders the importance of listening to these young people, as they put a face and a heart to the statistics that document the crisis and thus make it impossible to ignore these problems any longer.

Analysis: Sustaining Influence and Impact

In this case study, youth research and leadership has had a sustained impact on policy maker's decisions over time. The UC Berkeley Center for Community Innovation's final report on their baseline study on housing conditions in the San Francisco Bay Area Peninsula noted that the EPAPA students taught the Berkeley researchers that local knowledge provides insights that secondary data misses. In the report, Chapple et al. (2020) credited the students' processes and recommendations, and noted that their work "shifted the focus of the study to look more in depth at how dynamics related to real estate speculation shape conditions on the ground," and that "this report provides support for the policy recommendations that the [EPAPA] students put forth and continue to recommend in ongoing engagement" (Chapple et al., 2020, p. 3).

This ongoing engagement continued beyond the publication of that final report, and on August 11, 2020, in the middle of the global COVID-19 pandemic, the Menlo Park City Council invited them to co-present the housing study they worked on as interns along with Professor Karen Chapple from the UC Berkeley Center for Community Innovation. Jessica, one of the Y-PLAN youth leaders stated before the Mayor, City Council, and dozens of attendees who joined this digital discussion that "our research showed the importance of maintaining not only affordable housing but the local culture and honoring residents who have lived here for many years." These young scholars were given nearly equal presentation time to Professor Chapple, who was presenting the overall study, and they were recognized by all council members for the important insights they brought into local housing decisions in the heart of Silicon Valley. Furthermore, the Council and partners at Facebook invited these young leaders to continue their work by joining an

"Opportunity Fund" committee to help decide how $1 million, donated by the tech giant, should be invested in the local community.

The young planning scholars from EPAPA, designers from the Resilient by Design | Bay Area Challenge, university-based scholars, and civic, tech, and community leaders from Silicon Valley formed a powerful, intergenerational community of practice that has already withstood the test of time, and of a global pandemic, economic disaster, and historic social uprisings. All the student proposals prioritized protecting and enhancing the environmental and social fabric of the community and folding new folks into that identity without hastening the eradication of the existing culture. Students' recommendations for ownership, both literally (through a proposal of assistance programs for low-income locals to purchase condos) and figuratively (through their vision of a *plazita* driving the local economy and culture), demonstrated options for stabilizing the community in the face of rising costs of housing and elevating sea levels. Critically, students advocated for increasing the stock of affordable housing units before the community identity they seek to preserve is lost forever.

Only by forging relationships and professional and social networks that transcend race, class, income, and educational attainment, will we begin to develop the movement necessary to unravel centuries of de jure segregation and racism, or at least to disrupt its ability to displace another generation of low-income BIPOC residents. Despite the increasing understanding of the importance and potential of such networks, their development remains limited. Through engaging in urban planning, young people, with their unique blend of lived experience, hope, and openness, emerge to provide the spark.

Bayview: Mixed-Income Housing Adjacent to School

Why Plan for the Bayview in San Francisco?

When the San Francisco Mayor's HOPE SF (Housing Opportunity for People Everywhere) housing redevelopment process began, aiming to transform several of San Francisco's most distressed public housing sites, there was much antagonism in the Bayview neighborhood. Residents of the existing public housing development, Hunters View, were wary of the city, the government, the developers, and others involved in the project. Residents feared that they were going to be immediately displaced by the construction, relocated elsewhere and never moved back, or that they would be gradually run out of the neighborhood by the gentrification resulting from the redevelopment. Tenant groups were also concerned that proper measures were not being taken to account for hazards to residents' health, including construction dust, debris, and toxins, as many residents suffered from asthma. Those groups and individual members of the larger Bayview community (mostly African American and American Samoan) were also lobbying for more employment for locals during the construction process.

Intergenerational Community of Practice

Given this backdrop, third- and fourth-grade students from Malcolm X Academy (MXA) elementary school engaged directly in the HOPE SF housing process. The children, most of whom identified themselves as Black or American Samoan, met with HOPE SF officials, administrators from San Francisco Unified School District (SFUSD), the developers (John Stewart Company), architects, and landscape architects working on the plans. This fledgling community of practice offered these children their first opportunity to access professional practices and it also marked the first time many of the professionals could access the children's worldview.

Prior to the project, some of the adults had never set foot on the school campus, even though MXA neighbored the Hunters View HOPE SF site. The ongoing collaboration between the developers and many of the City's HOPE SF Program partners influenced the decisions that were made about housing development in the Bayview community and modeled how they could be replicated. Each step of the way, over seven years, this project involved and centered MXA students, all of whom traversed the neighborhood to attend school, and many of whom ended up living in the new housing units.

As the students set out to navigate their community through a professional lens, they canvassed and analyzed community needs; mapped neighborhood assets; learned about the proposed development plans; studied blueprints and renderings; and generated their own series of policy and design recommendations. The bulk of the student work over seven years focused on indoor and outdoor common spaces, public spaces, and connections between the school and the Hunters View development.

During the early years, one fourth-grade student, Sulu, enthusiastically engaged with the project. He was living in housing that was slated to be demolished and he embraced the opportunity to weigh in on the design

Image 5.3 These San Francisco fourth-grade students showcase their topographic scale model featuring ingredients they say will infuse public spaces in the HOPE SF housing community with connectivity, playfulness, and joy.

Source: UC Berkeley Center for Cities and Schools.

and function of the public spaces in the new housing development. He was particularly interested in environmental sustainability and was captivated by the images of best practices introduced by the adult partners as sources of inspiration. The student and his team sought to incorporate wind and solar energy strategies as well as rain water capture and reuse into their proposals. During one of the final presentations, the student turned to the adults in the room and said, "If these 'green' strategies are so good, and so important, why don't we see them being used in the buildings anywhere in the city?" The adults in the room were both dumbfounded and humbled. The answers they gave were both wishful and apologetic. But they also congratulated the student on his ability to navigate the planning process, ask the question, and bravely challenge the adults in the room. He responded by telling everyone he wanted to be president someday.

The public presentations to various civic leaders and other adults throughout the process provided a forum for rich, intergenerational dialogue that proved transformative over the seven years. Students were able to make compelling pitches for specific features, such as barbeque pits for community gatherings; water features to offer peace and calming effects; small business development to generate jobs; features to attract tourists to the neighborhood; and more. This process prompted many adults and students to think differently about the process of housing development, as well as the physical contours of the development itself.

The students engaged with a different aspect of the project each year, conducting an analysis of the process and their progress, articulating the needs of residents of all ages and generating a set of planning, design, and policy recommendations for each focus. Each year, students presented their imaginative and innovative work in several public forums to the civic leaders, the development team, and to representatives of the various tenant and community groups. The children's models, drawings, and words were optimistic, compelling, and hopeful. They moved many of the local residents in attendance. Several of the adult community members made comments, such as "Wow, these children are so positive;" "We are inspired;" "They can work together so well;" and "We are embarrassed that as adults, we cannot get along with each other as well as third and fourth graders did." The students helped identify the critical issues necessary for housing justice without displacement and pushed the adults to make the necessary changes.

In one particularly poignant forum, the developer team members asked the students living in Phase I of the new housing development for their feedback. They expected glowing reviews. Instead, one of the boys said, "The new housing is nice, but it is really cramped." The ensuing intergenerational exchange highlighted what both adult professionals and young residents bring into the equation. The developers discussed costs, square footage, cost/benefit analysis, and other technical constraints in a way the children could understand. The students had the confidence to speak out about their experiences and to lobby for the developers and architects to take their feedback into consideration in Phase II of the development.

In one of the later years, one of Sulu's cousins was participating in Y-PLAN as a fourth grader. By then, the HOPE SF Hunters View Phase I was complete and people, including Sulu, were living in the new housing. The new group of students were discussing their ideas for Phase II of the housing development when Sulu's cousin piped up: "You see the buildings that were just built over there? When he was in fourth-grade, my cousin Sulu designed those buildings." The pride in this statement is a testament to the legacy, continuity, and sense of empowerment imbued in the students as a result of their participation in Y-PLAN.

Image 5.4 At their culminating event, students present their models, maps, and drawings to civic leaders from the City of San Francisco and the HOPE SF developer team. The adults have enthusiastically embraced the students' visions and incorporated many of the features into their completed project.

Source: UC Berkeley Center for Cities and Schools.

Analysis: Sustaining Influence and Impact

This ongoing, multi-year collaboration underscores the importance of including young students in city planning and community development. It also highlights the role local universities can play in anchoring this work and offering high-level institutional legitimacy to it as well. During that time, UC Berkeley was instrumental in bringing civic partners to the table, formulating project questions and scaffolding the technical aspects of the children's research and proposal development. In general, the student participation in the planning, design, and development process humbled many of the adults who witnessed their presentations and saw their work. The young scholars' emphasis and modeling of community building transformed the process, and in this way, helped to build trust between the various players on the project. Over several of the early years of the planning, design, and building process, the students at MXA interfaced with various phases of the project. They helped to ease the antagonism and build bridges between the various parties and build a social network founded upon mutual respect. Everyone in attendance could see the powerful role young students can play as coalition builders.

After focusing on housing policy and design for seven years, the principal, teachers, and students at MXA continued to collaborate with UC Berkeley, civic leaders, professional associations, and non-profit organizations on a series of community development projects. Teams of students have focused their analysis and visioning processes on healthy public spaces, climate change education, and environmental justice in shoreline development. During these years, the Y-PLAN team worked with five principals, six teachers, and school staff and community volunteers. Additionally, the team was supported by the contributions of the following organizations, civic leaders, and clients: John Stewart Company, HOPE SF, Mithun Architects, GSL Landscape architects, San Francisco Planning Department (SF Planning), Education Outside, Urban Strategies, Inc., local and national journalists, community members, and various foundations. Through all the changes, the UC Berkeley Y-PLAN team has been the constant factor, building trust and carrying institutional memory from year to year. The Y-PLAN projects at MXA have focused on housing while also addressing the public space, health, well-being, green infrastructure, and more. Additionally, UC Berkeley and Y-PLAN have earned a reputation in the MXA community for constancy, high-quality pedagogy, authentic engagement, and academic and professional skill-building.

Building upon that legacy, in 2018, the San Francisco Planning Department selected MXA as a site to pilot one of a series of citywide efforts to institutionalize inclusive community engagement through youth-driven input. The goal of this multi-year process was to build the internal capacity of SF Planning to engage children and youth in ongoing planning initiatives throughout the city, form a bridge between planners and families, and diversify community input about specific planning projects. Additionally, SF Planning aspired to strengthen career pathways for BIPOC youth to diversify the department and the planning profession itself. SF Planning is now modeling how to meet this challenge to make the power and promise of youth engagement integral to the city planning process by compiling a resource bank with specific tools to effectively engage youth and building stronger relationships between city departments and the school district.

Concurrently, this reciprocal learning experience has enabled teachers to create opportunities for students to apply academic skills in math, history, environmental studies, and more to "real world" challenges with meaning for the students. Authentic projects have brought additional rigor and professional skills into the school setting and have showcased, validated, and honored the perspectives and voices of young students. This blending of professional practice and lived experience has provided new opportunities for each group to access and navigate the other's world, ultimately transforming the result for everyone.

Brooklyn: Elevating Students in Temporary Housing

Why Plan for Brooklyn

By the fall of 2015, homelessness was one of the key issues facing New York City (NYC) as a whole and Brooklyn in particular. Since Hurricane Sandy in 2012, student homelessness has been a major issue for schools. According to the Institute for Children, Poverty, and Homelessness, approximately one in nine students in the NYC Department of Education system has experienced homelessness. Schools with high levels of chronic absenteeism (20 or more absences during the school year) have a harder time meeting education goals. Children and youth were and still are facing extreme rates of instability, poverty, and homelessness in New York City. Students in temporary housing struggle more academically and face higher rates of absenteeism. Elementary students living in shelters have the highest rates of mid-year transfers and chronic absenteeism district-wide. As a result, students in temporary housing are disproportionately missing the education they need in order to succeed academically and go onto higher-level education.

Intergenerational Community of Practice

In response, the New York City Department of Homeless Services (DHS), in collaboration with the NYC Department of Education's (DOE) Office for Students in Temporary Housing, enlisted Y-PLAN students from the High

School for Enterprise, Business and Technology in Brooklyn (EBT) to examine the impact of the lack of housing on high school students and to offer recommendations to better support students in temporary housing. During that first year, DHS asked students in the After School Leadership program to answer the following question: *How can NYC leverage its resources and provide students in temporary housing with the tools they need to graduate from high school and become college and career ready?*

Early in the project, the NYC DOE's liaison for Students in Temporary Housing invited the EBT planning students and teachers to the annual conference of the Institute for Children, Poverty, and, Homelessness,[6] introducing them to the professionals leading the City's efforts to combat homelessness and the original data they had compiled. During the one-day conference, students worked alongside adults in a variety of workshops and sessions. The young scholars then returned to their classroom equipped with current information regarding educational access for students living in temporary housing. The impact of that project compelled EBT to create the first-ever Urban Planning elective at the high school level and the Brooklyn Borough President's Office to join forces with the students during the following school year. Honing in on the impact of absenteeism, students in the second cohort responded to the questions: *How can we support students in temporary housing so that they can consistently attend and succeed in school?*

Image 5.5 Students from the High School for Enterprise, Business, and Technology come to the NYC Department of Homeless Services headquarters to present and discuss their proposals with their civic clients.

Source: Benjamin Deibert.

How does homelessness contribute to absenteeism (absent from school)? In what ways does homelessness affect a student's ability to succeed in school?

These young planners were well-positioned to support their peers, as they understood the struggles of their unhoused peers and often had firsthand experience themselves. As one student explained during the second year of the project, "From personal experience, when I was younger, I had to go through the shelter, and miss a lot of school – like half of third-grade and I got held back." She then continued, "I had speaking problems and I had social problems. So, we felt like the school website would show that we really want to help them out."

Students quickly recognized the need for resources to support homeless students, not only in shelters but also at their schools. With their civic clients' support and guidance, they conducted site mapping at their local shelter as well as at their own school library and counseling center to examine what services were available to homeless students. Students analyzed the strengths, weaknesses, opportunities, and threats (SWOT) of the current condition of the library concerning supporting students in temporary housing. They interviewed the school social worker about her experiences working with students in temporary housing. To ground-truth and provide greater context, students interviewed shelter staff as well as unhoused students.

After completing their research, the EBT students moved into a charrette process, co-facilitated by their teacher and NYC Y-PLAN Coordinator, to explore and imagine new, youth-centered ideas to support students in temporary housing at their school. Students broke up into their research groups and their teacher Ms. Chon passed out paper, colorful markers, and post-its. Based on the information gathered during the urban inspiration tour and SWOT analysis, the scholars then dove into a more in-depth brainstorming session where they utilized these materials to vision ideas within three categories: academic support, social/emotional support, and parent outreach.

From this work, the young planners generated the following recommendations for their professional clients, primarily addressing either policy or community aspects of the crisis. They called on leaders to first acknowledge the challenges faced by unhoused students, to provide access to college and career counselors, and to mitigate social exclusion. They recommended hosting social events during and after school to reach out to students in temporary housing, as they would help those students feel needed and would encourage them to stay in school. In a similar vein, the Y-PLAN students recommended a citywide graduation ceremony for high school students living in temporary housing to ensure these students feel supported and encouraged by their community as they move forward on their educational journey. Students also recommended policy changes, including extended library hours, weekly opportunities for students in temporary housing to sign out equipment like laptops, and safe places to complete assignments. Additionally, they recommended that shelters revisit their policies preventing minors from entering the premises without a parent, as they have had the unintended impact of eliminating any space for teenagers to do homework after school until their parents were out of work. They proposed a paid peer-mentoring, after-school program for students in temporary housing and a centralized resource hub for all high school students in NYC to access college and career readiness and support resources for teens.

EBT students visited Brooklyn Borough Hall multiple times throughout this project. That May, before students returned to present their final recommendations at Borough Hall, their Civic Client, DHS, hosted them for a roundtable discussion in their offices. At this point in their process, the students shared many ideas with four DHS representatives and the group of adults and students proceeded to workshop those ideas together, each sharing equal footing as stakeholders and participants. Mutual respect permeated the room, as students began to develop as planners and agents of change. The students incorporated all of DHS's feedback successfully into their final presentations two days later at Borough Hall, where DHS would announce that they had already secured thirty laptops to contribute toward fulfilling the students' proposal.

During the next academic year, two students from the first year presented as keynote speakers during the citywide Y-PLAN launch, welcoming the next Y-PLAN NYC cohort from twenty schools across the city. As the year progressed, the new group of Y-PLAN EBT students conducted a similar process and returned to Borough Hall to present their recommendations at the Y-PLAN Final Proposal Review. They followed that presentation with a final trip to Borough Hall to share their policy brief with the Deputy Borough President and Deputy Policy Director during a roundtable meeting held exclusively for them. At its conclusion, the Deputy Borough President shared that "What we come up with here is going to impact not just one school, but this could change policy for the whole City of New York."

These student scholars from EBT raised funds to donate laptops to local shelters, helped the shelters to set up a distribution program to get the

Image 5.6 The EBT high school students present their in-depth proposals to improve college and career readiness for students in New York City temporary housing.

Source: Benjamin Deibert.

computers where they needed to go, and prompted the creation of a food pantry at Grand Street Campus to support students who are food insecure, another challenge faced by students in temporary housing. When given respect and the space to investigate an issue, these students were able to expand access to technology and food for students living in temporary housing, which they found to be key obstacles to student success.

Analysis: Sustaining Influence and Impact

Throughout this multi-year project, EBT students never stopped at the proposal stage, instead pushing to implement their vision in collaboration with their civic clients. The young planners from EBT emphasized the need to take steps to create a sense of belonging for their unhoused peers and focused their recommendations around that goal. When given the access to investigate an issue and promised respect for their conclusions, these students navigated civic and professional domains to transform the experience for their unhoused peers and the processes for major city departments.

Conclusion

The housing recommendations from young planning scholars, such as those in the three case studies presented in this chapter, reveal that all ages can grasp the intricacies of the debates occurring in planning today and master the subject matter of the field. Furthermore, students deeply enrich the conversation by bringing their lived experience as community members; young people know what is happening on the ground and their experience of housing is not dissimilar to that of their adult counterparts. In discussions about our housing crisis, they identify the same core causes as the adult experts: the lack of affordable housing supply, support for unhoused people, and the need for innovations in housing policies to stabilize communities and protect tenants. But as young people, they also inject a commitment to building a sense of joy and generating shared hope in their surroundings.

They speak in support of popular interventions when they see them as efficacious (e.g., revising zoning codes to expedite the production of ADUs, new and increasing funding streams for affordable housing). They also argue that policies like rent control are insufficient as currently implemented, suggesting new ideas when they see a gap in the planning discourse. Students challenge the boundaries drawn between planning sectors, recognizing housing as part of a larger ecosystem and advocating for a holistic approach, with integrated services that support people in their entirety.

As these young planners navigate housing policy, their shared vision emerges. They envision a range of right-sized housing options to accommodate our diverse population, with each having enough for their needs. Students are not naive, however. They know that even when adequate housing exists, policies are needed today to protect the right to adequate shelter for our most vulnerable residents. They recommend a robust range of policy proposals to secure that protection as well as a range of amenities that they deem essential for homes that are both just and joyful. They simultaneously chart a path forward, sharing ideas to support the development of a too-often overlooked sense of community, mutual respect, and understanding with an eventual promise of protecting the dignity of all. Luckily for us, they not only propose such essential community-building measures, but through their process, they model its potential.

The housing crisis facing our nation is acute and we will need radical interventions to solve it. In service of that goal, participating young planners urge us all to think of ourselves as part of a community, plan together for our collective well-being, and value the insights of all. In the wise words of students from a fourth-grade classroom in Santa Rosa, California, "Share your space!"

Notes

1 Names of all young people are pseudonyms.

2 EPAPA was a middle and high school, administered by Aspire Public Schools until 2018. The next school year they no longer had enough students to sustain high school enrollment, so it became only a middle school.

3 The US Department for Housing and Urban Development uses the 30% rule to assess if a household is struggling with housing costs. Households are defined as cost-burdened if they "pay more than 30 percent of their income for housing" and "may have difficulty affording necessities such as food, clothing, transportation, and medical care." There is dispute in the field if the 30% rule is the most effective measure of housing affordability, as it implies affordability remains relative across income levels.

4 The Child Friendly Cities Initiative (CFCI) is a UNICEF-led initiative and network that supports municipal governments in realizing the rights of children at the local level using the UN Convention on the Rights of the Child as its foundation.

5 The HOPE VI Program, originally known as the Urban Revitalization Demonstration (URD), was developed as a result of recommendations by the National Commission on Severely Distressed Public Housing, aiming to eradicate severely distressed public housing.

6 The Institute for Children, Poverty, and Homelessness is a New York City-based policy research organization focused on addressing family and child homelessness through research, policy briefs, and interactive data tools.

References

About Us. (2015). Growing Up Boulder. Retrieved January 22, 2021, from www.growingupboulder.org/about-us.html

Aviles, A. M., & Grigalunas, N. (2018). "Project Awareness:" Fostering Social Justice Youth Development to Counter Youth Experiences of Housing Instability, Trauma and Injustice. *Children and Youth Services Review, 84*, 229–238. https://doi.org/10.1016/j.childyouth.2017.12.013

California Housing Partnership. (2016). *Confronting California's Rent and Poverty Crisis: A Call for State Reinvestment in Affordable Homes*. http://chpc.net/resources/confronting-californias-rent-poverty-crisis/

Chapple, K., Armour, C., & Zhang, L. (2020). *Investment and Disinvestment as Neighbors: A Study of Baseline Housing Conditions in the Bay Area Peninsula*. Center for Community Innovation. www.urbandisplacement.org/sites/default/files/images/investmentdisinvestment-report-200117.pdf

Derr, V., & Kovács, I. G. (2017). How Participatory Processes Impact Children and Contribute to Planning: A Case Study of Neighborhood Design from Boulder, Colorado, USA. *Journal of Urbanism: International Research on Placemaking and Urban Sustainability, 10*(1), 29–48. https://doi.org/10.1080/17549175.2015.1111925

Ginwright, S., & James, T. (2002). From Assets to Agents of Change: Social Justice, Organizing, and Youth Development. *New Directions for Youth Development, 2002*(96), 27–46. https://doi.org/10.1002/yd.25

Mackie, P. K. (2016). Young People and Housing: Identifying the Key Issues. *International Journal of Housing Policy, 16*(2), 137–143. https://doi.org/10.1080/14616718.2016.1159273

McKoy, D., Kobler, A., & Buss, S. (2005). *The HOPE VI: Youth Leadership for Change Initiative* (p. 35) [Formulative Evaluation Report]. The Center for Cities & Schools. University of California, Berkeley. https://y-plan.berkeley.edu/assets/img/about-us/McKoy_et_al_2005_HOPEVI_Youth_Leadership_Eval.pdf

Office of Governor Gavin Newsom. (2019, August 15). *In San Francisco, Governor Gavin Newsom Highlights Major Actions Taken to Confront Housing Crisis & Says More Must be Done*. California Governor. www.gov.ca.gov/2019/08/15/in-san-francisco-governor-gavin-newsom-highlights-major-actions-taken-to-confront-housing-crisis-says-more-must-be-done/

Our Impact. (n.d.). Growing Up Boulder. Retrieved February 4, 2021, from www.growingupboulder.org/our-impact.html

Sherry, C. S. (2017). Accommodating Children's Activities in the Shared Spaces of High Density and Master Planned Developments. In *Designing Cities With Children and Young People*. Social Science Research Network. https://doi.org/10.2139/ssrn.3252282

Spotlight on Transportation

Introduction

"I'm going to tell you a little story." Brianna,[1] a Skyline High School senior from Oakland, California, opened the Transportation Panel at the UC Berkeley Center for Cities and Schools' Civic Learning Symposium in 2019 to an audience of planners and educators. She began:

> A couple of years ago, they were going to take away the buses that we take to Skyline and home after school. And it caused a lot of chaos and panic because a lot of us depend on those to go home. If you don't know, Skyline is located up in the hills which is a beautiful area. It's a beautiful school. It's so far away from where most of us live. So, it's really hard to get up there and to get back down from there. So, we petitioned. We did a whole lot, we talked to the Superintendent. We fought and we fought so hard so that we could keep our buses and they eventually gave us our buses.

The only student on the panel, she was joined by her teacher and planners from the San Francisco Planning Department and the Metropolitan Transportation Commission (MTC). The audience applauded as if she were done, but Brianna continued, her voice capturing the audience's attention. She argued:

> If that doesn't show you how powerful youth voices are, I don't know what will. We fought so hard for that and we really, really needed it. It was really important for me, and specifically for my mom. My mom

DOI: 10.4324/9781003141778-8

> is the only parent I have, and she works two jobs to make ends meet. So, there is very limited time for her to take me to school and take me home. She has to go from East Oakland all the way up to Oakland Hills and then all the way to San Leandro, to her job, and then all the way up to Lakeshore, to her second job. It's a lot of work, and she can't really do it all. So, I have to ride on the bus. And so, you can imagine my worry, [when the buses were going to stop during] my sophomore year. I would have two more years of school and my mom is working so hard, and I would have no way to get home. And there's only one way, one bus that gets me to the second bus and to get me to the third bus that gets me home.

Many adults in the audience, shocked by Brianna's tale, followed up with questions, prompting her to elaborate:

> There are about ten-ish buses that come up and line up right after-school, maybe around like 3:15 or 3:20 depending. So, you get on those buses. There's one bus, just one, that's a 39. And that one will take you down to the 54. And from the 54, you can take whatever buses that go from [the transit hub]. So, usually after school activities like sports and dance, clubs and stuff, you usually have to catch the 39. But the hard part about that is if I have to catch the bus, I can't go to activities like that because that later 39 does not have the same route that it takes me to get to East Oakland. And all of the times when people have after school activities, their parents usually come and pick them up or they have to rely on Uber or Lyft. But it is super hard to have to rely on those things because they're so expensive. I've had times when my mom told me, "You can't do this [activity]. I can't afford this right now. You just can't. You have to catch the bus. You can't do this right now." So, there are times like that, and it's super hard, but it is what it is.

Brianna's experience spotlights the ways in which the distinct experiences of young people as they navigate (and struggle with) our transportation networks often differ categorically from those of adults, even their parents. Like the preceding chapters on resilience and housing, this chapter includes a review of research in transportation planning, as it directly impacts and is impacted by children, youth, and schools. This chapter then features three important, in-depth case studies of youth engagement in the transportation sector driven by the UC Berkeley Y-PLAN (Youth-Plan, Learn, Act, Now) methodology. These examples and case studies showcase our theory of change in action and highlight the powerful role that young people can play in expanding our understanding of the issue of transportation in the planning of just and joyful cities.

Transportation is so integral to the planning of our cities that the very language we use to describe our transit systems drives our theory of change itself. Navigating the city is key to everyone's experience of the city and thus is central to any approach to city planning. In Y-PLAN programs, as young people critically examine challenges about transportation in their communities, they gain access to information about the dynamics of the transportation systems to which they demand equitable access and upon which they rely in their daily lives. Moreover, students learn how to navigate those planning processes, just as Brianna described her ability to navigate intricately complicated bus routes and times as her only option to transverse her city. Along the way, young people become advocates for change and agents in the creation of more equitable cities. In doing this, they begin to transform their communities by educating the adults who have been working professionally in transportation-related fields for many years.

Throughout this chapter, young people share their powerful visions for safe, reliable, and equitable transportation in our cities. Through their own words and actions, they advocate for new transportation improvements, technologies, and alternatives to equitably link schools, services, resources, and public spaces. Additionally, young planners emphasize the critical role transportation systems play in fostering independence, as well as community and connectivity, among all city residents.

Setting the Stage Through Literature and Practice: Transportation

The literature and practice review that follows begins by exploring what it means for transportation to contribute to a child- and youth-friendly city, including its potential to provide access to opportunity, its role in fostering independence and identity formation, and its capacity to drive or impede equity. The review then considers emerging best practices that have been recommended to help illuminate a path toward achieving such a youth-friendly city, including cross-sector integration, regulatory levers, effective and equitable public engagement, and most critically, the inclusion of young people throughout the process.

In defining a youth-friendly city, our young people clearly emphasize that transportation is about opportunity. As Brianna noted during the aforementioned symposium, and as her peers in multiple projects and schools have commented many times, limited accessibility impedes the ability of teenagers and their parents to access school, work, and needed services. It also creates obstacles to attaining a high-quality education, both inside and outside of the classroom. In addition, "school travel in the United States contributed 5%–7% of vehicle miles traveled and 10%–14% of all private vehicles on the road during morning peak period" (Makarewicz, 2020, p. 299). Despite the fact that school accessibility and transportation systems impact almost every resident, regardless of their personal school affiliation, Bierbaum et al. (2020) articulated that "absent from many of these conversations about transportation equity and accessibility are questions of school access" (p. 3).

Transportation is also about independence and identity development, as access to opportunity enables young people to see themselves as part of a broader, more connected community. As transportation determines both opportunity and independence, it plays a vital role in defining individual and community identity. As a result, "it is difficult to overstate the importance of accessibility in making urban living more affordable and socially just as limited accessibility prevents many low-income people from finding work, reaching medical services, or shopping at well-stocked supermarkets" (Cervero et al., 2017, p. 6).

Mode choice is part of the equation as well. Private automobiles have dominated the North American transportation landscape for the last century. People own more cars than ever before, more people are driving, and individuals are taking more trips per day by car (Gross, 2019). Families with access to a car are more likely to secure and keep a job, suggesting the central importance of car ownership to economic success (Blumenberg, 2002). However, as most of our young people do not have access to a car, the resulting limits on their access to opportunity can impede their burgeoning sense of independence and its role in their identity development.

Imagine instead a community in which the streets belonged to the children and youth. Our young planners envision exactly that joyful ideal, even though it is not a reality they have yet experienced. Instead, with a large percentage of public space claimed for the automobile, to which they have no access, youth (and other residents of low-income communities) enjoy fewer places to gather, interact, and develop a sense of community. As Deakin noted, "studies have shown that values such as the emphasis put on individualism versus communitarianism shape attitudes toward policy interventions and policy preferences" (Deakin, 2020, p. 589). That emphasis both fuels and is fueled by the supremacy of automobile culture.

Fortunately, young people are beginning to shift those values, opting increasingly for mass transit over cars and ushering in a shift that could provide needed support for our environment as well as our communal access to opportunity and education. A 2016 Pew Study found that young adults, aged 18–29, are almost twice as likely as any other age group to utilize public transit. When looking at travel choice by race and ethnicity, that same study found that in urban areas Black and Latinx residents are at least twice as likely to utilize public transit as their white peers – 34% of Black, 27% of Latinx, and 14% of white residents use public transit (Anderson, 2016). Additionally, patterns of employment for contemporary young adults are categorically different than they were for previous generations. Due to the global financial crisis and high rates of unemployment or underemployment among young adults, "many young adults start and end work outside traditional work periods, [are] without reliable car access [and] will face lower levels of transit service that may, in turn, restrict their employment options" (McDonald & Peng, 2020, pp. 12–13). This lack of opportunity is likely to persist unless transit schedules, which are typically optimized for peak commute hours, are made more accessible (McDonald & Peng, 2020).

Since transportation affects access to opportunity, to goods and services, and to jobs and schools, it is deeply enmeshed in debates about equity. Discussions of transportation systems that are more youth- and student-friendly and oriented also must focus on equity and efforts to improve conditions for other marginalized residents. As Bierbaum et al. (2020) has noted, "Education and transportation equity have an obvious affinity. In foregrounding questions of access and accessibility, both fields highlight the often-disparate landscape of opportunity faced by historically marginalized groups" (p. 9). Currently, despite this natural affinity, planning and policy discussions rarely integrate the two, and when they do, they often only consider simplistic variables like commute distances between school and home. Bierbaum et al. further emphasized the importance of integrating the two more closely to uncover and resolve complexities. The outcome of this approach is "that students have an opportunity to reach their full potential through high-quality educational experiences that they can reach affordably, reliably, and safely" (Bierbaum et al., 2020, pp. 9–10). In this way, mobility justice, a concept that imagines and works toward a world where everyone has safe and fluid access to transportation resources, must include equitable access to high-quality educational facilities for all young people.

Additionally, as referenced in the preceding chapter, transportation is closely tied to the environmental justice movement, given that the reduction in car use and CO2 emissions are primary concerns of both environmental and transportation planning. These issues will only become more urgent as the threat of climate change intensifies and poor and non-white communities face the imminent risks first. Moreover, "equity implications arise because the negative social impacts of transportation and land use disproportionately affect economically-deprived neighborhoods and certain racial and ethnic groups," (McAndrews, 2020, p. 35). As a result, it is transportation together with land use that "shapes the landscape of poverty and segregation through inter-governmental policies that determine infrastructure, investment, employment and housing patterns in regional economics, and local land-use decisions" (McAndrews, 2020, p. 37). As "the share of marginalized city dwellers with poor access to essential facilities and services, such as public transport and clean water, is increasing worldwide" (Cervero et al., 2017, p. 219), any attempts to plan and design more equitable and just cities must consider transportation advancements to improve access to opportunity for all residents.

Regardless of our definition of a youth-friendly city, the path toward achieving it must include regulatory levers that address the lack of integration between disparate sectors in our cities and embed equitable engagement throughout the process. As in housing, since regulations created this situation in the sphere of transportation, they must also be a necessary component in any solution. In transportation planning, this means solutions must advance multiple positive outcomes, including pollution reduction and the alleviation of poverty. Transit-Oriented Development (TOD) has the potential to reduce the need for automobiles and extensive research on TOD around the globe points toward a range of benefits, particularly noting the positive impacts on children and youth. Nevertheless, Cervero (2017) noted, "Although integrated transport and land development can relieve congestion, cleanse the air, and conserve energy, its potential to reduce what remains the gravest problem facing the Global South – extreme and persistent poverty – is every bit as important" (p. 225).

Over the past decade, several researchers and national think tanks have begun to look more deeply into the often-overlooked connection between housing, transportation, and schools – drawing inspiration particularly from international contexts. Cervero and Sullivan (2011) called attention to "Kid Friendly TOD," which showed how several European TOD developments replaced parking lots with gardens, playgrounds, and open space to reduce heat-island effects and water pollution while increasing pedestrian safety by both removing the cars and increasing the "'natural surveillance,' the ability of residents to keep an eye on who is using community spaces" (Cervero & Sullivan, 2011, p. 1).

Yet schools themselves still remain notably absent from this dialogue. As housing remains segregated, sometimes by freeways and other forms of transportation infrastructure, so do schools. As stated in the previous chapter, the reciprocal nature of housing and schools makes them impossible to separate conceptually or pragmatically. In an attempt to bring schools into this dialogue, the National Center for Transit-Oriented Development (CTOD), the UC Berkeley Center for Cities and Schools (CC+S) and other national players developed a best practice guidebook titled *Creating Families and Transit-Oriented Development – Creating Complete Communities for All* (Vincent et al., 2012). Bierbaum and Vincent (2013) broadened this work in a study revealing ten core connections between TOD, households with children, and schools, ranging from multimodal transit alternatives improving access to the school options landscape to TOD designs fostering walkability and bringing family-serving amenities and services closer to residential areas. After all, so long as quality and resources remain unevenly distributed, students will continue to face the challenges that Brianna shared at the outset of this chapter, including "long distances and travel times to choice schools or segregated neighborhood schools and attendant negative effects" (Bierbaum et al., 2020, p. 3). Students without access to automobiles, like Brianna, face additional struggles in choosing the former option and the latter confines them to the segregated, under-resourced schools that plague our nation.

Researchers also point to unexpected tensions that arise when active transportation priorities such as walkability are brought into the dialogue in ways that pose a direct conflict with other educational and housing priorities such as school integration. PolicyLink, a national social justice think tank, led an interdisciplinary initiative in 2013 that joined together public health calls for increasing walkability for all students to reduce childhood obesity, with housing advocates fighting for more racially and economically integrated schools. Working with CC+S and other national organizations, PolicyLink declared:

> All children should have access to high-quality, diverse, and walkable public schools within their neighborhoods, no matter their race, ethnicity, or income, and these schools should promote superior academic outcomes, enhance the relationship between schools and the community, support active and healthy lifestyles, and support the economic and cultural well-being and social cohesion of communities.
>
> (PolicyLink, 2013, p. 9)

Additional research strengthens the calls for walkable public schools for their potential to not only promote active lifestyles, but also develop social capital and even contribute to joy or happiness. According to O'Brien (2008), one method of improving safety for young children walking to school, Walking School Buses, would "contribute to more 'eyes on the street' and appear to build social capital as neighbours and children become better acquainted" (p. 292). Additionally, an Ontario Walkability Study surveyed more than 6,000 elementary students and found that almost three-quarters of them would prefer to walk or cycle to school regularly. As O'Brien (2008) asserted, walkable schools "could tap into this latent desire for active transportation – which is both sustainable and appears to be a source of delight for those who choose it" (O'Brien, 2008, p. 292). This vision refutes popular positions that characterize calls for walkable neighborhoods as inherently contrary to school integration strategies that send students across towns to higher-performing schools.

Until that vision becomes a reality, we cannot ignore the dominance of the yellow school bus to the American educational experience. Today, there are more than 480,000 yellow school buses across the nation, transporting an estimated 26 million students to and from school. As we look more closely into the relationship between transportation access and universal access to high-quality education and gainful employment, it is important to recognize the aspects of the transportation landscape that might bring new opportunities and innovations for schools and the students who attend them.

Vincent et al. (2014) have discussed the various ways cities are beginning to innovate on how to support student travel, while increasing local ridership of public transit systems, including discounted city bus passes, new technologies to support increased carpooling, and vehicle sharing between school districts and cities. In the work conducted by CC+S, young people have expressed great interest in the "micro-mobility revolution," the influx of bike and scooter-share options, that is creating more choices for how people navigate their lives (Ajao, 2019). As "the integration of transportation modes, real-time information, and instant communication and dispatch – all possible with the click of a mouse or a smartphone app – will continue to redefine auto-mobility," it is crucial to ensure all those choices are available to all people (Shaheen et al., 2020, p. 259). Our youth planners have told us time and again how that is currently not the case. Many young people's proposals simply ask to offer their communities advances that are present in wealthier neighborhoods, from electric buses to comfortable seating at transit stops.

Successfully integrating transportation, land use, and environmental planning requires us to "engage everyone and expect everyone to contribute" because "for broad social problems like the lack of affordable housing or climate change, it is neither equitable nor likely to be workable in the long run to depend on the actions of only a few," (Deakin, 2020, p. 592). Engaging everyone means "transitioning from highly antagonistic, counterproductive encounters to interactions of agnostic debate. Such an objective – with its focus on convergence among opposing parties – could assist local areas, regions, and states in moving forward," (Frick, 2020, p. 544). As we have seen many times, engaging young planners in dialogue with a diverse, intergenerational community of practice with access to power naturally accomplishes such an objective, paving the path to the engagement necessary for integrated planning.

Bringing Together Young People and Transportation Planning

When young planners are invited into the transportation conversation, they interrupt historically antagonistic processes; share new, powerful visions that address many of the issues raised by the research; and present important insights and directions for future transportation and policy making.

Fortunately, young people are playing an increasing and more visible role in how we think about our city transportation systems. One powerful methodology for enhancing that role is through Youth-led Participatory Action Research (YPAR). Through YPAR, youth gain important access to new information and understanding of the systems that frame their lives as well as insights on how to navigate these systems in new ways.

This process of youth engagement through YPAR ultimately can lead to transformative changes in individuals as well as in the systems that govern our communities. Thomas (2008) leveraged three diverse YPAR case studies from around the world to call on Canadian government leaders to increase youth engagement in transportation planning. The first elevated case study, led by the St. Lucie Transportation Planning Organization in Florida, taught young people to use the tools of the trade before inviting them to the transportation planning table to fully and effectively incorporate them into the process (Bonet, 2004, as cited in Thomas, 2008). Through listening to guest speakers and interviewing experts, students developed their own long-range transportation plan using the YPAR methodology and presented it to local and state leaders, leading to the creation of a Municipal Service Taxing Unit to fund long-term transit costs. The second case study – "Catching Them Young" in Manchester, UK – featured an effort to influence young people's modal choice and encourage active transportation through a short-term, intensive educational intervention. Utilizing YPAR, young people collected travel data, developed marketing materials, and tracked changes in modal choices. The authors reported significant changes in participant attitudes due in large part to their involvement in creating the materials. A third case study, Canada's "Offramp" encouraged youth to change attitudes around active transportation, leading to the implementation of school-based active transportation projects (Orsini, 2003, as cited in Thomas, 2008). Reflecting upon all three case studies, Thomas (2008) argued, "Educating young people about the political processes associated with transportation can change their perceptions and encourage action-oriented civic participation. Long-term transportation systems change can and should be informed by engaging youth in a range of action-oriented projects and research" (p. 17).

Another more recent example of a city effectively engaging youth involves the Growing Up Boulder (GUB) collaboration, based at the University of Colorado in Boulder. In the 2013–2014 academic year, organizers engaged over a hundred K–12 students, community leaders, city planners, and university students to develop their Transportation Master Plan for the city. In this project, the City of Boulder's transportation department partnered with GUB to better understand opportunities for and barriers to transportation options, such as biking and walking, as part of developing their Transportation Master Plan Update. GUB engaged middle and high school youth in mapping activities and conducted "walk audits" that provided specific feedback about local conditions. The planners and students used a range of tools to analyze and determine whether and how active transportation and independent mobility were closely connected to bike facilities, schools, parks, and other youth-identified social spaces. This project also offered young people opportunities to learn about the City of Boulder's sustainable transportation issues. They engaged youth using a range of age-specific qualitative methods, including map annotation, interactive presentations of different walking and biking environments, and information-gathering walkabouts around the neighborhood. This project analyzed the positive impacts of youth engagement in three areas: research, planning, and the decision-making process. This work also yielded important insights for other cities wanting to promote active transportation for underserved communities (*Transportation Master Plan: Young People's Use and Views of Transportation in Boulder*, n.d.).

The following section will build on the previously mentioned literature and practice by offering three in-depth case studies that demonstrate the critical and powerful role of young people in transportation planning. In each case, students gain access to and learn to navigate within the transportation planning processes as they help define a more youth-friendly city and begin to transform both their identities and their communities.

UC Berkeley Y-PLAN in Action Transportation Case Studies

Aligned with Y-PLAN's Theory of Change, described in Part I, the following case studies represent three (out of more than 50) transportation-related projects facilitated by UC Berkeley over the past two decades, including an analysis of how each demonstrated the key aspects of youth engagement work: access, navigation, and transformation. From brightening the Broadway Corridor in Brooklyn, NY, to exploring active transportation in Sacramento, CA, to planning "For the Culture, By the Culture" with students from the African American Male Achievement Initiative classes in Oakland, CA, each case exemplifies the youth planners' constant interest in finding ways to achieve both justice and joy in their communities. Through their activities in their own communities, students have used the Y-PLAN process over time to deepen their engagement and facilitate significant changes in their own communities.

Bushwick: Brightening Broadway

Why Plan for Brooklyn's Historic Broadway Corridor?

The East Bushwick Campus High School for Public Service (EBC) is located in the Bushwick neighborhood of Brooklyn, New York. One block away, the Broadway Corridor features an above-ground train line that stretches from East New York to Williamsburg. The stretch was decimated in 1977 during a massive blackout, during which fires, looting, and violence destroyed 250 buildings and residences. As a result, nearly half of the businesses along the commercial hub closed. This crisis was followed by decades of disinvestment through policies of redlining and urban shrinkage in the historically working-class neighborhood, populated primarily by residents of Puerto Rican and Dominican descent. The Broadway Corridor continues to suffer from deficient economic growth, with high vacancy rates and chronically underutilized prime retail space. There are several issues perpetuating these problems: the elevated train line running above casts shadows on the street below, the area is poorly lit, the sidewalks and public spaces are poorly maintained, and there are ongoing issues contributing to the relatively high incidence of drug overdoses.

More recently, Bushwick has been undergoing rapid gentrification, with spikes in rental prices, increased numbers of bars and other nightlife venues, and the appearance of high-end retail and cafes catering to middle-class, young adult newcomers. The Broadway Corridor, with its great access to transit, has become the epicenter of this struggle, and many long-term residents are fighting to maintain the existing community and cultivate affordable retail, housing, and services. With no "one size fits all" solution to combat gentrification and displacement, or revitalize the corridor, stakeholders from Community Board 4, City Council, and local nonprofits have been increasingly pressed to take action.

Intergenerational Community of Practice

In 2015, EBC High School for Public Service students requested that their closed subway station be reopened but instead learned that it had been shuttered for safety reasons and would remain closed. The students were not satisfied with this action; they felt it was unfair to force them to walk even farther to and from school through an area deemed unsafe to access the train. In response, the EBC teacher and their local council member committed to a Y-PLAN project in early 2016 that continued for three years.

The goal of the project was to inject youth-driven insights to "brighten" the Broadway corridor, literally and figuratively. Students initially discussed the safety challenges associated with Broadway being poorly lit, since they had to walk through this darkened corridor to and from school. By this time, the aforementioned subway entrance had been closed for years, limiting their access to the system ostensibly designed to provide regional connectivity to all residents and visitors. The young planners quickly made the connection between transportation access and connectivity, street lighting, and safety. Their teacher was excited to bring her policy and government curriculum to life and the council member's office found a new way to engage his constituents. Over time, reciprocal trust developed between young people

Image 6.1 In collaboration with local civic leaders, high school students map the Broadway Corridor as they generate imaginative and actionable proposals to infuse Bushwick with cultural meaning, color, and life.

Source: Emmanuel Moran.

and adults, and each gained new access to the daily lives and knowledge of the other.

During the spring of 2016, EBC students began with a community study that explored four core categories: public safety, affordable housing, transportation, and mixed-use development. Students personally recognized the need for capital improvements to improve the safety of the corridor, noting the extremely cracked sidewalks, large pieces of trash littering every street corner, and poor lighting as they walked to and from school. In addition to their own insights, students attended Community Board 4 meetings and they hosted two town hall meetings to reach out to community members about the most pressing problems on Broadway. Students then presented their recommendations to Brooklyn civic leaders and community members. Their recommendations called for repaving the full stretch of sidewalk along the corridor, emphasized the importance of maintaining their bodegas and inexpensive coffee, and proposed a free physical public or private space to hang out without feeling criminalized or surveilled.

During those presentations, students also pitched the creation of a Broadway Merchants Association to organize the current business owners and leverage their collective power. Students proposed an overarching concept to use the Merchants Association to "Brighten" the Broadway Corridor by turning it into an "Art Walkistrict" that would encourage active transportation by bringing in more foot traffic to businesses, which would ultimately improve public safety. The students continued their partnership with their council member's office and brought the Brooklyn Chamber of Commerce to the table during the 2016–17 school year.

In the second year of the Y-PLAN project, students built on the previous work and grappled with the question: *How do we create a Merchants Association for the purpose of Brightening the Broadway Corridor?* Students surveyed shop owners along Broadway and facilitated three meetings to bring merchants together. By the end of the spring semester, the charter for their proposed Broadway Merchants Association was in process and several businesses organized the first Broadway Block Festival. Students continued to coordinate and facilitate meetings for the fledgling Broadway Merchants Association; they were proud of their role in creating it to revitalize the economic state of the corridor and maintain local businesses in light of gentrification and increasing property values. As demonstrated time and again in similar projects, the presence of young people in such meetings prompted adults to reduce animosity and act more "adult" themselves. The civic partner from the Brooklyn Chamber of Commerce reflected on the impact of working with Y-PLAN students during a presentation of the project at the APA Annual Conference in 2017:

> I have to say that the way that these children – I'm sorry, these young adults – really came and attacked the situation, was second to none. They created their own Facebook page for the Merchants Association, they were out every day with me handing out fliers for our merchant meetings, they were out there recruiting their parents to come to these merchant meetings. I have to say, I wouldn't be able to have the same results that I've had with this merchants association without the help of Y-PLAN and these students.

For their teacher, the greatest highlight of the second-year project was watching her students begin to realize their agency: "They are important agents of change. Not just saying it to them, but having them actually see it. You know what's going to happen. They're going to come back to visit, and they're going to see it all."

When the teacher who led the program left to teach at another school the following year, the power of this project continued for a third year with a new teacher, in continued partnership with the council member's office, and with new support from a community artist. The third year's "Artervention" project reimagined existing statues in NYC through the perspective of young people around the themes of diversity, immigration, and community in an attempt to improve the transportation corridor and make it safer by enhancing it as a community space. To execute this complex task, students took photos of inspirational statues around NYC and worked in partnership with the artist to alter and enhance the pictures using Photoshop. Students dove into the project, researching statues and monuments around NYC and using the NYC Parks and Recreation Department website in search of any that felt relevant and important to them. This research culminated in a trip to the Upper West Side of Manhattan, where students photographed statues and displays inside the American Museum of Natural History. They also mapped sites along Broadway to determine the best locations to place their art pieces. Culminating this three-year project, students returned to Brooklyn Borough Hall to present their posters and copies of their final art pieces.

Just a few short months later, in October 2018, these young planners and their civic partners unveiled their final art pieces in a ribbon-cutting ceremony and press conference. Several local news outlets covered the event. As the local council member shared his reflections on the three-year partnership, he explained, "These kids are taking ownership of Broadway. It doesn't belong to the drug dealers or people who are causing trouble. It belongs to these students. And that is truly remarkable" (Leonhardt, 2018). Ultimately, the Brighten Broadway project and partnership transformed the school and the space in a wide range of ways. This included attracting half a million dollars of investment to their neighborhood.

Empowering young people to tell their own stories and experiences of Broadway revealed innovative recommendations to tackle complex community challenges such as gentrification. Although gentrification is an inherently complex issue with no silver bullet solution, the process of enabling EBC students to tell their own stories about what they value about their neighborhood revealed small-scale but key priorities in the fight against gentrification. Emboldened by their new sense of agency, the students began to question their own process for project development. One student, Ricardo, said plainly, "Doesn't street art create more gentrification? Art draws people into places, and on Broadway I see art popping up in places where nobody used to go, but now there's bars and hotels, and housing is way more expensive." His comment launched an ongoing discussion among the adults and young people in this community of practice about the relationship between public art and gentrification, as well as the significance of monuments, particularly in light of recent news about the removal of oppressive statues representing white supremacy. In these discussions, students voiced their fears about gentrification and displacement in Bushwick, especially in the context of disappearing cultural and commercial spaces. One student explained that "white people especially want to move into areas with art that is trendy" and expressed her fear that "when we say 'Brightening Broadway', we're not just talking about brightening with art and better lighting, we're going to brighten with people – white people will move in."

At this point, the professionals encouraged students to use the Artervention Project as a tool to tell their own narrative about Bushwick & Broadway and rebuke the changes they saw happening. By the end of these discussions, students felt greater ownership over the project because they felt it was actually relevant to their values and priorities. Students created the hashtag *#LetBrooklynBeBrooklyn* to represent the theme of their art pieces that celebrated the diversity, immigration, and inclusivity of the Broadway Corridor that they themselves value.

Simultaneously, through engaging with the young planners, the professionals in the community of practice learned not only how to reimagine school spaces but also how to navigate the places they already occupy in a new way. As a speaker at the Y-PLAN NYC Summit in May 2018, their civic client from the council member's office shared:

> The leaders that go to City Hall, the levers of power, how are they going to be able to advocate for policy and laws that are reflective of their communities if they're not listening? I was reminded [by the students] about the changes that happen in Bushwick that they care about – that they felt anger that Party City, the long-term community partner that gives to community events, was no longer going to be in the neighborhood, and we're getting a Starbucks and we're getting other coffee shops that are charging $5 that make no sense when the bodega folks are charging $1.

In this way, as the professionals learned to navigate communities through the eyes of our young planners, they learned to see those communities in a whole new way.

Analysis: Sustaining Influence and Impact

Students took the reins in the project to use art pieces, social media, and writing to articulate their narrative about Bushwick, gentrification, and uplifting Black and Latinx figures who represent home. Their pushback on the project and analysis of street art's contribution to gentrification and displacement of their community brought a much more explicit social justice lens to the project. They realized they could use public art as a platform to argue for affordable housing and against gentrification, leading to greater buy-in throughout the project. In the course of their work together, they changed both the project itself and the Broadway corridor.

Three years and half a million dollars later, the transformation ignited from this project transcends the fiscal, physical, and even attitude changes: a novel, authentic partnership between the school and the local council member emerged. Students grew to know and respect their client for both his status as an insider who knows and loves Bushwick and as a

Image 6.2 In response to their clients' project question, students worked in teams to collate and analyze data, brainstorm possible solutions, and conduct a cost-benefit analysis of their proposals. Here, they showcase their imaginative, actionable ideas to Brighten Broadway for politicians and community members.

Source: Benjamin Deibert.

rare adult who genuinely listens to and hears youth. In part, the strength of this partnership enabled the project to persist through a change in teachers, even as the school administration was only tangentially involved. The power of this partnership promises to transform the relationship between these systems into the future while cultivating open, safe spaces for young people to speak up and share their lived experiences, inside and outside of the classroom.

When Ricardo raised his question about street art causing gentrification, he was hesitant and seemed a little worried about the adults' reactions. In persisting to ask it, he bravely reminded the adults that he and his peers had perceptive questions and particular insights to share. The adults then created space to continue these conversations that allowed students to discuss their concerns about the project and whether it was perpetuating the changes in Bushwick they dislike. While this may have been the first time the EBC young planners challenged the professionals, it was not the last. Cultivating a structured and reflexive space to talk about gentrification and street art made students feel safe enough to discuss their reservations about the project. Open dialogue and interconnectedness between youth and adults, modeled in the Brighten Broadway project, are central to the theory of change in creating just and joyful cities for everyone.

Sacramento: Forging a Walkable Path

Why Plan for Sacramento's Walkability?

The city of Sacramento has grown rapidly in recent years and this population growth and corresponding housing development have gentrified its low-income communities, displacing long-term residents. Leveraging the state capital's existing cadre of non-profit and civic agencies ready to protect the most vulnerable populations from displacement, The California Endowment (TCE) and the Sacramento City Unified School District (SCUSD) brought the UC Berkeley Y-PLAN initiative to Sacramento during the summer of 2015. Their shared goal was to build and maintain a healthier, more equitable Sacramento by engaging young people, especially those farthest from opportunity, in the planning process from the start. To accomplish that goal, they partnered with community-based non-profit, WALKSacramento, whose organizers work with transportation and land use planners, elected officials, and community groups to create safe, walkable environments that encourage active mobility for all citizens, especially for children, seniors, the disabled, and low-income individuals. To that end, they wanted to use the Y-PLAN process to expand their engagement to include younger residents.

Intergenerational Community of Practice

As a lead partner, SCUSD identified two veteran English teachers to spearhead the partnership effort. Hiram Johnson, a large, comprehensive, and historically underperforming school with many promising educational programs working to improve the rigor and relevance across curriculum, located Y-PLAN within their Health and Medical Sciences Academy.[2] Across town, Health Professions High School, a newer, much smaller school with a school-wide health focus, used the Y-PLAN to address the social determinants of health. Both teachers conducted the project in 10th-grade English classes during this first pilot year, engaging a total of 90 students across the two schools. The project posed the question: *How does the design of a community affect young people's health?* and encouraged students to consider three primary areas: access to healthy food, physical activity, and personal and physical safety. With that, students set out to identify opportunities to advocate for policy or design changes to promote better health outcomes for teens and youth.

After a brief introductory phase, WALKSacramento led the young planners on walk audits around their schools. During these walking tours of the neighborhoods, the youth observed the streets, local parks, and public amenities. They conducted a needs assessment, with a goal of identifying how the existing buildings and spaces have been designed, how those design decisions affect the health of young people, and if they meet or do meet their needs. The walk audit of the built environment and following debrief provided the first opportunity for students to navigate the city they knew in a new way. The students learned about how people in power enact plans, designs, and policies that affect their health, well-being, and opportunities. From there, they learned to survey their community to gather additional input about needed change. They weighed the costs and benefits, evaluated qualitative and quantitative data, and generated graphs as professionals.

Working with these young planners not only expanded the age included in WALKSacramento's engagement efforts, but also diversified the input from a racial and socio-economic perspective. More than 90% of the 1,543 students enrolled at Hiram Johnson for the 2015–16 school year were classified as "Socioeconomically Disadvantaged,"[3] as were 83% of Health Professions' students. Additionally, at Hiram Johnson, 44% identified as Hispanic or Latino, 31% Asian or Pacific Islander, 14% African American, and 8% white. At Health Professions, half identified as Hispanic or Latino, a quarter African American, 15% Asian or Pacific Islander, and 8% white. Nearly a quarter of the students at Hiram Johnson and 14% at Health Professions were considered English Language Learners (California Department of Education, 2021).

The students' final recommendations not only focused on redesigning key elements of the community to improve the health of the neighborhood residents but also linked public space, active transportation, and public health. This conceptual linkage highlighted the interconnected nature of these spheres for their peers, their audience, and the young researchers themselves. Student recommendations fell into three broad categories: healthy food options, public park facilities and bus stops, and active mobility, such as walking or biking. In terms of improving healthy food options, students recommended transforming vacant lots into farmers markets, expanding produce sections in local supermarkets, and adding organic produce sections. Once these enhancements were established, they called for educating local citizens about the enhanced healthy food options in their neighborhood. In improving public park facilities, students focused first on basic needs. Noting that park restrooms were critically important to people experiencing homelessness as well as other residents enjoying the parks, they recommended keeping restrooms clean, providing baby changing areas in all restrooms, adding doors to stalls, upgrading facilities to include proper lighting for better safety, and ensuring that sufficient bathroom tissue and soap is available throughout the day.

Many student proposals revolved around bus and active transportation improvements. While Health Professions students focused on improving bikeability by adding bike lanes, Hiram Johnson students advocated for upgrades to bus transit citywide. They recommended installing benches to provide comfort for people waiting at bus stops and to eliminate sidewalk crowding. In their research, they discovered that many of their peers sat on the curb of

Image 6.3 Y-PLAN students pose for a photo prior to going into City Hall to present their Healthy Sacramento proposals to the Mayor and city leaders.

Source: UC Berkeley Center for Cities and Schools.

the sidewalk while waiting for the bus, thus putting themselves dangerously close to road traffic. The Hiram Johnson students also recommended building shelters at high-use bus stops to protect people from intense sun or rain. They recommended upgrading the lighting around bus stops to make it safer to wait for the bus in the evenings and during shorter winter days. Additionally, they proposed posting accurate time schedules for bus routes and providing community information brochures at stops to keep community members informed and updated on relevant changes. Overall, their goal was to convey to their community that their safety and comfort do matter.

Analysis: Sustaining Influence and Impact

This pilot year of Y-PLAN Sacramento set into motion the transformation of individuals as well as public health and public transportation systems within their community, for years to follow. It afforded students, teachers, and planners access to each other, often for the first time. It laid the groundwork for students to learn about the planning process and how they could play an active role in it. In addition to the access enabled by introductions to people and places within their city that had previously been hidden to them, students reached people and spaces beyond the original project design, leading to lasting changes on a broader scale. For example, the Health Professions students presented their Bike Lanes on Broadway proposal to members of the Sacramento Bicycle Advisory Group. By the end of the meeting, members of the citywide committee emphasized their newfound understanding of the importance of teenage voices in the planning process. This expanded thinking occurred in two directions; as young planners learned about their city through the lens of city planning, civic partners learned about the lived experiences of the young people and how the city works (or does not work) for them.

As WALKSacramento explained in a 2016 letter to the students upon completion of the project:

> Having never worked with student consultants, we were not only impressed by your work products, but the critical thinking and teamwork that you exhibited throughout the process. Your ability to think outside of the box was critical to your success and an inspiring reminder to us here at WALKSacramento that we should always strive to expand the realm of what is possible. Your projects were interesting,

> well thought through, and demonstrated a strong understanding of the impacts of urban design on health. Through individual conversations with each of you, it was clear to us that your understanding of health and your ability to impact change has grown significantly. Finally, your abilities to professionally communicate your process, recommendations, and overall goal to a broader audience were outstanding.

Through their collaboration, WALKSacramento staff began to understand the city through the eyes of the young people living in it. They learned to recognize the value of young people's insights, the extent of their abilities, and the imperative of listening to what they have to say.

Shortly after the students' final presentations to their client, the school year ended. Students knew their teachers intended to introduce a new planning project the next semester but one Hiram Johnson student was compelled to pursue her own agenda. She contacted her civic client independently and learned that their regional transit authority had the power to install benches at the bus stop near her school. She then emailed the new head of the transit authority that afternoon, explaining her project, their findings, recommendations, and why it mattered so much to the young residents. The reply from the head of the transit authority, committing to install benches, came within hours. By the start of their junior year, two public bus stops had been upgraded with seating, signage, and landscaping to create greater comfort and usability for local bus users and pedestrians.

WALKSacramento was so impressed with the students' presentations and recommendations that they decided to continue engaging youth throughout all their projects to reach a broader community whose important insights were often left out of the conversation. As they explained to the students in their letter following that initial project:

> Simply put, without your assistance this past year, WALKSacramento's work to analyze and solve issues related to safety, active transportation, and access to healthy foods would not nearly have been as successful. Additionally, as your work continues to inspire and influence change in your communities, your involvement in this project has really shifted our thinking about working with and engaging youth in the future. . . . We are honored to have been assisted by each of you and are looking forward to expanding this "pilot" project to an even more successful program in the future.

Image 6.4 In Sacramento, students collaborate with their community partners to promote health and mobility from a socio-economic and cultural perspective. Here, they present their proposals featuring buses, active transportation, and public space to Mayor Darrell Steinberg.

Source: UC Berkeley Center for Cities and Schools.

That work did continue. In the spring of 2018, the students presented to Sacramento Mayor Darrell Steinberg at City Hall. Speaking to students from both Hiram Johnson and Health Professions, he stated, "I am so pleased and proud that as young people, you are choosing to spend real time and effort in . . . community-based problem solving." He spoke to how their efforts would help them beyond the project itself, which the young people already understood. The student who had secured the bus stops two years earlier had also completed an internship with the City. She shared that "My work with Y-PLAN helped me realize I can be an advocate for change and help create equity. As students, our voices can and will be heard" (Thanpaeng & Salias, 2016).

The success of the pilot sparked a renewed interest in youth participation from the SCUSD. Since that project, hundreds of young planners from five SCUSD high schools have conducted more than two dozen Y-PLAN projects in partnership with dozens of civic leaders across the city, from the Sacramento Housing and Redevelopment Agency to the Mayor's Office to the Planning Department. The school district has institutionalized the process of engaging youth in local planning processes, embedded within their school day, by investing over half a million dollars from their Career and Technical Education funding to expand district-wide. The City of Sacramento has continued to partner on this work, engaging youth in their General Plan update, Climate Action Plan, housing development planning, and mental health service planning to help support students manage through the global COVID-19 pandemic.

Oakland: For the Culture, By the Culture

Why Plan for a Transit Hub for BART?

East Oakland was once a flourishing, middle-class community. Over the past century, however, discriminatory housing policies; an exodus of industry and high-wage, low skill jobs; and disenfranchisement have profoundly changed this neighborhood. Now liquor stores, check-cashing agencies, and hair and nails shops stand where thriving commercial thoroughfares, banks, and restaurants once reigned. "According to the Alameda County Public Health Department, a child born in East Oakland will live on average 10 years less than a child born in the Oakland Hills" (Shrimali, 2018). Today, half of East Oakland households earn less than $30,000 per year and the unemployment rate is double that of the city overall (Youth Uprising, 2021). Through it all, East Oakland has remained an exceedingly resilient community, with many residents who are active in community and religious organizations. Many families have lived in the neighborhood for generations. However, as described by well-respected youth serving community organization, Youth Uprising, the lived experiences of East Oakland's youth "are sobering. Over 40% of local young people are not enrolled in school, the rate of teen pregnancies is three times that of Alameda County, and the murder rate is seven times higher than the national average" (Youth Uprising, 2021). Meanwhile, East Oakland is also a transportation hub boasting many regional connections. Its Coliseum Station serves as a rail stop for

Amtrak as well as half a dozen AC Transit bus lines, provides the rail connection to Oakland International Airport, and was one of the first segments of the Bay Area Regional Transit (BART) system to be constructed.

In 2016, BART faced a major challenge: ridership was declining, particularly during off-peak hours. BART sought to expand their market to include people outside of commuters, especially young people, who were not riding the system in high numbers. In order to attract more riders, they knew they needed to connect with segments of the population that they had not reached before. Meanwhile, CC+S was just beginning to work with the nationally-recognized African American Male Achievement Initiative (AAMA)[4] within the Oakland Unified School District (OUSD) and recognized this opportunity to bring locals confronting myriad social and economic challenges together with BART to address how to better connect the stations to their surrounding community. The team was formed with AAMA students, known as "Kings," from both Skyline and Oakland High Schools and BART as their civic client.

Intergenerational Community of Practice

After curriculum alignment, planning, and training sessions throughout the fall, the official project launched in January of 2016. Nearly 100 young Black men from 9th-12th-grade Manhood Development classes at Skyline High School and Entrepreneurship and Computer Science classes at Oakland High School worked under the guidance of their facilitators, with the support of CC+S undergraduate mentors, to develop proposals for BART. Before the official launch of the project, the Kings and BART representatives visited UC Berkeley together to join the college students for their seminar on campus. Many of the young men had never been to a university campus before and fewer had participated in a college lecture. In addition to empowering the young men, the visit also allowed for power-sharing between the college students and the professionals. While the BART representatives had all attended college and many had advanced degrees, on campus, the college students confidently guided the professionals in navigating their space.

When BART representatives and the college mentors met at Skyline and Oakland High a week later to introduce the project, their nervousness was clear. Most had not spent time in a high school classroom since their teens, and for many of them, who had grown up in more privileged communities, their schools and classrooms looked different than this one. However, their demeanor shifted quickly when the Kings started asking difficult and insightful questions. Instead of finishing the long PowerPoint filled with professional terminology, the outsiders morphed their lecture into a discussion about housing equality in Oakland, as they recognized how the students' interest was piqued after the BART team shared that they were considering developing housing on the surface parking lots surrounding their local station. When the BART representatives posed the central question of the project – *How can BART better connect the stations to the communities they serve?* – students were ready with follow-up questions about housing affordability and parking access. More crucially, the students posed their central question – whether this neighborhood investment would simply facilitate gentrification and exacerbate the displacement they already witnessed around them. The BART staff were immediately impressed and shared the fact that they asked themselves and their colleagues these questions daily. The Kings pressed them to take action on issues from housing to security to affordability of transit. They specifically highlighted questions about security on transit and about fearing for their lives due to police brutality more generally. BART representatives were surprised by the Kings' openness and questions, and the Kings were equally surprised that the professionals' interest seemed genuine.

BART's presentation not only introduced the project questions and expectations but also offered students direct access to those who can have a significant impact on the lives and communities of these students. Due to the unique college-city-school nature of this collaboration, the access granted by the project was multi-dimensional. High school students, in this case, young Black men, gained access to the people and places of power in their city and the nearby institution of higher learning. College mentors gained access to the lived experiences of low-income, Black youth and simultaneously those same people and places that held civic power. Finally, the professionals gained access to the city's schools and to the experiential insights of the high school and college students who live in and traverse them. These insights included the painful reality of violence for the young Black men of East Oakland. Tellingly, four students associated with this project lost their lives before it was completed.

When BART planned and prepared an elaborate site mapping and inspirational tour for the students, the Kings stepped into a world that was new to them. In one day, they toured the newly redesigned (and now infamous,

Image 6.5 Mentors from the University of California, Berkeley work with the Skyline High School students in Oakland as they develop presentation boards reflecting their creative visions for the BART transportation hubs.

Source: UC Berkeley Center for Cities and Schools.

given the murder of Oscar Grant by BART police) Fruitvale Station with representatives of a local non-profit before taking BART to the agency's headquarters in downtown Oakland. There they enjoyed a catered lunch during a college and career panel before taking BART to the Coliseum station, where a housing developer discussed emerging plans and proposals with them. As the day progressed, the young men learned to navigate the city they already knew so well through a new perceptual lens and they were able to contribute directly to the plans for their project site. All the while, the professionals and mentors were also learning to navigate the city through the lens of the Kings.

Throughout the next month, as university student mentors supported the AAMA classes several times a week, excitement grew for the culmination of their project: a presentation of their proposals at Oakland's City Hall. From their extensive primary and secondary source research, they developed several short- and long-term recommendations that would make BART a more attractive way to travel for young people by better aligning it with the local community. While these recommendations centered around the young people's own experience, the young planners asserted their belief that the changes they proposed would make the BART experience better for all users.

Specific examples included station beautification; safety enhancements; inclusion of arts, history, culture; and affordable housing. First, students recommended BART create a more comfortable and welcoming station atmosphere by improving the availability and quality of seating, altering ticketing machines to facilitate easier use by individuals without credit cards, investing in digital boards to fluctuate between advertisements and showcases of student achievements, and providing "hang out" spaces like parklets to attract young people and encourage them to geotag themselves to provide informal advertisement. Although the Kings described the need for lighting improvements as well, the hallmark of their safety proposal was their "Community Protectors Program." Students noted that security guards and armed police are not the only way to improve rider safety in BART stations and instead suggested hiring a cadre of Community Protectors to oversee station safety. They would be trained in nonviolent conflict mediation, unarmed and unaffiliated with the police. They envisioned community protectors as being local people who know the area and care about its safety and wellbeing.

Illustrating the need for station beautification, the Kings provided a sketch of a mural, done by one of their classmates. It featured two suns shining over both sides of the tracks at Coliseum station. The young planners asserted that the murals should be about more than mere aesthetics. They should honor Oakland youth who have been killed, Oakland heroes, and neighborhood history and identity in order to generate community pride. They commented that they had read BART's *Art in Transit* policy and argued that their mural project was in alignment with its stated goals.

Finally, students called for affordable housing to be included in BART TOD projects, both at the Coliseum BART and system-wide. They explained that all of the enhancements would make BART more attractive, which in turn would make neighborhoods with this upgraded BART access more attractive and potentially raise housing costs. As residents of Oakland neighborhoods served by BART stations, they stated that they wanted to stay in Oakland and were concerned about the displacement they observe in their community every day as rent prices continue to rise. The young planners concluded that BART should exist not only for the well-to-do but for people of all incomes and all ages.

When the Kings presented these and other final proposal ideas at Oakland City Hall in April of 2017, they shared their visions, their ideas, and their experiences with their university mentors, their peers from another high school, UC Berkeley professors, their BART clients (including the General Manager herself), their school district Superintendent, and their Mayor. Embedded within their proposals were tributes to their classmates who had lost their lives during the project. They also brought in and set up plants representing each deceased young man's spirit to adorn the conference room. Just as the young men were transformed by presenting in this place of civic power, they also transformed and expanded the consciousnesses of the adults present, leading them to a fuller understanding and appreciation of the experiences of our marginalized youth and

Image 6.6 Student scholars from Oakland work closely with artists and transportation administrators to bring cultural pride, accessibility, and safety into the local transit hub. In August 2020, they unveiled the mural they designed.

Source: UC Berkeley Center for Cities and Schools.

of the importance of holding space both for grieving and for honoring the peers they had lost along the way.

Analysis: Sustaining Influence and Impact

UC Berkeley undergraduate mentors noted that during post-presentation reflection sessions, the Kings seemed happier, more confident, and proud of the work they had done. The Kings asked about next steps and how they could stay involved and some stated that they wanted to work for BART in the future because they want to transform their communities firsthand. They believed in their ability to induce change. When BART invited them to present at their quarterly managers' meeting, they were eager to do so, and on May 17, 2017, four Kings represented their classmates, presenting to more than fifty BART managers from departments across the agency. When they finished, the General Manager took the microphone and announced, spontaneously, that she would fund internships for these young men to implement their ideas over the summer. She called for volunteers to host those interns and the Director of the Arts Program eagerly agreed. On June 26th of the same year, seven Kings began their paid summer internships to implement their recommendation of a community mural at Coliseum BART and one UC college mentor was hired to help facilitate the process, thus maintaining representation across all levels of this intergenerational community of practice. Throughout the summer, the Kings designed the scope of the mural, put out a call for artists, reviewed submissions, and selected a muralist to complete the project.

After obstacles typical of planning processes caused three years of delays, their mural "For the Culture, By the Culture" was unveiled in a ceremony at the Coliseum station in August 2020, during the COVID-19 pandemic; it was viewed then through smoke-blackened air from nearby wildfires, surrounding the city. Despite the trying times, the BART Art Director, the mural artist, the mentor who helped facilitate, the UC Berkeley CC+S Y-PLAN team, the AAMA Director, the teachers, and four of the seven interns – now college students themselves – came together to celebrate. This project cultivated deeper understanding and enduring relationships as the diverse members of this intergenerational community of practice became true partners in innovation, each bringing their knowledge, skills, insights, and abilities, and recognizing those unique talents in each other.

Conclusion

This chapter features a wide range of literature and practice demonstrating how and why to incorporate young people into transportation planning. The findings of the research and youth in planning case studies discussed in this chapter reveal that students can understand the issues and the tools being used in the transportation planning field today. As one teacher from Sacramento's Health Professions High School eloquently posed "Who better to ask about public transit than kids who take the bus?" Students whose families have been displaced due to gentrification often commute great distances just to attend their original neighborhood schools. Whether by necessity or choice, young people are more likely to depend on non-car transportation modes, including transit, walking, biking, and other types of micro-mobility. They navigate our transportation networks under different constraints and can easily identify shortcomings that are invisible to more privileged residents. As a result, they are strategically situated to offer valuable insights regarding the shortcomings as well as potential solutions for our current transportation landscape.

Combining the knowledge gleaned from their lived experience with data gathered using professional planning tools, young people can productively collaborate with civic leaders to produce substantive transportation policy recommendations. Furthermore, when students are equipped with planning expertise through intentional youth planning studios and classes, such as GUB and Y-PLAN, they can draw on their lived experiences to identify challenges and opportunities that might be invisible to others. These youth planning initiatives connect students with industry and civic leaders as well as elected officials. Together they form intergenerational communities of practice ready to learn from each other and to change transportation policies and practices to become more efficient and effective.

Ultimately, young people call for transportation networks to be safe and accessible, with improved technologies to fluidly connect public spaces, and foster community and independence for all. To the young planners, all components of a city can and should promote mutual respect, engagement, and understanding across diverse populations and transportation can be a key ingredient toward realizing this goal. As in other policy areas, young people see transportation as having the potential to bring people together in positive and aspirational ways, by inviting and encouraging them to share public space. When youth engage in the planning process, they both model that potential and call for it to be realized, and they invite adults to do the same.

Notes

1 Names of all young people are pseudonyms.

2 Health and Medical Sciences Academy at Hiram Johnson High School is a small learning community grounded in work based learning and authentic curriculum.

3 Students are classified as Socioeconomically Disadvantaged if they were migrant, foster, homeless at any time during the academic year, or they were eligible for Free or Reduced-Priced Meal (FRPM) Program (also known as the National School Lunch Program), or if neither parent has graduated from high school.

4 See OUSD's AAMA Program www.ousd.org/Page/495 and more on the Kingmakers philosophy – https://kingmakersofoakland.org/who-we-are/story/.

References

Ajao, A. (2019, February 1). Electric Scooters and Micro-Mobility: Here's Everything You Need to Know. *Forbes*. www.forbes.com/sites/adeyemiajao/2019/02/01/everything-you-want-to-know-about-scooters-and-micro-mobility/.

Anderson, M. (2016, April 7). Who Relies on Public Transit in the US *Pew Research Center*. www.pewresearch.org/fact-tank/2016/04/07/who-relies-on-public-transit-in-the-u-s/

Bierbaum, A. H., Karner, A., & Barajas, J. M. (2020). Toward Mobility Justice: Linking Transportation and Education Equity in the Context of School Choice. *Journal of the American Planning Association*, *87*(2), 15.

Bierbaum, A. H., & Vincent, J. M. (2013). Putting Schools on the Map: Linking Transit-Oriented Development, Households with Children, and Schools. *Transportation Research Record, 2357*, 77–85. https://doi.org/10.3141/2357-09.

Blumenberg, E. (2002, May). *The Travel Behavior and Needs of the Poor: A Study of Welfare Recipients in Fresno County, California*. Mineta Transportation Institute. https://transweb.sjsu.edu/research/Travel-Behavior-and-Needs-Poor-Study-Welfare-Recipients-Fresno-County-California.

California Department of Education. (2021). DataQuest—Student & School Data Reports (CA Dept of Education). https://www.cde.ca.gov/ds/sd/cb/dataquest.asp

Cervero, R., Guerra, E., & Al, S. (2017). *Beyond Mobility: Planning Cities for People and Places*. Island Press.

Cervero, R., & Sullivan, C. (2011). Green TODs: Marrying Transit-oriented Development and Green Urbanism. *International Journal of Sustainable Development & World Ecology, 18*(3), 210–218. https://doi.org/10.1080/13504509.2011.570801.

Deakin, E. (Ed.). (2020). *Transportation, Land Use, and Environmental Planning*. Elsevier.

Frick, K. T. (2020). Citizen Mobilization in Digital and Analog: When Regional Planning Lands in Marin County, California, Is It a Carrot or a Stick Painted Orange? In *Transportation, Land Use, and Environmental Planning* (pp. 523–555). Elsevier.

Gross, A. (2019, February 27). *Think You're In Your Car More? You're Right. Americans Spend 70 Billion Hours Behind the Wheel*. AAA Newsroom. https://newsroom.aaa.com/2019/02/think-youre-in-your-car-more-youre-right-americans-spend-70-billion-hours-behind-the-wheel/.

Leonhardt, A. (2018, October 1). *Bushwick Students "Brighten Broadway" with Colorful Street Signs | BK Reader*. www.bkreader.com/2018/10/01/bushwick-students-brighten-broadway-with-colorful-art-signs/.

Makarewicz, C. (2020). Balancing Education Opportunities with Sustainable Travel and Development. In *Transportation, Land Use, and Environmental Planning* (pp. 299–331). Elsevier.

McAndrews, C. (2020). Transportation and Land Use as Social Determinants of Health: The Case of Arterial Roads. In E. Deakin (Ed.), *Transportation, Land Use, and Environmental Planning* (pp. 35–54). Elsevier.

McDonald, N., & Peng, K. (2020). The Changing Nature of Work and Time Use: Implications for Travel Demand. In E. Deakin (Ed.), *Transportation, Land Use, and Environmental Planning* (pp. 3–16). Elsevier.

O'Brien, C. (2008). Sustainable Happiness: How Happiness Studies Can Contribute to a More Sustainable Future. *Canadian Psychology/Psychologie Canadienne, 49*(4), 289–295. https://doi.org/10.1037/a0013235

PolicyLink. (2013). *Managing Walkability, Diversity and Educational Equity in US School*. https://citiesandschools.berkeley.edu/uploads/WALKBILITYAND DIVERSITY_FINAL.pdf.

Shaheen, S., Cohen, A., Chan, N., & Bansal, A. (2020). Sharing Strategies: Carsharing, Shared Micromobility (Bikesharing and Scooter Sharing), Transportation Network Companies, Microtransit, and Other Innovative Mobility Modes. In *Transportation, Land Use, and Environmental Planning* (pp. 237–262). Elsevier.

Shrimali, B. (2018). *Community Close-Up: East Oakland*. Federal Reserve Bank of San Francisco. https://www.frbsf.org/community-development/publications/special/community-close-up-east-oakland/

Thanpaeng, A., & Salias, T. (2016, November 30). *Sacramento High School Students Recount Their Experience with Y-PLAN*. http://y-plan.berkeley.edu/blog/sacramento-high-school-students-recount-their-experience-with-y-plan.

Thomas, R. (2008). Engaged or Disinterested? Youth Political and Civic Participation in Canadian Transportation Planning. *Critical Planning, 15*(1), 2–21.

Vincent, J. M., Bierbaum, A. H., McKoy, D. L., Rhodes, M. P., Zimbabwe, S., Britt, K., & Wampler, E. (2012). Families and Transit-Oriented Development: Creating Complete Communities for All. *Transit-Oriented Development Best Practice Guidebooks, 1*(205), 1–28.

Vincent, J. M., Makarewicz, C., Miller, R., Ehrman, J., & McKoy, D. L. (2014). Beyond the Yellow Bus: Promising Practices for Maximizing Access to Opportunity through Innovations in Student Transportation. In *Center for Cities & Schools*. Center for Cities & Schools. https://eric.ed.gov/?id=ED558542.

Youth Uprising. (2021). *East Oakland*. Youth UpRising. https://www.youthuprising.org/issues-responses/east-oakland

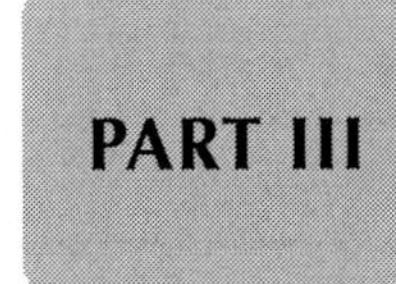

PART III

Call to Action

The Essentials

Introduction

The nine in-depth case studies from UC Berkeley's youth in planning initiative, Y-PLAN, as well as others described in Part II illuminated powerful opportunities as well as thorny challenges facing civic leaders who aspire to authentically engage young people and schools in the city planning process. While the featured nine case studies focus on resilience, housing, and transportation, the underlying theory and practice apply to other realms of city planning, such as public infrastructure, health, sustainability, civic services, and more. Decades of research and experience in the field reveal how intergenerational communities of practice, which include youth in schools alongside adult professionals in planning and government, can facilitate a meaningful process for all participants while yielding positive outcomes for our cities. Integrating the resulting actionable planning proposals and recommendations into city planning processes, projects, and policies can begin to change the way civic leaders and decision-makers understand the role of young people in our cities.

As cities are working to combat one crisis after the next, city planning theory and practice need to converge, seeking innovative ways to move big ideas into immediate action. This dilemma is not new for city planning. Nearly forty years ago, de Neufville (1983) warned that:

> Planning theory not only provides little guidance to the practitioner but that it also contributes to a sense of frustration and can hinder practice . . . [therefore] it is a matter of considerable urgency to

DOI: 10.4324/9781003141778-10

> develop theories of planning that will both mesh with the realities of practice and be useful and inspiring to the practitioner.
>
> (p. 35)

A decade later, Alexander (1997) presented the possibility that "the planning theory-practice gap is unbridgeable" (p. 5). After crossing into the new millennium, the Review Editors for The Journal of the American Planning Association identified the importance of such bridging saying that recent trends represented "not a one-time convergence but a healthy and enriching merger of theory and practice" (Nedovic-Budic, 2003, p. 193).

Despite that recognition and optimism, research-practice gaps still divide city planning. More recently, Hurley et al. (2016) recognized that "exchange between planning researchers and practitioners is essential to the development of both disciplinary knowledge and professional practice" (p. 447). In response, they crafted a dialogue between researchers and practitioners to explore whether bridging is "an achievable objective or a bridge too far" (p. 448). They identified collaboration between researchers and practitioners as both the most challenging barrier to overcome and the most important. They found potential to foster collaboration in cases with "a strong shared sense of purpose and outcome," those that build "personal relationships and trust between researchers and practitioners," and those that foster "open dialogue and . . . understanding of the drivers and needs of different actors seeking to collaborate" (p. 472).

Interestingly, this solution is reminiscent of communities of practice, defined by Lave and Wenger (1991) as groups of people who share a concern or a passion for something they do, a shared practice, and learn how to do it better as they interact regularly. Wenger (1998) further argued that "building complex social relationships around meaningful activities requires genuine practices in which taking charge of learning becomes the enterprise of a community" (p. 272). In this way, this chapter points once again to the power of the community of practice introduced in Part I and driving the case studies in Part II, not only for its importance in planning with and for young people but also for its potential to bridge the research-practice divide. Doing so, however, will also require stepping back and recognizing the essentials that emerge from the research in Parts I and II to lay the groundwork for productive, positive, authentic engagement in practice.

Facilitation of diverse partnerships can remain daunting, but laying the groundwork to foster success does not have to be complicated. Consider for a moment the survival items that wilderness guides advise hikers to take for safe travel in the backcountry. Sometimes known as the "Ten Essentials" (*Ten Essentials (US National Park Service)*, 2020), they are considered necessary before people set out on trails or even day hikes. From hydration to illumination to insulation, these essentials both inform a novice's first foray into nature and remind the expert backpacker to take the necessary preparations for safe exploration.

Similarly, the "Six Essentials for Planning Just and Joyful Cities" emerge from the research discussed throughout this book as prerequistes to effectively plan with and for young people and public schools in practice. Introduced here with case snapshots and guidance for planners, this chapter will dig into these six essentials: basic needs, mutual understanding, trust and relationships, power of all ages, responsibility, and connectivity. Together, these Essentials offer planners a foundation to guide the field forward.

Six Essentials for Planning Just and Joyful Cities

Basic Needs: Attend to First Things First

Many young people live with fear and uncertainty. They have experienced violence, displacement, and instability that curtail their access to healthcare, work, healthy food, education, transportation, social services, and recreation. They are particularly qualified to speak directly to these issues, offer strategies to ameliorate them, and contribute to planning vibrant, healthy, and resilient cities. They remind adults that before planning for the future, we need to ensure that the current basic needs of all residents are met. For them,

Figure 7.1 Basic Needs: Attend to First Things First.

Source: UC Berkeley Center for Cities and Schools.

physical safety and a sense of well-being starts with freedom from violence, including guns, gangs, drugs, and the police. Additionally, they speak to the need for safe housing, transportation, and access to healthy food and water. Once students feel secure, they may fear a return to the unsafe conditions. In the face of displacement, young people yearn for stability in their homes, in their schooling, and in the people who surround them.

While teacher turnover is a challenge nationwide the instability it creates for our young people is the greatest in schools serving the most vulnerable populations. Teacher turnover is 50% higher than the national average in Title I schools, which by definition have high percentages of children from low-income families, and 70% higher in the quartile of schools serving the most students of color than in the lowest such quartile (Title I, Part A Program, 2018; Carver-Thomas & Darling-Hammond, 2017). Meanwhile, some urban schools are closing their doors forever as family displacement causes a decline in school enrollment. This instability is exacerbated by mass incarceration and murder rates, forcing a turnover in students' homes as well. By high school, many urban teenagers have dealt with a revolving door of peers and adults in and out of school, and they approach new faces with caution. Even when a student's family can withstand the social and economic strains around them, our urban youth are still living amid chronic instability with many of their basic needs in continual jeopardy. They seek to make constant the variables in their lives.

Case Illustration: East Palo Alto, California

Students from East Palo Alto Phoenix Academy (EPAPA), featured in Chapter 5, poignantly demonstrates how critical it is to directly acknowledge and address issues of safety, security, and stability when engaging low-income BIPOC (Black, Indigenous, People of Color) youth in the planning process. EPAPA is in Silicon Valley, which hosts high-tech campuses such as Facebook, Apple, and Google. Here highly-paid workers in search of housing and services have pushed their way into, or in effect eradicated, many low-income BIPOC communities. As residents of one of the few remaining such neighborhoods surrounded by high-income communities, these students were hyper-aware of how gentrification and the ensuing displacement and decimation of neighborhoods impacted them personally.

One week after the UC Berkeley Y-PLAN (Youth-Plan, Learn, Act, Now) project at EPAPA launched in 2017, the school announced it would permanently close its high school at the end of the year, due to declining enrollment. This instability directly affected these students and engendered intense feelings of hopelessness, insecurity, and pain. The young people asserted that the immediate issues around safety, stability, security, and displacement had to be prioritized. With the students' input, the focus of the project shifted to consider the role of schools and resilience through the lens of lived experiences. Before any discussion about climate change or sea level rise, the top priority for them was to address issues associated with stability and security. To that end, they emphasized that affordable, safe housing is the bedrock of a resilient community. The adults on their team acknowledged this truth and supported the students to develop proposals to ensure the basic needs of East Palo Alto residents were met.

Throughout their research and planning process, the students eloquently described the challenges in their daily lives. They infused cold statistics with powerful stories, heartfelt feelings, and human faces. They described the devastation imposed on their community by the lack of affordable, reliable, and comfortable housing. Some students reported living in severely crowded or partitioned rental housing. Others said they occupied homes in disrepair, with substandard appliances and utilities. Some revealed that their families were subject to illegal rent increases and shady landlord tactics. Many had witnessed friends and neighbors driven out by escalating rents.

Mixed into their painful stories of displacement and degradation was also a deep pride and connection to the people and places of East Palo Alto. Many of these students' families had lived here for generations and were deeply ingrained in the fabric of this community. While conducting research, the students named, honored, and celebrated the strengths and admirable qualities of their community, despite the challenges people faced every day. The EPAPA students' proposals built upon these assets. They prioritized protecting and enhancing the environmental and social fabric of the community. The young people translated their local knowledge into innovative design and policy solutions focused first on the housing crisis. Their visions also emphasized leveraging their community's greatest strength: the people themselves. Generously they proposed strategies to familiarize newer residents with the local culture and welcome them into it. As one student, Jessica[1] explained, "Our research showed the importance of maintaining not only affordable housing but also the local culture while honoring residents who have lived here for many years."

These young scholars from EPAPA wisely knew that safety, security, and stability are the foundations of not only a resilient city but also a just and joyful one as well. They had adult allies in their community of practice who listened to their desire to take care of the present-day challenges and meeting basic needs before asking young people to help plan for their future. In this unsettling time of transition this effort offered the students continuity and a level of stability in their relationships.

Mutual Understanding: Listen and Share Across Boundaries

People's personal and collective identities are deeply rooted in their experience of the places they live. The lived experience of low-income BIPOC young people, one of our most vulnerable groups, provides them with a specialized perspective on both the built and the natural environment. Many have an acute understanding of the dangers, the bright spots, and the nuances of their environment. Listening to diverse young people, validating their experiences, and integrating their voices and insights into action plans cultivates the mutual understanding necessary for young people and adults to learn from and with each other. Deep and respectful listening on the part of adults creates a climate of dignified mutuality and opens the door for productive two-way exchange.

Figure 7.2 Mutual Understanding: Listen and Share Across Boundaries.

Source: UC Berkeley Center for Cities and Schools.

Mutual understanding is a reciprocal dynamic. When the youth engagement process grants students and adults access to each other, it centers the students' voices and bolsters their capacities to effect change. It also provides adults with fresh insights and approaches, grounded in and inspired by a deeper appreciation of the lived experiences and perspectives of young people. As adults participate alongside young people during this process, they develop greater cultural sensitivity and humility. Young people gain a better comprehension of, and respect for, the wisdom and experience it takes to navigate social, economic, and political systems to pull the levers of power and make change. Youth and adults together begin to understand that city planning can be a powerful interactive process in which diverse groups care and support each other while striving to make their shared communities better.

Case Illustration: Oakland, California

The Oakland case study, featured in Chapter 6, underscores the importance of mutual understanding as a critical prerequisite for effective planning with young people. The reciprocal collaboration between Black male students from two Oakland high schools (known as Kings), college student mentors from UC Berkeley, and professionals from the Bay Area Rapid Transit (BART) revealed the challenges and opportunities in fostering mutual understanding over time. Several key factors helped deepen those relationships in this unique college-city-school collaboration.

While BART administrators sought youth-driven input about how to improve ridership, safety, and workforce development, the first challenge was to acknowledge and understand the myriad social and economic challenges facing these young Black men and their families in East Oakland. Violence and police brutality were at the front of their minds. Their feelings of vulnerability and uncertainty intensified as four students associated with the project lost their lives to violence during this time. These truths had to be heard, acknowledged, and validated, and the mistrust that resulted from their vulnerability had to be addressed.

To build mutual understanding, the college students, the adult leaders, and the young men held three-way forums in the public school classroom, on the university campus, and at the corporate headquarters. In these exchanges, the college students asked the Kings deep questions, and the young men spoke from their hearts about their experiences in the city. BART staff members were impressed by their knowledge and vision. During the planning process, once they came to believe in the earnestness of their partners, the Kings felt empowered to press BART to take action on a range of substantive issues from housing to security and affordability of transit. BART planners designed paid internships to further develop their capacity as emerging professionals and committed to integrate student recommendations into BART's future planning strategies and current practices.

BART planners, the Kings, educators, and university mentors all became genuine partners in this process, each bringing their own knowledge, skills, insights, and abilities into the equation while honoring those qualities in each other. Connections between so many different members of this community of practice drove its success. Mutual trust, listening, and respect grew into a deeper understanding and enduring relationships. This project became a model for powerful, authentic adult-youth partnerships.

Trust and Relationships: Cultivate Genuine Connections

The capacity of individuals and communities to build trust, understanding, and connection is a prerequisite for democratic participation by people of all ages. In order to enlist young people's participation and deep engagement in civic planning, time and space must be made to allow relationships to form and trust to develop. Although trust is a necessary precursor for relationships, forging these relationships also requires honesty and authentic connection. Take the time needed and embrace the tensions to develop trust and build genuine relationships capable of driving intergenerational collaboration and partnerships.

Figure 7.3 Trust and Relationships: Cultivate Genuine Connections.

Source: UC Berkeley Center for Cities and Schools.

Successful youth engagement requires multiple layers of trust: trust in the students, trust in the teachers, trust in the civic leaders, and trust in the process. In a community that has legitimate, multi-generational skepticism of government, city leaders must establish trust through repeated interactions. When well-meaning city leaders visit a classroom for the first time – even if they attended the very high school they are visiting or even if they come from a similar background to the students – they will likely be met with caution. Students are used to people coming into their classroom, talking to them for half an hour, promising to return, and never coming back. Adults know the reasons for these broken promises are not about the young people. Changes in staffing, funding, and organizational or political priorities often preempt an individual adult's ability to return. However, that message rarely makes it back to the students. As a result, it takes repeated interactions over time to establish the foundational trust necessary for successful collaboration with youth. The second time students meet a city leader, they might even ask why that leader has returned. By the third or fourth time, their expressions change. They relax their guard. They are ready to engage.

Case Illustration: Brooklyn, New York

The Brighten Broadway case study, featured in Chapter 6, exemplifies the importance of building trust over time when engaging young people in the planning process. Students from East Bushwick Campus (EBC) High School for Public Service collaborated with civic leaders to take on a challenge in a neighborhood suffering from the impacts of disinvestment, weak economic growth, high vacancy rates, and chronically underutilized retail spaces. The goal of the three-year youth planning effort initiated in 2016 was to inject youth insights into the campaign to literally and figuratively brighten the Broadway corridor, a poorly maintained public space beneath the train line near their school.

The teacher saw Y-PLAN as an opportunity to bring her policy and government curriculum to life while the council member viewed it as a new way to engage his constituents in community improvement. The challenge was to motivate the students, many of whom mistrusted politicians and were anxious about the impacts of gentrification on their everyday lives. Some felt anger about having to walk along dirty, crumbling sidewalks past a train station deemed too "unsafe" for use, in order to get to and from school. Others resented that they were subject to surveillance or criminalization if they lingered in this public space. They felt that adults who controlled the levers of power were not willing to listen to their voices, and hence would not advocate for policies reflective of their own or their families' needs.

However, over time, trust developed between the young people and the adults, as each gained new access to the daily lives and knowledge of the other. Several key strategies contributed to this trust-building process. During the early stages, adults encouraged and supported the students to take leadership roles in coordinating and facilitating meetings for the fledgling Broadway Merchants Association. This participation allowed for a civil, respectful, and productive climate during those meetings, as adults felt pressure to match the same sense of decorum proffered by the students. Additionally, their teacher, the Y-PLAN team, and the council member cultivated open, safe spaces, both in and out of the classroom, for the young people to speak up and share their lived experiences of the corridor and the neighborhood. In response, the students shared their values and priorities. They grew to know and respect the council member as an adult who genuinely listened to and heard them. As they voiced their fears about displacement, they were able to articulate small-scale recommendations to tackle complex community challenges.

Through their active engagement, the students took the reins of the project. The resulting student-led, adult-supported efforts engaged young people more seriously in the work, cultivating their sense of ownership over the project and their continuing role in civic change. Students, who initially said they didn't care or thought it was just another regular assignment, realized over time that the adults, as one student put it, "really care what we think." She went on to explain "I took it more seriously when I realized we could make an impact."

Power of All Ages: Engage Across the K–12 Spectrum

When young people of all ages feel heard, understood, and genuinely included, they are eager and able to take on the challenges facing their cities. Elementary and secondary students offer distinctive insights and equally important visions for civic challenges. Engaging across the entire age spectrum deepens discourse and cultivates civic capacity. Older youth have more tangible skills, longer attention spans, and the ability to articulate their ideas with more sophistication. They are capable of conducting more complex research and data analysis. They are more acutely aware of the political forces around them and can speak to the impact that issues such as violence, displacement, and environmental racism have on their daily lives. Older teens are also more likely to rightfully demand to address the pressing questions of basic human needs

Figure 7.4 Power of All Ages: Engage Across the K–12 Spectrum.

Source: UC Berkeley Center for Cities and Schools.

in their community before they will actively engage in contemplating the future.

Meanwhile, younger children also have the ability to grapple with complex issues, such as transit, housing, and sustainability, with intensity, intelligence, and creativity. When they are encouraged and supported to engage in projects in authentic and meaningful ways, students as young as 5 or 6 years old have contributed powerful insights about the environments they inhabit. Participating in these projects boosts their confidence and whets their appetite for higher learning and lifelong civic activism, and their proposals are consistently imbued with optimism and hope.

Our youngest residents have a distinctive view of the dynamics of their local community. Because of their age and size, they are often among the most vulnerable residents of our cities. They see and hear minute details and revealing clues in their homes, neighborhoods, and schools that adults might overlook. Hence, they are keenly sensitive to the intricate impacts of planning policy and design. Concurrently, they have clear, creative visions of how their community could better respond to their own and their peers' needs for features such as enhanced safety, mobility, access to nature, and joy.

Case Illustration: San Rafael, California

In 2018–2019, as described in Chapter 4, forty-six children from Laurel Dell Elementary in San Rafael, California worked with architects, planners, and artists from Y-PLAN, Youth in Arts, and the Bionic design team as part of the Resilient by Design (RbD) Youth Challenge. These fourth- and fifth-grade students, 95% of whom were first generation immigrants from Mexico and Central America, lived in lower-income neighborhoods projected to be the most severely impacted by sea level rise in the next twenty years. Since many adults in the San Rafael community expressed the view that sea level rise was too overwhelming, too complicated, or too far in the future to be a priority, the professionals working with the students feared that the topic might be too abstract, complex, or depressing for children to confront in a meaningful way. Instead, the elementary students approached the challenge with vigor. They wanted to be engaged in authentic real-world issues, were not daunted by real, thorny problems, and ultimately embraced the challenge.

The young planners eagerly studied best practices to respond to climate change in cities around the world. They were inspired by images of beautiful waterways and floating buildings in Amsterdam and the protective strategies being proposed for New York City in the wake of Hurricane Sandy. They interviewed fellow residents and analyzed the predictions for their city. They translated their research into models and posters featuring vibrant interventions to protect the low-lying areas of San Rafael from flooding, while increasing accessibility, livability, and fun. Students wanted to learn, act, and contribute. They used real tools to analyze data, create models, and generate imaginative, insightful, and humane solutions, and they presented their work to stakeholders at various community forums. Engaging with real challenges activated their sense of purpose and imbued them with a sense of pride and an investment in their community.

The elementary students' visions and recommendations were integrated into the Bionic proposals to RbD, displayed in the city administrative offices, and featured in articles and OpEd pieces in the local newspapers. Subsequent cohorts of students built on their proposals by participating in the City of San Rafael 2040 General Plan process and submitting their written recommendations for the public records.

Responsibility: Professionalize Partnerships with Real Tools

Professionals seeking to engage young people in the process of city planning may initially wonder how to introduce technical terms, tools of the trade, and complex concepts to young people. However, students of all ages are capable of analyzing data, creating models and maps, employing technical vocabularies, proposing solutions, and providing leadership to help meet contemporary urban challenges. Gaining access to and knowledge of rigorous, authentic practices, and being held accountable to that rigor is an empowering experience. Rather than engaging young people as "window dressing," it is both possible and highly useful to introduce authentic professional terms, practices, and responsibilities to participants of all ages.

Figure 7.5 Responsibility: Professionalize Partnerships With Real Tools.

Source: UC Berkeley Center for Cities and Schools.

When working with young people, professional discourse is both a tool for empowerment and, at times, a barrier to participation. City planners use terms and acronyms unfamiliar to the general population, from TOD (transit-oriented development) to AMI (area median income). Using specialized terms with young people can create an obstacle to their engagement. However, simply removing the professional vocabulary and syntax entirely, especially with teenagers, can be limiting. Therefore, it is important for professionals to recognize that while these terms may be unfamiliar to students, they are eager and able to learn and understand them. When young people deploy professional language, it legitimates and amplifies the power of their ideas. Once professional relationships have formed, students deserve the opportunity to shine, impress, excel, and be held accountable. Raising the bar of expectations, praising students' early efforts, and letting them know how they can improve supports the growth of our young people, improves their projects, and is most importantly a valuable investment in our shared future.

Case Illustration: Tohoku, Japan

As described in Chapter 4, each year for eight years after the 2011 Great East Japan Earthquake and Tsunami devastated Tohoku, Japanese high school students flew across the world to the UC Berkeley campus to participate in an intensive urban planning studio. The program was designed to develop professional skills to address the challenges of rebuilding their communities back home. Adults (city planners, designers, social workers, and educators) played a critical role in this process, as architects, environmental activists, artists, community organizers, and business people introduced the students to the range of professional skills and tools needed to bring about change and move the levers of power. Through guest lectures, forums, interviews, desk crits, hands-on demonstrations, and site visits, the professionals exposed the Japanese students to an array of best practices and processes necessary to add substance and rigor to their proposals for changing communities, both in the US and in their own hometowns.

Through dynamic dialogue with the youth, these adults helped the high school students learn to use sophisticated tools to analyze data, create models and maps, conduct interviews, and craft proposals. With this professional guidance, the young people found their voices and respectfully began to speak their truths to each other and to adults, as they navigated multiple systems of governance and education, new cultural contexts, and two languages.

Presenting in a high-level civic arena on a university campus brought gravitas and credibility to the students' work and impressed adults. As students gave inspiring speeches and read their powerful personal statements, fortified with rigorously collected information, technical tools, and strong voices, the students began to navigate their new access to the city planning, governmental, and organizational systems responsible for community redevelopment and rebuilding. This amplified the strength and transformative potency of the young people's proposals for change in both the US and Japan. Through this eight-year partnership, the students have left a lasting impact on their home communities, proving that a real partnership with real tools created real change.

Connectivity: Bridge Gaps Between Disparate Networks

Professional planners often work in silos and generally see the school system as being outside their domain. They often do not have the time, resources, or capacity to engage with more diverse groups of people, especially with children and youth. Young people have the desire and capability to connect diverse groups, but they, and their public educational institutions, are often excluded from networks of power, particularly when it comes to planning, designing, and maintaining our cities. Structuring access to decision-makers and places of power for young people leverages their ability to serve as connectors.

Figure 7.6 Connectivity: Bridge Gaps Between Disparate Networks.

Source: UC Berkeley Center for Cities and Schools.

Public schools also operate within silos, with starkly different policies, standards, and objectives than the cities in which they are situated. Teachers and students often toil away in their classrooms in isolation. Educators may have little time or limited opportunities to bring students into the civic arena. School projects are often academic simulations with little or no connection to the "real world." Within this context, students often become frustrated, thinking that they and their ideas don't matter.

However, when children and youth have access to people and places of power, they have the power to motivate adults and break down these barriers. When planners and educators capitalize on young people's social power and potential as community connectors and activists as discussed in Chapter 2, the results are impressive. Authentically involving them in the planning process has a transformational impact on everyone involved. Young people's participation in the planning process can be inspiring, heartfelt, and personal. They have the capacity to convey information to adults who by displacement or disenfranchisement have been removed from the process in an accessible, digestible, compelling way. Their activism, energy, and leadership can thus catalyze the engagement of the adults around them.

Including young people in community engagement invites a broader audience into planning conversations, as parents, teachers, friends, and family members become intensely interested in their children's presentations and events. In this way, engaging young people in planning serves as a prime gateway for more diverse participation in larger, more complex planning issues. In particular, as discussed in Chapter 2, engaging low-income or BIPOC youth in this process can offer newfound access to social and professional networks, opening doors to future college, career, and community opportunities.

Professionals in the planning world know how difficult it is for agencies, divisions, and organizations to communicate and collaborate across cities and regions, even when they have shared goals and missions. The beauty of youth involvement in the planning process is that it is more than just young people working together. It is the defining process for the emergence of an entire community of practice – students, their parents, teachers, city leaders, local businesses, academics, and community activists – recognizing, often for the first time, that they are all on the same side of a shared struggle, driven to improve their community by working together.

Case Illustration: Resilient by Design Youth Challenge Regional Summit at UC Berkeley

In the spring of 2018, more than 200 students, educators, professionals, academics, and city and regional leaders convened on the UC Berkeley campus for the Y-PLAN Resilient by Design Youth Challenge Regional Summit.

Elementary and high school students from Oakland, Richmond, East Palo Alto, San Rafael, and San Francisco came together to share design proposals and visions for a more climate resilient region. These students represented almost 1000 youth from the San Francisco Bay Area, all of whom had participated in the Youth Challenge during that school year.

Using the Y-PLAN methodology, these students had spent the previous semester engaging with experts and local stakeholders to co-design innovative and implementable solutions to the challenges posed to the San Francisco Bay Area by climate change and sea level rise. Each of the student teams had worked with engineers, architects, and planners from nine professional adult teams, who were part of the Resilient by Design | Bay Area Challenge. These civic partners, many of whom were in attendance at the Summit, had provided expertise and guidance to student teams throughout the year. They had also served as role models and sources of inspiration for pursing higher educatation and various careers.

During the Summit, students presented their imaginative ideas and substantive proposals through poster sessions, lightning round pitches, models of resilient shorelines, and a panel discussion about how and why to engage young people in planning. They shared innovative visions of floating houses, buses, and solar-powered buildings; of healthy, accessible, and educational parks, museums, shorelines, and grocery stores; and of resilient housing models for unhoused people and low-income families. These young people presented as experts, lifting their voices across the campus community, to the convened city and regional leaders, proving to themselves, their peers, and adults the advantages of including them in the planning and visioning processes. One Oakland student explained, "At first I wondered why they are having us do their job for them. Do these people even live in these areas? They don't experience what we live every day." Her classmate added, "Young people are thoughtful. Their words can make people pay more attention and are more powerful in this situation [with climate change]. More people should listen." Their peer from Richmond added, "I'm proud to be a part of something bigger than myself. We can think ahead and [identify] issues that you can improve."

At the Summit, elementary school students from San Francisco brought an infectious optimism, and positive energy. Their proposals for pop-up learning stations and outdoor public "rooms" focused on educating people about the issues of sustainability and climate change while enhancing appreciation of the Bay. They gave tours of their beautifully constructed models and received insightful feedback from high school students and adult professionals. The young students also circulated throughout the Summit, asking the high school students incisive questions about their proposals. During the lightning round, in which student representatives from dozens of Bay Area classrooms provided proposal overviews, the fourth graders and high schoolers alike confidently stepped up to the podium together, presenting to the larger audience with aplomb.

Connecting youth and adults in public convenings such as this regional Summit highlights the role youth can play in bringing previously disconnected people and networks of power together. In a dignified, high-powered all-day event such as this, young people find that they have an opportunity to shine and showcase their value and expertise as connectors. Being on a university campus with college students and a range of adult leaders elevates and validates the children and youth by bringing them into a higher-level academic context, in which they are not just taking a tour as passive observers, but actually taking on the role of the expert themselves (Eppley et al., 2021). It creates an important opportunity for them to communicate with adults and to network, making connections between ideas, people, and places. It also grounds the adults in the real life of their cities and communities. Respectful interaction with young people encourages older people to step back and remind themselves why they are doing the work they are doing and how they can match the students' optimism and creativity in their respective professional lives. San Francisco's Sea Level Rise Project Manager reflected, "seeing their work and hearing their voices fills me up with hope and good energy."

Conclusion

The 2018 Resilient by Design Youth Challenge Regional Summit built on dozens of prior events like the 2014 National Youth Planning Summit in Washington, DC (discussed in Chapter 1) and the 2017 Y-PLAN New York City Summit atop the World Trade Center (discussed in Chapter 3). Like those before it, the power of connectivity among geographically, racially, and socioeconomically diverse young people and professionals heightened the experience for everyone. The power of those connections did not emerge simply by colocating these individuals in the same space. Instead, it was

Image 7.1 Students gather together for a group photo to memorialize their contributions to the Resilient by Design Youth Challenge Regional Summit at UC Berkeley in April 2018.

Source: Kingmond Young.

made possible by the work of intergenerational communities of practice that took the time to consider basic needs first, develop mutual understanding, build trust, cultivate relationships, embrace differences across the age spectrum, establish and maintain high expectations of each other, and prepare for and demand success, together. Embracing the six essentials for planning just and joyful cities is core to interrupting historically entrenched patterns of unequal access to opportunity for so many young people. This shift will require humility, resource-sharing, and retooling on the part of planners throughout the profession, local community developers as well as federal leaders, for decades to come.

Note

1 Names of young people are all pseudonyms.

References

Alexander, E. R. (1997). A Mile or a Millimeter? Measuring the "Planning Theory – Practice Gap". *Environment and Planning B: Planning and Design, 24*(1), 3–6. https://doi.org/10.1068/b240003

Carver-Thomas, D., & Darling-Hammond, L. (2017). *Teacher Turnover: Why It Matters and What We Can Do About It* (p. 60). Learning Policy Institute. https://learningpolicyinstitute.org/sites/default/files/product-files/Teacher_Turnover_REPORT.pdf

de Neufville, J. I. (1983). Planning Theory and Practice: Bridging the Gap. *Journal of Planning Education and Research, 3*(1), 35–45. https://doi.org/10.1177/0739456X8300300105

Eppley, A., Gamez-Djokic, B., & McKoy, D. (2021). Cultivating Inclusion: Belonging and Agency in Young Black Men through Civic Action Research. *Canadian Journal of Action Research, 21*(2), 72–90. https://doi.org/10.33524/cjar.v21i2.513

Hurley, J., Lamker, C. W., Taylor, E. J., Stead, D., Hellmich, M., Lange, L., Rowe, H., Beeck, S., Phibbs, P., & Forsyth, A. (2016). Exchange between Researchers and Practitioners in Urban Planning: Achievable Objective or a Bridge Too Far? *Planning Theory & Practice, 17*(3), 447–473. https://doi.org/10.1080/14649357.2016.1190491

Lave, J., & Wenger, E. (1991). *Situated Learning: Legitimate Peripheral Participation* (1st ed.). Cambridge University Press.

Nedovic-Budic, Z. (2003). Bridging Theory and Practice. *Journal of the American Planning Association*, 69(2).

Title I, Part A Program. (2018, November 7). [Program Home Page]. US Department of Education (ED). https://www2.ed.gov/programs/titleiparta/index.html

Wenger, E. (1998). *Communities of Practice: Learning, Meaning, and Identity*. Cambridge University Press.

Forging Justice and Generating Joy in Our Cities

Introduction

Our cities today are at a crossroads. Low-income and well-to-do communities are increasingly divided along social, economic, racial, and ethnic lines. As the final *New Yorker* edition of 2020 titled "The Plague" declared, "We've seen how our country has failed in so many different ways. And the pandemic has been kind of like an X-ray into the broken places in our society" (Wright, 2021). How we plan for the future of our nation and the world must enable us to overcome the increasingly devastating challenges of inequality and difference. City planners and civic leaders can no longer afford to exclude our cities' vulnerable and marginalized populations who bear the greatest burdens of our current inequities but also offer many of the answers we need to create a more just future.

This chapter speaks to city planners as well as all civic agencies in positions of power, and it offers a more holistic approach to improving cities for everyone. While not exclusively responsible, two of the major actors in shaping our cities are the institutions of city planning and public education. This chapter explores their historic roles and responsibilities in creating some of our current conditions. It then presents a two-pronged approach to creating a just and joyful future: first, inviting low-income, Black, Indigenous, People of Color (BIPOC) children and youth into planning and policymaking; and second, calling on higher education to reflect this change in its curriculum and pedagogical practices. Finally, to illustrate what diverse and age-inclusive planning can precipitate, this chapter discusses exciting changes taking place in states ranging from Washington, DC to Minnesota to California. It concludes with a call to action for planners, educators, and

DOI: 10.4324/9781003141778-11

researchers to move past historically established planning sector siloes, to recognize the critical roles young people and schools play in our cities and to recognize the power of the theory of change for planning cities with and for young people.

It is increasingly clear that meeting the growing challenges in our cities in a siloed, isolated fashion risks reproducing current social, economic, and racial inequalities rather than ameliorating them. Partnerships with other fields from public health and architecture to civil engineering respond to rising global public health crises, social and racial unrest, and economic turmoil. Progressive planners who heed the call to confront challenges and injustices facing cities agree that approaches today require new partnerships and collaboration among diverse fields (American Planning Association et al., 2017).

While it is critical for planners to move beyond their silo, it is also important to recognize the roles that diverse civic sectors play in building equitable and vibrant cities. As described in the opening chapter, planners can inspire people – young and old – to re-imagine and re-vision future possibilities for their communities. As demonstrated in the case studies in Part II, young people can bring out the best in planners and allied fields, inspiring mayors, planners, councilmembers, designers, activists, and city agency leaders to open up to new ideas and new possibilities. By focusing on cities through a community of practice lens (Lave & Wenger, 1991), city planning practice can cross generational, geographical, and disciplinary lines.

Just and joyful cities offer everyone, especially those who have been marginalized, to speak out freely and ask critical questions about their experiences. Those questions need to find their place both at the core of planning discourse and within a broader context recognizing the diverse sectors that shape the future of our cities. There are many definitions of a "just city," from Plato to progressive planners today (Griffin et al., 2015). Nevertheless there is general consensus that a just city is one in which "public investment and regulation would produce equitable outcomes rather than support only those already well off" (Fainstein, 2010, p. 3). What is missing from that definition of a just city is a broad and inclusive vision that spans generations and recognizes the important role and power of how young people experience the city in their everyday lives, prioritize issues, and envision the future. That is, a new definition that includes a vision encompassing not just the challenges young people face but also the sense of well-being they seek and prioritize. As Enrique Peñalosa Londoño, former Mayor of Bogotá, famously said about his work, "We had to build a city not for businesses or automobiles, but for children and thus for people. . . . All our everyday efforts have one objective: happiness" (Walljasper, 2004). When young people think of the cities they want, they describe access to better options for learning, employment, housing, and mobility as well as spaces to have fun and to connect joyfully with those around them.

For two decades, the UC Berkeley Y-PLAN (Youth-Plan, Learn, Act, Now) initiative, located at the Center for Cities and Schools (CC+S), has encouraged young people, city planners, educators, and civic and community leaders to assert that community participation in civic change is a right. Until the field of planning shifts from the position that community engagement, particularly with young people, is simply "nice to have" rather than "necessary to have," the impacts of such engagement will remain largely relegated to the sidelines and margins of planning. Doing so also requires a critical consciousness by all adults to not co-opt young people's activist agendas and use them to further their own goals either intentionally or unintentionally (Clay & Turner, 2021). As Lansdown (2014) explained:

> Ultimately, meaningful participation is about a commitment to concede a degree of power. It is easy to take account of children's views when those views coincide with those of adults. The challenge arises when they contradict or threaten adult assumptions.
>
> (p. 187)

Authentic, meaningful collaboration between adults and youth within an intergenerational community of practice must begin with a new inquiry process, one which first asks and answers two essential questions: *Why is a change in priorities integral for the future success of cities and schools?* and *How do we achieve that change?* These questions lead us to other provocative but equally important questions:

- Why and how can cities consider the needs of their current and most vulnerable residents before seeking to attract new development or wealthier potential residents?

Image 8.1 Educators, planning professionals, university mentors, and K–12 students come together as a community of practice at the 2019 UC Berkeley Regional Youth Planning Summit.

Source: Robinson Kuntz.

- Why and how can schools interrupt the centuries-old traditional public schooling by injecting authentic civic projects into their standard operations?
- Why and how can higher education institutions prepare future planners to instigate the diversification of the field itself?

The answers to these questions begin to emerge through the case studies and literature presented in Part II, and highlighted throughout this chapter. As Figure 8.1 illustrates, when people within three major communities of practice engage with each other, all reap beneficial impacts and outcomes. As each stakeholder group benefits individually, overlaps also develop. Those in K–12 and higher education gain access to authentic learning opportunities. Higher education and the civic community expand and diversify the academic and professional pipelines. Civic communities and K–12 education work together to promote and forge more child- and youth-friendly cities. When stakeholders within a community of practice reap the

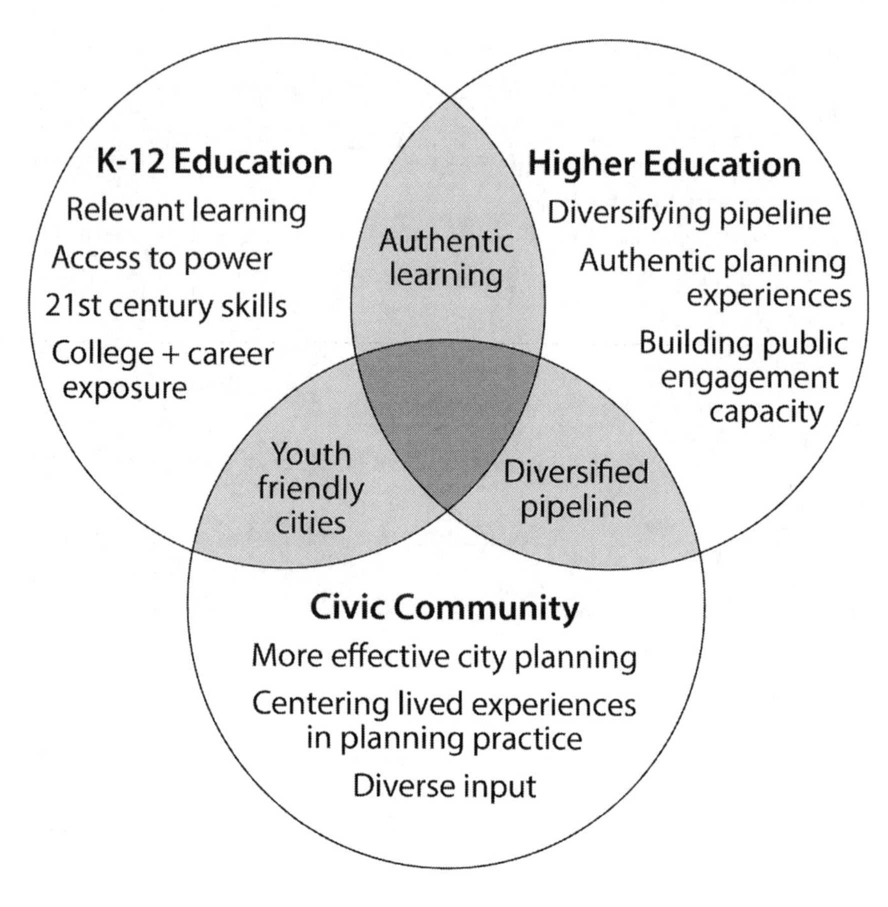

Figure 8.1 Community of Practice: Impacts and Beneficial Outcomes.
Source: UC Berkeley Center for Cities and Schools.

benefits of deep collaboration with others, they are more likely to return to the table in the future.

The Roles and Responsibilities of Cities and Schools

City Planning

Historically, city planning decisions have created and perpetuated segregated and unequal communities (Rothstein, 2017). These fissures run throughout the lives of the young people described in the case studies in Part II. For example, consider the experiences of young people at the East Palo Alto Phoenix Academy (EPAPA) from Chapters 5 and 7. As one of the few remaining low-income communities in the Silicon Valley area of the San Francisco Peninsula, these young people have watched their families and friends priced out of their homes. They have suffered the closure of their school, a charter school serving a community long abandoned by traditional public schools, due to declining enrollment. The current conditions confronted by those students in East Palo Alto, like many across the nation, were the result of racist planning practices such as redlining. As Rothstein (2017) explained, "federal and state housing policy had created a slum in East Palo Alto" (p. 13) by creating laws that restricted Black families from buying homes in white areas.

Since 2017, the young planners from East Palo Alto have been working alongside adult leaders from diverse sectors to ameliorate the situation. Together they investigate why circumstances in their own neighborhoods differ so dramatically from ones in the neighboring, predominately white, and high-income city of Palo Alto, and they study how those divisive inequities can be remedied. In doing this work, the concerns of young people shift from the margins of community participation to the core of a new line of inquiry in planning the future of their cities. The adult leaders in this process include forward-looking professionals, community leaders, and elected officials who work in collaboration with the young planners.

In its Silicon Valley location, East Palo Alto struggles to balance community stabilization for long-term residents with a dramatic influx in access to high paying technology-related jobs. According to Schragger (2016), instead of encouraging cities to compete for mobile capital, as if they are "merely vessels to be filled with [new] desirable people or investments" (p. 3), planners should develop the capacity of their existing residents. As Jacobs (1961) noted a half century ago, that approach to building capacity "means considering the city's people valuable and worth retaining, right where they are, before they become middle class," (p. 282).

The young planners from EPAPA have watched for years as high-paid technology workers, many of whom are recent college graduates trained in computer programming, move into their neighborhoods and displace their families and friends. The young planners, who presented their recommendations for stabilizing their community in a boardroom at Facebook headquarters in August of 2018, called for computer science training, comparable to what technology workers have received, to be made available to themselves and their parents. Speaking truth to power about this issue, they also presented to mayors, council members, city staff, and local residents at city council meetings in both East Palo Alto and adjacent Menlo Park. These young leaders' proposals went beyond planning for future housing in their community. They also called on civic leaders to consider how basic needs, services, schools, and the sense of community contribute to young people's well-being and ability to actualize their potential. They were simply requesting that Jacobs' vision be fulfilled.

Civic leaders, and planners in particular, must answer for and strive to remedy past actions – both intentionally racist acts and the unintentional mistakes that caused disproportionate harm to low-income communities of color. City planning needs to join forces with allied agencies and take on this new agenda while remembering that many of the most effective policies are those that ensure good basic services to all current residents, including healthcare, public safety, education, and sanitation. This policy reorientation requires the consideration of what constitutes success, as suggested by Jacobs and Schragger, rather than declaring communities deficient because they do not provide jobs. They can be labeled deficient because they do not provide even a baseline of welfare. Changing this paradigm requires "shifting the city's attention away from trying to attract the tech industry, the creative class, the middle class, or any other desirable demographic" (Schragger, 2016, p. 217). It is time for the field of city planning – and all sectors of our cities – to prioritize existing residents. As demonstrated throughout this book, one of the most effective ways of bringing current residents into the equation is to directly engage youngest people – their future leaders – in the process of planning our cities today.

Public Education

Like city planning, the public educational systems and structures over the last hundred years have created and replicated the inequities that persist to this day. For example, in 1958, during East Palo Alto's rapid shift from an entirely white to predominantly Black population, its school district created a second local high school to meet the need generated by the booming population (Rothstein, 2017, pp. 12–13). They located Ravenswood, the new high school, in East Palo Alto and reassigned the Black students from the integrated Palo Alto High School to it, effectively re-segregating the schools in the area. In 1976, Ravenswood High School closed due to declining enrollment after a failed attempt at integration. Outside of one or two charter schools, like EPAPA, nearly all high school students from East Palo Alto have endured long commutes across city limits in order to access the opportunity for free, public education that this nation promises its youth (Jan, 1996).

Perhaps the most persistent obstacle to rectifying unjust public education policies is the unyielding "grammar of schooling" that has defined the institution since its inception. This so-called grammar enabled the processing of large numbers of students at many locations in a standard easily replicable manner. Over time, the generations who had themselves been schooled in this system, assumed, protected, and perpetuated that the grammar of schooling, such as uniform school structures from blackboards to period bells that "embodied the necessary features of a 'real school' (Tyack & Cuban, 1995, p. 107). This was nothing new – John Dewey warned a century ago against "dismissing the way schools are organized 'as something comparatively external and indifferent to educational purposes and ideals.' He declared, 'the manner in which the machinery of instruction bears upon the child . . . really controls the whole system.'" (Tyack & Cuban, 1995, p. 85). The contrast between its form and function that Dewey warned of more than a century ago, persists to this day.

Fortunately, things have been changing in recent decades. As described in Part I, a wide range of school reforms are taking root in classrooms across the US These proposed reforms call on educators to reach out beyond the walls of their classrooms to engage with and learn from their students and the places in which they live, learn, and play. National curriculum efforts, such as Common Core, recognize the need for consistent, real-world learning goals and the importance of ensuring that all students, regardless of where they live, graduate from high school prepared for college, career, and life (National Governors Association, 2010). Another evidenced-based secondary education reform along these lines (and particularly well aligned to city planning) is the career academy model. Offering students small learning communities, contextualized with career themes of interest to the students, has been most effective when paired with partners in the broader community – both employers and higher education (Stern et al., 2010). "Community Schools" offer a broader and equally important, evidence-based national strategy (Oakes et al., 2017) aiming to align public education, supportive services, relevant curriculum, and community development (*What Is a Community School?*, n.d.). With decades of experience reenvisioning schools as comprehensive community centers, Community Schools are poised to inform the diverse sectors whose contributions and expertise are essential to forging more just and joyful cities.

Such reforms to democratize public education are key steps towards creating a more democratic society. Such a role of public education is described by Tyack and Cuban (1995) as "a kind of trusteeship, an effort to preserve the best of the past, to make wise choices in the present, and to plan for the future" (p. 142). Ultimately, both the fields of city planning and public education have played active roles in creating and even increasing the chasms that now exist among different groups within our contemporary society. Working in tandem, as called for in the national educational reform efforts cited earlier, promises the greatest potential to begin to close those gaps.

A Two-Pronged Strategy for City Making: Diversifying the Pipeline and Transforming Curriculum

Planning cities for and with young people, especially low-income BIPOC, holds the potential to remedy existing inequality when shifted to the core of city planning, and can be achieved through a two-pronged approach. First, as described in Chapter 2, our theory of change, providing K–12 students, specifically those who are furthest from opportunity, access to the fields of planning and policy making and support navigating them. When young people engage in the planning process at a young age, they can see the potential to transform a piece of their city and develop the agency to sustain participation in the democratic process. This process can also diversify the pool of future professionals, as these young people begin to see civic-minded careers as an option. Hundreds of national and global projects, many of which we have profiled throughout this book, have demonstrated the potency of this theory.

Secondly, higher education institutions that teach city planning can actively attract and retain racial, ethnic, and socio-economic diversity in the student bodies and faculties as well as embedding youth engagement as a required element of city planning curricula. In doing so, future professionals will begin to view themselves as members of an intergenerational community of practice, not as isolated actors. They will also gain access to the lived experience of diverse city residents from the start of their professional training. Additionally, they will develop the tools, experience, and confidence to navigate cities, build relationships, and cultivate transformative communities of practice throughout their careers.

While it is important to recognize the historically racialized and socially divisive roles of both city planning and public education, we also recognize the unique and important roles both of these fields can play to the future of our cities. City officials can consider the needs of their current and most vulnerable residents before looking to attract new development or future potential residents, accepting that it is their responsibility to promote the public good and economic equity. Moreover, public schools can interrupt the conventional grammar of schooling by injecting authentic civic projects into core pedagogical practices, as a result of the recognition that education for the public good is more than simply promoting economic advantage for those who can afford it.

Importantly, this two-pronged agenda fits squarely into the self-interest of the field of planning, as it both addresses declining enrollment in university planning departments and re-establishes city planning as a more inclusive, ethical profession. In 2018, only 1109 students were enrolled accredited bachelor degree granting, constituting a 17.4% decline over a decade (Palazzo et al., 2020, p. 1). Two years prior, the decline in enrollment, particularly among students from underserved communities, was so dramatic that the presidents of national professional planning organizations formed a "Joint Task Force on Enrollment" to address this issue (American Planning Association, 2016). In a succinct statement, it set out "to promote more inclusive and equitable communities through a planning profession as diverse and inclusive as the many communities we serve" (American Planning Association, 2019). Among other factors, they recommended increasing the socio-economic, racial, and ethnic diversity of applicants to planning programs and more effectively connecting all planners to the array of communities they will ultimately serve. The process of planning cities for and with young people, particularly those who identify as low-income or BIPOC, would cultivate a cadre of potential applicants to accomplish this very mission.

Diversifying the Pipeline

As the multi-agency Joint Task Force on Enrollment acknowledged, students from underrepresented communities, "especially those that may not be traditionally be the benefactors of generational wealth and social capital" (American Planning Association, 2016, p. 5), face serious barriers to joining the profession, including barriers to enrollment in and the completion of graduate degree programs of any kind. Simultaneously, the Task Force emphasized that "a clear career path and pipeline into the planning field for diverse populations is critical to the long term stability, relevance, and effectiveness of the profession" (American Planning Association, 2016, p. 5).

More recently, and in alignment with the Task Force's recommendations, the *APA Equity, Diversity, and Inclusion Vision Mission, and Strategy Report* set its first strategy to "continually expand the representation and understanding of diverse and inclusive perspectives within the organization and throughout the profession." The Report also called for creating a professional culture where advancing equity is at the forefront and advocates for integrating equity, diversity, and inclusion training into the organization's leadership development resources for APA staff and leadership (American Planning Association, 2019). Successful diversification of the planning field requires a proactive stance to create opportunities for young people to be active change agents in their neighborhoods. It must grant young people who have been excluded from it access to the planning profession and to BIPOC planners so they can see people who look like them in the field.

Responding to this challenge facing the field, Palazzo et al. (2020) contended that university urban planning programs and their home departments have a responsibility to create Design and Planning Language Programs. These authors call on such programs to work directly with high school students, their counselors and teachers, and local design and planning professionals to increase awareness of different career pathways related to the planning of our cities so that students will see the array of civic minded careers available to them. They have also outlined the specific skills that they feel young planners need to be exposed to, including public speaking,

Image 8.2 San Francisco Planning Commissioners come down off the rostrum to engage with students and study their models featuring their design and policy proposals to revitalize the Mission Street corridor.

Source: UC Berkeley Center for Cities and Schools.

policymaking, budgeting negotiation, research, critical thinking, writing, and more. These are exactly the skills that developed in the planning processes described in Part I and demonstrated in Part II of this book.

Professional planning and design associations are also starting to engage youth directly in planning processes. The Washington State chapter of APA has developed a Youth in Planning Task Force to raise awareness of the valuable role of youth in cities across the state. They created a civic engagement graphic novel, *Washington, By and By* (Lyon et al., 2019), modeled on award-winning graphic novel, *No Small Plans: A Graphic Novel Adventure Through Chicago* (Lyon et al., 2017), which is now used in public school curricula throughout Chicago. At a national level, the National Organization of Minority Architects (NOMA) offers Project Pipeline, an intensive summer camp for BIPOC middle school students interested in architecture, design, and planning. Project Pipeline is a powerful model for how to nurture future design professionals, civic leaders and changemakers while advocating for increased diversity, equity, and excellence in our cities.

Similarly, the Y-PLAN project in East Palo Alto, CA, illustrates the multifaceted potential of programs. First, the young planners from EPAPA became aware of a wide range of potential careers in planning, including those within a city department, a technology giant, and an academic institution. Next, these students learned professional skills through working on an authentic city planning project. These young planners navigated in diverse environments, such as research labs and presentation halls at UC Berkeley, boardrooms at Facebook, and hearing rooms at City Halls. Moreover, many of the adult planners guiding this process were BIPOC themselves, sharing their background and journey to the profession with the high school students. Seeing people who looked like them and learning stories of their similar upbringings enabled the students to envision a future for themselves in the field.

During a 2019 Center for Cities and Schools policy symposium at UC Berkeley, an EPAPA student shared her insights with a room full of planning practitioners, two university undergraduates slipped into the back of the room. They quietly listened to the presentations and then approached the high school speakers. These college students, now pursuing an education in public health and urban planning, informed participants they had participated in the Climate Action Plan project at Richmond High School (as described in Chapter 4). They described how that experience had led them to pursue planning-related fields of study at the university. This was an example of the tangible and intangible workings of the diversity pipeline. One of those college students was so moved by seeing this work continue that he later shared:

> Y-PLAN is a revolutionary program that has mobilized many underprivileged students, those currently in higher education and other pathways, to reflect on the past and focus on what we can do in the present to shape the trajectories of the future. It has definitely served as one of the significant roots to why I am here at UC Berkeley. . . . This is such a humanizing experience that empowers youth.
>
> (Eppley & McKoy, 2020)

The UC Berkeley CC+S have heard many similar anecdotes and experiences over the past two decades. During that time, more than 10,000 K–12 students have participated in more than 275 projects across dozens of cities around the US and the world. The overwhelming majority of these students identify as African American, Latinx, or Asian and live in low-income communities.

Evolving Higher Education Curriculum to Engage Diverse Populations

While diversifying the pipeline of potential planning students comprises one component of the strategy, expanding the city planning curriculum itself forms the other crucial element for the field's future. As Booher and Innes (2002) noted nearly two decades ago, "significant rethinking of what is taught will be required" for city planning (p. 232). They asserted that to prepare future planners to leverage the power of networks, their education must include these key ingredients: collaboration, negotiation, authentic communication skills, greater self-awareness and reflection, responsiveness to others, and a willingness to constructively embrace conflict. "Most of all, planners and educators need to embrace rather than shrink from what is new and experimental. That is what planning is all about after all" (Booher & Innes, 2002). More recently, the American Planning Association (APA) also highlighted the need to "build the capacity of planners to practice inclusive, culturally competent, and equitable planning practices" (American Planning Association, 2019).

As a result of this shift in thinking, the APA recommended sharing educational resources and tools for non-planners in schools and the most affected communities, requiring social equity understanding within credentialing processes, creating opportunities to facilitate communication and information across diverse constituents, and developing academic planning curricula related to issues of equity, diversity, and inclusion. Unfortunately, the APA's explicit statements remain limited to the area of reading, learning, and information sharing. To reap all of the potential benefits of equitable planning, professional preparation must extend beyond such distant, safe steps to include authentically collaborative engagement with diverse residents, including young people, in historically marginalized communities. The field must regard all participants as partners who each bring different strengths to the table, as they meet shared civic challenges together.

Professional training for planners includes experiences of deep engagement with young people, especially those from under-resourced neighborhoods, has many potential benefits. Jacobs (1961) worried that planners might be less well equipped for considering and understanding the needs of ordinary people and their neighborhoods. In Jacobs (1961) view, "city dwellers, indeed, are commonly great informal experts in precisely this subject" while "planners are the ones who are at the disadvantage. They have inevitably come to regard 'unaverage' quantities as relatively unimportant because these are statistically inconsequential. They have been trained to discount what is most vital" (p. 443). As a result, embedding diverse youth engagement within the planning process simply makes for better cities. It provides planners with access to vital truths of city life that previously went unrecognized by many of them. Authentically and equitably engaging young people enables planners to diversify their methods and explore new lines of reasoning necessary to optimally engage with all the neighborhoods within a city, particularly those that they all too often overlook.

Conclusion

Diversifying the fields responsible for planning our cities is essential to re-imagine and create more equitable places to live, work, go to school, and play. When scholars and practitioners recognize the need to incorporate

Image 8.3 At a 2019 Policy Symposium on the UC Berkeley campus, a student from East Palo Alto Phoenix Academy challenges practitioners, private and public sector leaders, city officials, and academics to engage with young people in authentic and substantive planning processes.

Source: Robinson Kuntz.

training about youth participation in city planning and policy making, they help current and future planners overcome the systemic challenges driven by a lack of age, racial, and socio-economic diversity within the field. Yet future planning education, practice, and policy must go further. Realizing these powerful aspirations, necessitates learning more, asking more, and fostering an interdisciplinary research on the changing role of young people and public schools within city planning.

At the same time, adults should embrace their own roles as learners by elevating the ideas envisioned by our cities' young people. We need to heed their calls to re-imagine our cities as vibrant communities that are woven together with an equitable and inclusive social fabric. We must redefine what makes a community truly resilient, driven by social connection and bonds, rather than new engineering advances. We must hear their urgent calls for affordable, right-sized housing in areas where they and their families can find jobs, good schools, and youth friendly spaces. Moreover, city leaders, planners, and those in positions of power need to listen, learn, and understand the central role transportation plays in young people's ability to be independent, to seize opportunities, and to enjoy each other.

As planning professionals in the field and in higher education begin to open up to the possibility of welcoming young people and public schools into the planning field, it is not enough to say that young people should be at the table or even leading the conversation. Instead, civic leaders and policy professionals must be prepared to cede power, to be humble, to listen to young people's voices and ideas for change, and to change their own practices, assumptions, and priorities in response. As demonstrated by over two decades of collaborative practices in cities from Berkeley to Brooklyn, young people and adults can come together in powerful and transformative ways. Reimagining and reconfiguring the planning of our cities as cross-generational, cross-geographical, and cross-sector communities of practice will take us one step closer to realizing the vision of just and joyful cities – now and into our shared future.

References

American Planning Association. (2016). *Joint Task Force on Enrollment Report*. https://cdn.ymaws.com/www.acsp.org/resource/collection/055FFFC1-636E-4B9C-9587-6D4FED91A23C/Planning_Enrollment_Trends_2015.pdf

American Planning Association. (2019). *APA Equity, Diversity, and Inclusion Vision, Mission, and Strategy*. https://planning-org-uploaded-media.s3.amazonaws.com/document/APA_Diversity_and_Inclusion_Strategy.pdf

American Planning Association, American Institute of Architects, American Public Health Association, American Society of Civil Engineers, American Society of Landscape Architects, National Recreation and Park Association, US Green Building Council, & Urban Land Institute. (2017). *Promote Healthy Communities: Joint Call to Action* (p. 2). https://planning-org-uploaded-media.s3.amazonaws.com/document/Promote-Healthy-Communities-Joint-Call-to-Action-rev.pdf

Booher, D. E., & Innes, J. E. (2002). Network Power in Collaborative Planning. *Journal of Planning Education and Research, 21*(3), 221–236. https://doi.org/10.1177/0739456X0202100301

Clay, K. L., & Turner, D. C., III (2021). "Maybe You Should Try It This Way Instead": Youth Activism Amid Managerialist Subterfuge. *American Educational Research Journal, 58*(2), 386–419. https://doi.org/10.3102/0002831221993476

Eppley, A., & McKoy, D. (Eds.). (2020). *Y-PLAN Voices 20 in 2020.pdf*. Center for Cities + Schools. http://y-plan.berkeley.edu/uploads/Y-PLAN_Voices_20_in_2020.pdf

Fainstein, S. S. (2010). *The Just City*. Cornell University Press. www.jstor.org/stable/10.7591/j.ctt7zhwt

Griffin, T., Cohen, A., & Maddox, D. (2015, October 19). *The Just City Essays: 26 Visions for Urban Equity, Inclusivity and Opportunity*. https://nextcity.org/features/view/just-city-essys-toni-griffin-theaster-gates-angela-glover-blackwell

Jacobs, J. (1961). *The Death and Life of Great American Cities*. Random House.

Jan, T. (1996, September 11). *Ravenswood Revisited, Reunited*. www.paloaltoonline.com/weekly/morgue/cover/1996_Sep_11.COVER11.html

Lansdown, G. (2014). 25 Years of UNCRC: Lessons Learned in Children's Participation. *Canadian Journal of Children's Rights/Revue Canadienne Des Droits Des Enfants, 1*(1). https://doi.org/10.22215/cjcr.v1i1.12

Lave, J., & Wenger, E. (1991). *Situated Learning: Legitimate Peripheral Participation* (1st edition). Cambridge University Press.

Lyon, G., Bayer, K., & Mawdsley, D. (2019). *Washington By and By*. American Planning Association Washington State Chapter.

Lyon, G., Mawdsley, D., Bayer, K., & Lin, C. (2017). *No Small Plans*. Chicago Architecture Foundation.

National Governors Association Center for Best Practices. (2010). *Common Core State Standards*. Publisher: National Governors Association Center for Best Practices, Council of Chief State School Officers.

Oakes, J., Maier, A., & Daniel, J. (2017). *Learning Policy Institute National Education Policy Center* (p. 29). National Education Policy Research Center.

Palazzo, D., Hollstein, L., & Diko, S. K. (2020). Urban Planning as a Career Preference for Students: Efforts to Improve Awareness about the Profession. *Planning Practice & Research*, 1–19. https://doi.org/10.1080/02697459.2020.1782056

Rothstein, R. (2017). *The Color of Law: A Forgotten History of How Our Government Segregated America*. Liveright Publishing Corporation.

Schragger, R. (2016). *City Power: Urban Governance in a Global Age*. Oxford University Press.

Stern, D., Dayton, C., & Raby, M. (2010). *Career Academies: A Proven Strategy to Prepare High School Students for College and Careers*. CASN.

Tyack, D., & Cuban, L. (1995). *Tinkering Toward Utopia: A Century of Public School Reform*. Harvard University Press.

Walljasper, J. (2004, October 31). *Cities of Joy*. www.pps.org/article/november2004 joy-2

What is a Community School? (n.d.). Coalition for Community Schools. Retrieved March 31, 2021, from www.communityschools.org/aboutschools/what_is_a_community_school.aspx

Wright, L. (2021, January 7). *How Mistakes, Missed Opportunities Allowed COVID-19 to Ravage the US* (T. Gross, Interviewer) [Transcript]. www.npr.org/2021/01/07/954387123/how-mistakes-missed-opportunities-allowed-covid-19-to-ravage-the-u-s

Index

Note: Page numbers in *italics* indicate a figure on the corresponding page. Page numbers followed by "n" indicate a note.

Why include youth?

Agents of change

1/4th of population

Pg 32 - children's ability to change
social dynamics

Creativity

Ability to offer insight
into lived-experiences that
is need to transform society